Becoming A Skilled Negotiator

D1502434

Kathleen Reardon
University of Southern California

WILEY

John Wiley & Sons, Inc.

ASSOCIATE PUBLISHER *Judith R. Joseph*
SENIOR PRODUCTION EDITOR *Valerie A. Vargas*
PROJECT MANAGER *Jessica Bartelt*
NEW MEDIA EDITOR *Allison Keim*
MARKETING MANAGER *David Woodbury*
TEXT AND COVER DESIGNER *Madelyn Lesure*
PRODUCTION SERVICES *Pine Tree Composition*
COVER IMAGE *Herman Eisenbeis/Photo Researchers*

This book is being simultaneously published, with some difference in content, under the title *Becoming a Skilled Negotiator,* by Wiley College, ISBN 0-4714-2969-4.

This book was set in 10/12 Caledonia by Pine Tree Composition and printed and bound by Courier-Westford. The cover was printed by Phoenix Color Corporation.

The book is printed on acid-free paper. ∞

Library of Congress Cataloging-in-Publication Data

Reardon, Kathleen Kelley.
 Becoming a skilled negotiator : concepts and practices / Kathleen Reardon.
 p. cm.
 Includes Index.
 ISBN 0-471-42969-4 (paper/website : alk paper)
 1. Negotiation in business. I. Title.

 HD58.6.R433 2004
 658.4'052--dc22

 2004042234

ISBN 0471-42969-4

Printed in the United States of America

10 9 8 7 6 5 4 3 2 1

To Connie and Earl Noblet

Preface

Becoming a Skilled Negotiator is based on decades of learning through direct experience and study supplemented by observations of the negotiations of business-people, students, colleagues, friends, family and strangers. It's always a pleasure to finish writing a book. In this way, *Becoming a Skilled Negotiator* is no exception. In another way, however, it is very much an exception. There is so much to say about negotiation, so very much to learn, that I found deciding what to include in the book and what to leave out even more of a challenge than it has been for most subjects about which I've written. Any choice of focus runs the risk of omitting other important aspects, just as a painting focused on the foreground invariably does some injustice to the background. Similarly, the choice of negotiation study focus is, by its very nature, a distortion of sorts. Nevertheless, a choice had to be made. And in this case, the choice was to focus on language—the talk of negotiation. There is a good deal out there on negotiation strategy; far less on how the more skilled among us translate strategy into verbal and nonverbal action. Yet what negotiators actually say and do during negotiation makes all the difference in their outcomes.

The study of how we express what we mean, or fail to do so, has always fascinated me. I hope that some of my fascination rubs off on you as you turn the pages of this book. We human beings are so often our own worst enemies: allowing ourselves to speak too little, too soon, too much, or without consideration for the interests of others. We slip into patterns of talk that take us away from our goals, because we've taken our ability to communicate for granted. Skilled negotiators are different in this regard. They are intrigued by talk, connoisseurs of it, capable of detecting subtleties in manner and speech that novices fail to notice. They are themselves fascinating, so studying them has been a good deal of my life's work. Fortunately, there is no end to what can be learned from observations of people.

Becoming a Skilled Negotiator contains my thoughts regarding these observations. I hope you enjoy and benefit from this book as much as I've enjoyed and benefited from acquiring the expertise that made it possible. When you're through reading, your repertoire of options will have been expanded. With practice and fearless experimentation, you'll add to it. The development of negotiation expertise requires a trial-and-error approach to find what works for you. I've tripped and fallen in negotiation, as no doubt you have, but we've both learned from those times. I'm now, according to my family, friends, and colleagues, a negotiation force with which to be reckoned. When you finish this book, you will be one too.

▶ ACKNOWLEDGMENTS

My gratitude for their contributions to this book go, at Wiley, to Susan Elbe, Judith Joseph, and Jeff Marshall, and at Jossey-Bass, to Susan Williams, Byron Schneider, Rob Brandt, Akemi Yamaguchi, Carolyn Miller, Jeff Wyneken, and copy editor Kristi Hein. My agent, Peter Ginsberg, has my continuing gratitude. My husband, Chris Noblet, did critical background research, edited, and developed charts and figures from my chicken-scratch notes. He is a quiet genius. Devin, Ryan, and Shannon, you were wonderful.

About the Author

Kathleen Kelley Reardon is professor of management and organization at the University of Southern California's Marshall School of Business and visiting research professor of philosophy at University College, Cork, Ireland. A member of Phi Beta Kappa and a best-selling author, speaker, and consultant in negotiation and politics in business, Reardon is also a founding board member of the First Star Foundation in Washington, D.C., and was recently named Distinguished Research Scholar by the Irish Management Institute in Dublin.

Contents

Defining the Art

Negotiations are as varied as roller-coasters. Some are gentle; others, frighteningly fast and treacherous, with surprising twists and erratic turns. The person who consciously and carefully selects the type of roller-coaster and the seat location suited to his or her level of experience and then remains seated and belted in, leaning confidently into sharp turns, is likely to survive the ride unscathed and enjoy it as well.

Negotiation success and enjoyment are achieved in a similar way. The more complex forms change direction unexpectedly. Accomplished negotiators recognize this and so are not derailed by it. They also know that although negotiation occurs often in daily life, it is rarely a simple process. Ups and downs—gains and losses—must be expected. Managing these requires several skills, all harmoniously coming together to ensure progress toward the desired outcomes.

Reaching those outcomes also requires forging alliances, often between people with diverse interests, each determined to walk away with the lion's share of resources. In the best negotiations, there is a meeting of the minds, an allying, at least on what matters most, who gets what, and how these allocations will be achieved. In fact, business in general cannot profitably operate in the absence of alliances.

When Charles Handy, author and business expert, was asked what skills will be needed in organizations of the future, he emphasized the ability to ally with others: "Key skills will be the ability to win friends and influence people at a personal level, the ability to structure partnerships, and the ability to negotiate and to find compromises. Business will be much more about finding the right people in the right places and negotiating the right deals."[1]

Businesses in the future will be more shapeless, Handy adds. Unlike companies of the past, in which people with roughly the same purpose were bound together, businesses now and in the foreseeable future are more like "a collection of globules—partnerships and alliances."[2] When people form partnerships and alliances, they also negotiate the terms of those relationships. Little can be taken for granted in organizations whose people may not be housed together and, even if they are, often do not think alike. One's personal and professional success in organizations therefore requires skillful management of one's surroundings—not in

the old top-down way, but from all directions. This is only accomplished through skillful negotiation. Warren Bennis, a professor at the University of Southern California and a renowned business author, considers even leadership largely a function of alliance formations—and thus of negotiation.[3]

Just as business leaders must sell a shared vision to their various stakeholders, world leaders must forge alliances to solve global problems. When leaders fail to form alliances, their legitimacy is questioned. Even when their cause is just, they may be perceived as rogues. And however they are perceived, their work is made harder by the absence of allies willing to share the burden of the enterprise, including its costs.

The importance of alliances in business organizations, be they for profit or nonprofit, applies as well to the governing of people by heads of state and their associates. John Donne's declaration that "no man is an island" may have never been more true than it is today. Alliances are as essential to the daily life of the entrepreneur as they are to large organizations and governments, and alliances do not exist or succeed without negotiation.

Becoming a Skilled Negotiator focuses on how successful negotiation alliances are formed. The more skilled among us in this domain are people who have trained themselves to be versatile; who have studied their own habits and set themselves free from dysfunctional ones. They are both detectives and social scientists, searching for clues regarding their counterparts' interests and studying their communication. They are by nature inquisitive and by practice insightful. Their mastery of language is at the heart of their success—hence the subtitle of this book. The emphasis on language use in the chapters to come separates *Becoming a Skilled Negotiator* from many previous books. The *talk* of negotiation, informed by strategy considerations, is a consistent element throughout the book. I examine not only what the experts, both practitioners and academics, have taught us regarding strategy but also how the most skilled negotiators convert those strategies into words.

The term *engagement* in the subtitle refers not to war, as it is sometimes used, but rather to the active, tête-à-tête nature of negotiation. We use *engagement* because negotiation begins with a mutual invitation made by interdependent parties to grapple with shared concerns. People *engage* in negotiation, starting from different vantage points, interests, goals, concerns, and emotions. Through talk, they attempt to identify an avenue of alliance on at least some primary issues. A negotiator cannot become truly skilled without an understanding of how words and actions shape perceptions that stand in the way of such alliances. This requires what Harvard University psychology professor Ellen Langer describes as *mindfulness*—a rare level of attention to detail and subtlety. According to her research, people who are mindful live longer. Why? Because they pay attention to their surroundings and their own habits, some of which are dangerous. Langer explains: "In the 25 years I've been studying this, I've learned that the consequences of mindlessness include things like accidents, burnout, poor job performance, memory problems, interpersonal difficulties and health problems. Our mindlessness essentially turns the body off. On the other hand, when we are mindful, we are literally more alive."[4]

Skilled negotiators are literally more alive. They do not let the past determine their present and are not ruled by routine. They put in the extra effort it takes to be sensitive to their surroundings and notice not only how things are the same but also how they are different. It is this attention to differences, in particular, that keeps them alert. People generally do not pay attention to the same old things, so people who are not alert to subtle, otherwise unexpected differences walk around each day half asleep. It is largely in times of uncertainty that most of us pay more attention. For example, Langer explains, we pay attention to the sounds our new car makes but soon tune them out. We may tune back in when the car makes a loud grinding noise, by which time it's too late to do minor repairs.

Skilled negotiators don't stop listening and observing. They pay attention to subtleties and intentionally look for distinctiveness in people and events that others fail to notice. As a result, they are not caught unaware when things change—when the roller-coaster takes a dramatic turn.

It is, of course, one thing to tell negotiators that to be highly skilled they must be mindful; it is quite another to show them what that means in terms of assessing situations and selecting from a repertoire of words and actions. *Becoming a Skilled Negotiator* takes you on this journey. Its purpose is to provide you with insight into how negotiation works and to train you to notice the kinds of subtleties that are obvious to the highly skilled negotiator. Each chapter presents a step in the process of gaining such awareness, taking you from your present skill level to higher-level functioning—and thereby to greater negotiation success.

Chapter 2 explains in detail how we routinely abdicate our responsibility to communication and negotiation by allowing ourselves to slip into verbal and nonverbal habits that make us predictable and easy targets for the more alert. Expertise in negotiation requires versatility in word choice, emotional expression, and nonverbal gestures. This chapter explicates how expert negotiators free themselves from the restrictions, born of habit, that imprison so many of their less skilled counterparts. In this and subsequent chapters, I provide examples of how versatile negotiators decide what to say. Such strategies as timing, positioning, advancing, and retreating are important, but so is the less studied talent of using words to implement these and other strategies. This chapter is an eye-opening introduction to the extensive range of choices available to the astute negotiator.

Chapter 3 puts the concept of versatility into practice. Focusing on the steps to take in the intelligence-gathering stage of negotiation, I address a variety of interesting questions: How do skilled negotiators create a climate of inquiry that effectively informs language choice? How do they learn more than others about their counterparts? How do the more skillful formulate arguments and articulate them—and in doing so, how do they maintain versatility? How does negotiation style diminish or enhance this versatility of choice? Much of who we are conspires in our unconscious to limit choice. Negotiation at its best involves acute awareness of and adept management of such constraints. Negotiators use the predictability of others to inform their choices while endeavoring to avoid providing their counterparts with the same advantage. They do this by extensive preparation involving expansive thinking and the kind of careful selection of language options introduced in Chapter 3.

Chapter 4 describes how ideal and backup goals are developed. When negotiators identify goals too far afield of what can be achieved, they set themselves up for disappointment or failure. Here we look at ways of reducing the likelihood of that outcome by basing goals on the kind of effective intelligence gathering described in Chapter 2. We consider how to work with the other negotiator or team to jointly prioritize issues, as well as ways to keep the negotiation on track once this prioritization is decided. Finally, this chapter deals with the important issue of what to say and do when the other side will not accept your proposed issue priorities.

Chapter 5 addresses the important topic of ethics in negotiation. It's difficult to say exactly what separates the ethical from the unethical negotiator, so most discussions of this topic fall short for those who would like a lists of dos and don'ts. There isn't such a list in Chapter 5, but you'll find an overview of some excellent thinking on this subject, some ways to assess your own ethics, and guidelines for establishing ethical parameters. My own view is that negotiators should strive to stay on the high road—to reject deception, traps, trickery, and manipulation. Yet if you are of the same mind, you'll need to know how to deal with those who aren't. This is also part of Chapter 5, as are ways to bring a negotiation to a higher plane even if your counterpart is a snake in the grass.

Having discussed how negotiations can go down unethical roads, in Chapter 6 we delve into persuasion, an activity that, although central to negotiation, is often branded as devious. Persuasion is the heart of negotiation; ethics, its soul. It is possible to persuade without resorting to unethical practices; I offer some real-world examples. We then turn to the ordering of issues—agenda setting—and the art of positioning or "framing" issues. It is not sufficient for a negotiator to simply present the issues as if they are self-explanatory; this must be done persuasively. Successfully proposing the ordering of issues also requires persuasion. In fact, persuasion begins even before an issue is discussed, by virtue of its placement. Just as newspaper editors often place more important stories on the first page, negotiators often endeavor to place their most important issues early on. The agenda is therefore not a boring list of topics but an indicator of topic concern. It is the first line of a good negotiation offense and defense.

Chapter 7 focuses on the types of persuasion that skilled negotiators use once the actual interactive part of negotiation is under way. Persuasion at its best is not forceful or deceptive; rather, it encourages a counterpart to *choose* to adopt an advocated perspective or action. This requires skillful reasoning and appeals to emotion. I offer a repertoire of persuasion strategies, along with two shortcut methods for determining when and how to select among those strategies. We look at the role emotion plays in negotiation, how to employ emotional strategies effectively, and ways to ensure that you are aware when someone is trying to manage your emotions to their advantage. Next, we explore three forms of deception common in negotiation and ways to handle each of them. The chapter ends with several cases of deception and effective ways to return negotiation to a more productive track.

So much of what occurs in negotiation is rooted in perceptions of who has power. What is power, and how do you get it? Chapter 8 answers this crucial question. Power does not exclusively accrue from status, wealth, or expertise. All of us have the ability to create power. Skillful negotiation requires the rare ability

to look carefully, mindfully, at what one brings to the table. Ask yourself what the other side wants that you have—or what they might want if they knew you could provide it. Assess, too, what they fear that you might control. Power is, in many respects, in the eye of the beholder. Astute negotiators know this and are therefore not thrown off stride by the status of their counterparts or by any other indicator of static power. They craft their own power and thereby increase the odds of a profitable negotiation.

Chapter 9 addresses the important subject of conflict. Even if a negotiator takes all the steps advocated in previous chapters, things can still go very wrong. Obstacles and impasses are natural in negotiation, so negotiators must know how to anticipate them as well as know what to say or do when they occur. When negotiators treat conflict as a natural part of negotiation, they are not derailed by it. In fact, just as pain tells the body that something is wrong, conflict can serve as a useful warning that a change of approach is needed. The negotiator who knows how to handle conflict has greater confidence, and in negotiation, confidence—without arrogance—is a significant asset.

Cross-cultural negotiation is the subject of Chapter 10. Crossing cultures in negotiation calls for a high level of the kind of attentiveness and versatility described in earlier chapters. Success here depends on a willingness to learn how people from other parts of the world think about such issues as timing, trust, socializing, decision-making authority, who should speak with whom, etiquette, appropriateness of strategies, gender, and emotional expression. I look at several regions of the world in terms of these topics and offer examples of how cultural sensitivity proves a considerable negotiation advantage—of interest even if you never travel abroad.

Becoming a Skilled Negotiator ends with a review of key points from all the numbered chapters. At this point, you'll possess the capacity to be a skilled negotiator yourself. The only remaining ingredient—a very important one—is commitment to practice. With experimentation comes progress; this is especially true in the development of negotiation skill. Best and worst outcomes are equal teachers, honing the skills of student and expert alike. By the end of the book, you will be better able to craft alliances and to use language tactically in the service of your business, political, and personal goals.

The first step is to position your mind-set so that you are poised to dissect the negotiation process, to learn how to analyze the interests of others, and to select your words to bring about a desirable outcome. Let's turn now to those critical skills.

2

A Versatile Frame of Mind

Effective negotiators are adaptable. They do not become wedded to static approaches or strategies. They remain vigilant on the real issues from start to finish, all the while absorbing information about their counterparts' habits, speaking and presentation patterns, and personal style. They monitor themselves as well, making sure to avoid mere reaction to choices the other side presents. This level of performance, not easily achieved, is at the heart of what separates the skilled negotiator from the amateur.

We begin our discussion of these rarely developed talents with one of the first choices a negotiator makes: whether to take an integrative or distributive approach to negotiation—or an approach somewhere in between the two. Writers on negotiation have placed considerable emphasis on the mutual gain orientation. For decades, the trend in such writings has been away from the idea of winning in negotiation at the expense of others toward the concept of cooperative sharing. The former is called *distributive negotiation;* the latter, *integrative negotiation.*[1] Research has indicated that negotiators who more frequently use cooperative strategies achieve high mutual gain, whereas those who rely on competitive strategies tend to achieve less.[2] This finding suggests that negotiators should focus mainly on the establishment of cooperation. Yet research also shows that negotiators who view themselves as having considerable influence over the other party are more likely to assume a position of strength and to hold firm on issues of importance. Negotiators who perceive that they have little influence over the other party are more likely to make greater concessions.[3] Taken together, these research findings suggest that a cooperative, win-win focus is generally useful, but it is also important to know how much one is willing to concede to achieve that focus. If we look at this in terms of a continuum (see Figure 2.1), at one end is purely distributive negotiation, in which there is no regard for the needs and interests of the other side. Ultradistributive negotiators at this end of the spectrum are addicted to winning. They may lose sight of their original goals and trample on the aims of others, all in the service of being able to say, "I won." I recall speaking with a young businessman who had just returned from a negotiation in Japan. He proudly informed me that he hadn't let them "get the best" of him. He described how he'd stood his ground, pressed for his goals, and refused to back down. I

Figure 2.1 A Continuum: Competition and Cooperation.

asked whether he'd been successful. He responded, "I didn't get what I wanted and they didn't get what they wanted—but now they realize that I'm not going to back down, that I intend to win. That's important, so in that sense, I won." This businessman never returned to Japan because he was never invited back. Such is the fate of those who habitually focus on winning and disregard the process of give and take that is required to "win."

At the other end of the continuum are negotiators who focus almost exclusively on the needs and interests of the other side: ultraintegrative negotiators. Ensuring that the other side leaves with a sense of having won is imperative to these negotiators; they are willing to sacrifice a good deal to achieve it. Although the more productive side of the continuum usually is the integrative one, it is possible for negotiators to go too far—to give up too much merely to feel that both sides have obtained something. In one of my seminars, a junior executive complained of her supervisor, "Nice guy, but that's the problem. He wants to make everyone happy, so we get nowhere. The competition is walking all over us."

Somewhere near the middle of the continuum, moving as needed toward the integrative or distributive end—but never too far in either direction—are flexible negotiators. At their best, they are so well prepared in their goals prioritization that they know how much to give, how much to retain, and when to do either—or both.

Skilled negotiators are not committed to either win-win or win-lose. They know that while the former is typically preferable, understanding how to engage in the latter (or in some mode in between) is what enables them to achieve their goals. They are more versatile than their less competent counterparts. They don't memorize strategies and apply them in lockstep order; rather, they practice versatility. Total surprise is a rare experience for such skilled negotiators. Even when it does occur, they're prepared because they've trained themselves to adapt, to step back if need be in order to reinquire and reassess negotiation conditions before making the next move.

▶ DANGERS OF ASSUMPTIONS

For a negotiator to achieve versatility requires a clear understanding of the primary obstacles to successful negotiation inquiry—faulty assumptions. As humans, we tend to categorize. Many of us take in superficial information about others (their dress, manner, expressions, and so on) and decide that we know much more about them than in fact we do. We quickly determine whether they are like or unlike us—friend or foe.

Anthropologist Mary Catherine Bateson has spoken of the dangers inherent in our "myths of commonality" and "myths of disparity."[4] In the former, we assume that we know people (especially family members) when it is merely an illu-

sion to believe so. Given how long people live, they inevitably undergo a number of changes. Furthermore, Bateson explains, the stranger may be found not only across the breakfast table but in the mirror as well. If we understand ourselves as constantly evolving, then we must both recognize the need to continually get to know each other and continually appreciate the changes that have transpired. If we also recognize that like ourselves, other people are highly complex beings, we will be better prepared to truly understand them. Skilled negotiators do not impose assumptions of commonality or disparity on others. They study them and endeavor to make sense of who they are, how they think, and what they desire. The versatile negotiator is first and foremost a detective, skeptical of easy categorization and alert to the limitations of even the most astute judgments.

This kind of detectivelike sensemaking is what good managers and negotiators do for much of each day.[5] They bypass easy assumptions and instead operate in a mind-set that expects shifts in perception. They remain flexible even while powerfully destination oriented; they put a premium on observation and encourage frequent updating. They ask questions.

As leadership expert Karl Weick puts it, "Sensemaking is not about rules and options and decisions. Sensemaking does not presume that there are generic right answers about things like taking risks or following rules. Instead, sensemaking is about how to stay in touch with context."[6] At least as important as keeping a goal or destination in mind, when faced with inevitable uncertainty, is the capability that sensemakers have "to act their way into an understanding of where they are, who they are and what they are doing." They have the ability to make sense of others in the same way and, armed with this knowledge, are better prepared to influence the course of negotiations (see Exhibit 2.1).

This balance between observation and action is what negotiators need to achieve. Those who weigh more heavily on the observation side gain the advantage even in crisis. They do not refrain from action but charge into it when they have gathered enough information to make informed choices. For people to make sense of each other's actions and utterances, they must become apprised of expectations that guide each other's choices. *Rules of engagement,* as we might call them, create conditions that allow participants to make sense of what's being said and done in human interaction (how much to say, what to say, how to say it, and so on). Absent such rules, literally anything may be said or done at any time. An infinite set of responses would not *make sense* in any kind of human communication, including negotiation. When one wanders too far afield of expected behavior, an interaction and perhaps even an entire relationship may suffer irreparable damage. Indeed, most people will quickly stop talking to someone who strays far outside the range of sensible responses. Now, what the designation "sensible" means will vary within cultures and even more between them. In many instances, this meaning changes across gender and age as well. Despite such variations, however, parties to negotiation bring a set of general expectations. Expert negotiators understand this. They know they must identify these expectations or they risk speaking in ways that appear irrelevant or offensive to their negotiation counterparts. This is why the early stages of negotiation should involve considerable use of questions.

THE SENSEMAKING MENTALITY

Karl Weick gives the following example of a sensemaking mentality:

One of the five best wildland firefighters in the world is Paul Gleason. Much of his fame comes from his work in over five hundred serious fires, as crew chief in charge of nineteen other firefighters from the Interagency Hotshot Crew (the ZigZag Crew). Gleason said that when fighting fires, he prefers to view his leadership efforts as sensemaking rather than decision making. In his words, "If I make a decision, it is a possession, I take pride in it, I tend to defend it and not listen to those who question it. If I make sense, then this is more dynamic and I listen and I can change it. A decision is something you polish. Sensemaking is a direction for the next period."

When Gleason perceives his work as decision making, he feels that he postpones action so he can get the decision "right" and that after he makes the decision, he finds himself defending it rather than revising it to suit changing circumstances. Polishing an defending eat up valuable time and encourage blind spots. If, instead, Gleason treats and unfolding fire as a problem in sensemaking, then he gives his crew a direction for some indefinite period, a direction that by definition is dynamic, open to revision at any time, self-correcting, responsive, and with more of its rationale being transparent.

Gleason's commitment to sensemaking is striking. When crews fight fires, they post a lookout whose job is to monitor the relationship between the oncoming fire and the crew and to warn if the distance between the two gets too small. On some of Gleason's especially hazardous fires, where there is danger of rolling rocks or windblown spot fires, he has assigned as many as sixteen people to be lookouts, leaving only four people to actually fight the fire.

Source: K. E. Weick, "Leadership as the Legitimation of Doubt," in *The Future of Leadership*, ed. W. Bennis, G. M. Spreitzer, and T. G. Cummings (San Francisco: Jossey-Bass, 2001), pp. 95–96.

▶ USING QUESTIONS

Questions are critical in unearthing assumptions, but how exactly do they work? Skilled negotiators typically enter negotiations with a number of questions already prepared. Questions asked early in a negotiation should seek general information about

- What the other person thinks will be achieved
- What expectations he or she has regarding each side's goals
- Attitudes on key issues
- Relational perceptions (for example, advisory or friend)
- Interest in developing or maintaining a relationship

- Goals of his or her own
- Outside constraints—actual and perceived

Open-ended questions such as "How do you feel about X?" or "What are you hoping to achieve today?" should be asked in the early stages. As negotiation proceeds, conditional questions become more useful. These involve probing for specific information about proposals. Questions like "What would happen if we were to . . . ?" and "If we proceed as you suggest, what will that mean for . . . ?" are useful. Conditional questions don't pin either side down. They focus on hypothetical conditions. "If we develop a three-year contract, what would be the advantages and disadvantages for you?" This question doesn't specify that a three-year contract is the choice being made but rather explores what the effects of such an approach might be. "What if?" questions can be a good way to disagree when a direct "no" might damage a relationship. "Before we decide, we should ask ourselves whether the three-year approach makes us less committed to the project. Three years passes quite quickly. Do you think either of us will jump ship, knowing in year two that there is only one year left?"

Questions constitute a critical component of negotiation. They can be used to unearth hidden assumptions and to ensure that what was said is also what was heard. We're not referring here only to the denotative or dictionary meanings of words but also to the connotative or personal interpretations of words and nonverbal messages. Even phrases common in one community can be annoying in another. Claude Cellich, dean for academic affairs at the International University in Geneva, Switzerland, explains, "Certain words or phrases that may irritate the other side should be omitted. For example, phrases such as 'To tell the truth,' 'I will be honest with you,' 'I will do my best,' and 'It's none of my business, but . . .' convey a sense of distrust and make the other person more apprehensive and possibly less cooperative."[7] Cellich warns that "No problem" is another commonly used phrase that annoys those who do not use it.

Obviously, much goes on in communication in terms of meaning formation. Questions are a good way to ensure that interpretations of intended meaning are accurate. They are also a good way to test the progress of negotiation. Gary Tharp, president of GT Commercial in Orlando, Florida, advises negotiators to frequently test how the other side feels. "Are its interests being met? Does the other team buy into a particular solution?" He cautions, "If members of the other side aren't going down the same path you are headed, stop and find out where they are."[8]

Questions are also a means of influencing the other side to participate more in the discussion. Persuasion research tells us that when people are involved in a decision, they're more likely to be committed to it. As Tharp writes, "Good negotiators strive to do less than a majority of the talking, allowing the other side to make most of your side's points by asking questions that lead to the desired result."[9] "Have you considered approaching this from the vantage point of X?" or "If you were in our shoes, would you take this approach?" are questions of a somewhat leading type. "Were you as impressed as I was with the tactics used by X Company?" and "Do you think what they did could be a lesson for us?" are some

other examples of leading the horse to water to see if it will drink. Also, walking through the likely result of adopting an undesirable approach and then asking, "Would that be fair?" or "Would that result suit you?" is an indirect way of steering a negotiation away from an unfavorable result.

▶ MEASURING THE ENVIRONMENT

Optimism and confidence in negotiation emanate not only from a thorough examination of how the other side views things but also from a keen awareness of the conditions that surround the negotiation. Negotiations do not occur in a vacuum. They are influenced by such internal and external factors as time pressure, number of parties involved, proximity, and location. Like the firefighter who keeps apprised of prevailing winds, astute negotiators are aware of shifts in their surroundings. Nothing remains entirely static in human interaction, and nearly everything can be altered to some degree. The novice negotiator, for example, who examines a situation and determines who has power may quickly become intimidated. An experienced negotiator knows that power is not a static phenomenon. It can be altered favorably if conditions are managed. He is aware of the balance but not deterred by it.

A business executive who served on his company's corporate contributions committee told me of a case in which a simple, environment-altering tactic improved a grant applicant's leverage. Funding providers receive far more applications for financial support than they can respond to favorably. When service agency directors are able to obtain an appointment, they tend to arrive with hat in hand, allowing the power to rest entirely with the person on the "business" side of the desk.

The executive had agreed to meet an agency director who ran a small program (we'll call it "Born Free") that encouraged inner-city youths to avoid gangs and find other avenues of self-expression. He expected to go through the motions of meeting yet another hat-in-hand, well-intentioned, low-powered person. When the executive greeted Born Free's director, he was stunned to find the clean-cut man accompanied by a large, hulking, former gang member with a knife-scarred face, attired in "street" clothes and a skeptical attitude. While there was certainly no physical threat intended, the very presence of such an individual nonetheless proved intimidating. The executive quickly realized that what he expected to be a disposable sales pitch was going to be a very serious negotiation indeed. A similar effect would likely have derived from a Special Olympics agency director bringing along a handicapped athlete or a shelter director accompanied by a battered wife. It's much harder to dismiss a request for help when the human object of the entreaty is sitting in your office and looking into your eyes. It gives power to the otherwise powerless. Indeed, as it happened, the Born Free agency received a full hearing, on-site visits, and financial support for several years.

Power, like other negotiation conditions, is in this sense in the eyes of the beholder. It is negotiable. Once you believe that power is yours, it shows. Author and power expert Michel Foucault described how power "seeps into the very grain of individuals," reaching into their bodies, where it "permeates their ges-

tures."[10] Those who do their homework well, who studiously search for personal or team power advantage on key issues, go into negotiation with this type of power sense. They appear confident, not arrogant. They do not seek to win at every turn or at any cost. They seek to win when it counts the most. They know in advance what they're willing to sacrifice, when they're likely to accommodate, and when they are likely to press for accommodation from the other party. They are not easily impressed with surface indicators of power or advantage because they know that these can be located on their side as well. And when it seems that they possess the lion's share of power, they are pleased but not lured into comfort, for power is easily converted to powerlessness when one's guard is down. So once a negotiator has made sense of the other side's perspectives, his or her job is to consider ways to foster perceptions about environmental conditions that are conducive to success. We'll discuss other environmental aspects at greater length later in the book. The key point there is that nearly everything involved in negotiation—people and surroundings—is subject to alteration—to another interpretation besides the easy or prevailing one. To be a skilled negotiator, you need to start with this mind-set.

In general, to increase the chances of achieving desired goals by altering conditions or interpretations, a negotiator's orientation going in must be one of learning—of asking more than telling. The first of the following interactions demonstrates the wrong way, and the second, the right way, to do this:

Sid: You say we're looking for more than you're offering?

Karen: We're maxed out here. We've given up far more than you have.

Sid: By what measurement is that?

Karen: By any measurement.

Sid: Listen. We don't have the time or inclination to keep opening doors only to have them closed in our faces. We made a perfectly reasonable proposal, and you've come back with very little. We're miles apart.

Karen: Your proposals are one sided. What we're proposing is very generous.

Sid: To your side, anyway.

Karen: No—to yours.

Sid: This is getting us nowhere.

Karen: That's right. Because you won't budge.

Neither of the parties asks questions or seeks information, never mind searching for common ground. Each person is *telling* the other what he or she thinks. Each stridently presents his or her respective position with the intent of demonstrating how right it is. Compare this dialogue with one in which the negotiator attempts to learn how the other side thinks and to work with that:

Sid: We're looking for more than you're offering.

Karen: In what sense?

Sid: The delivery date is three weeks too late for us, and the price is still above what we can pay.

Karen: Which is the more critical of these two? It's hard for us to lower the price much if we have to meet such an early delivery date.

Sid: Most important to us is the delivery date. We need a lower price, though.

Karen: I can budge on price but not more than six thousand dollars, given the extra people we'll need to meet your deadline priority. Does that work?

Sid: It's in the ballpark. I think I can sell it back home.

Negotiation is a process, not simply an outcome. It is a process of making sense out of what is happening and then working with those conditions to bring about a desirable outcome. In the second dialogue, Karen asks Sid what matters most to him. With that information in hand, she offers to respond to his priority with a small reduction in price. If her greater concern is cost and $6000 is less than she expected to concede, she has done well while responding to Sid's stated needs, all because she listened and learned. She thought in terms of versatility, not intransigence. Certainly, negotiators who take a learning approach have outcomes in mind and work toward their achievement, but they realize that until they know what matters to the other side, they won't achieve what matters to them. They realize, too, that versatility fosters better relationships—and in negotiation, relationships are critical to success. Approaching negotiation with such a versatile mind-set, as negotiation scholar Linda Putnam puts it, "centers on the way that the task of negotiating can serve the relationship rather than the reverse. This perspective values relationship in its own right, not for instrumental gain."[11]

Contrary to common wisdom, not all aspects of negotiation are about rationality or even about strategy. Negotiation is about relating with one or more individuals with the intention of bringing about desired outcomes, but at any juncture in the process, the main focus is likely to be more on relating constructively—on sensemaking and managing—than on getting to the goal. If basketball players were to always take the halftime score as their cue to whether their team could win the game, many great and memorable victories would never have taken place on the court. Sure, a halftime score can affect the mood and attitude of the players as they return to the court, but in a competitive league, it's rarely a good indicator of the final outcome. Unlike negotiation, in sports, there is necessarily a winner and a loser, but in negotiation, as in sports, there is also a point at which the outcome is in sight and many points before that when the play at hand is what matters most. In negotiation, often the interaction at hand matters, and to measure it always against some ultimate goal can lead to premature judgments and faulty actions. The key is to keep on track generally but to place a high priority on understanding how the other side thinks and to identify ways to respond so as to advance your goal while appreciating and, where possible, responding to theirs.

Nelson Mandela has spent much of his life engaged in negotiations, with the ultimate goal of forging a united post-apartheid South Africa in which people of all colors could live freely and peacefully. Mandela treated negotiation as a learn-

ing process, as an art to be mastered en route to achieving an ultimate goal. "During my lifetime I have dedicated myself to this struggle of the African people," he told a judge during his 1962 trial. "I have cherished the ideal of a democratic and free society in which all persons live together in harmony and with equal opportunities. It is an ideal which I hope to live for and to achieve. But if need be, it is an ideal for which I am prepared to die."

Social movements, political change, and organizational policy changes are all long-term endeavors. They require a *learning process perspective* on negotiation—attention to the short term in service of the long term. An article about Mandela in London's *Independent* newspaper described him as follows: "Mr. Mandela knows when to attack and when to retreat. He knows too the difference between what is possible and what is desirable." In the same article, John Carlin described Mandela's life as "a patient preparation for the moment when he would engage the Government at the negotiating table."[12]

Mandela's patient yet dogged persistence served him well. He was known for his propensity to examine all sides of a question and to get to know the enemy. Even during his eighteen years as a prisoner at Robben Island, South Africa's Alcatraz, Mandela practiced negotiation. He arranged for interviews with each new officer posted to run the prison. He sized up his adversaries both in and out of prison in anticipation of needing such information in later negotiations. He managed interactions of the moment with the intention of using what he learned to ultimately derive the ends he desired. One of Mandela's prison victories was the result of such activity:

> He rapidly got the measure of a commanding officer appointed in the early Seventies called Colonel Badenhorst—"Kid Ruction" to the prisoners. The colonel ruled his little empire by terror, routinely ordering prisoners to be strait-jacketed and beaten in their cells. One day a contingent of judges visited Robben Island on an inspection mission. The judges conducted an interview with Mr. Mandela, who had asked to be allowed to make representations to them on the prisoners' behalf. The Colonel insisted on being present. Michael Dingate, a Robben Island prisoner at the time recalled the scene some years later in testimony for a book on Mr. Mandela called *The Struggle Is My Life*. Kid Ruction butted in and made threats to Nelson: "Nelson, did I ever order you to be punished since I arrived here?" "No," said Nelson, "not me personally, but what you have done to some of my colleagues affects all of us. You are persecuting us." "Nelson!" interjected Kid Ruction, fuming and shaking his finger at Nelson right before the eyes of the judges. "You'll pay for this." Nelson, with an eloquent dumb expression, turned to the judges. That was all that was needed. Words, Mr. Mandela's considerable courtroom experience told him, were superfluous. Within weeks, Kid Ruction was removed from his post.[13]

Mandela knew that success in negotiation requires a thorough understanding of "the enemy" or the other side. He recognized the need for patient determination backed by thorough research and a clear understanding of the ultimate goal. This is the hallmark of a great negotiator, the kind who can change the course of history.

The point is that negotiations are multifaceted, relational, and often long-term interactions. Categorizing them as win-win or win-lose distorts the true na-

ture of the process and limits the potential outcome. Such pigeonholing fails to capture the versatility negotiators require, the adaptations they must make in their expectations and strategy. Certainly many negotiations (or parts thereof) are win-win and many are win-lose. Yet rather than merely monitoring the degree to which actions move toward or away from a predetermined goal, a negotiator needs to focus on managing factors that influence the process of relating and succeeding in the interaction at hand. Negotiators set themselves up for failure when they constantly measure their moves in relationships against some endpoint. Yes, they should know where they're going, but their minds should be mostly focused on the choice at hand: the next move and how it will affect their own and the other side's subsequent moves.

▶ VERSATILITY IN ACTION

Versatility in the formulation of assumptions is crucial to information gathering. Versatility in action refers to having at one's disposal a repertoire of responses. Communication is like chess in its complexity and in its process as well. Each player's move in chess limits or expands the moves available to the other player. In this sense, negotiators are interdependent, even if one has more power or some other factor apparently in his or her favor. In chess, the more expert players think beyond the current move to subsequent ones, to what the other player is likely to do if they take a particular course and how their own options will be limited or expanded in turn. They observe carefully and make sense of the types of actions the other side takes. The effective negotiator then selects, from a repertoire of words and nonverbal behaviors, those that will influence the other player to make a desired selection among moves available to him. In contrast, amateurs are easily led. They react to the moves of their opponents without sufficient forethought and so are easily lured by more expert communicators into abandoning their goals. Observe how the novice negotiator can, by virtue of limited action versatility, easily be taken off track:

> *Jim:* My review is coming up, and I thought it would be a good time to talk about my salary. I understand that several of my colleagues have had their scales upgraded.
>
> *Bob:* You know I can't talk about individual personnel issues, Jim. Those are confidential.
>
> *Jim:* I understand, but I know it's being done for them, so I'd like to move upscale as well.
>
> *Bob:* Have you gone over your written performance objectives?
>
> *Jim:* I thought we'd do that at my review. In the meantime, though, I've taken on new responsibilities, and I think I should be compensated accordingly.
>
> *Bob:* And it's great that you can still find time to think about those things. It seems like I spend most of mine lately trying to keep people on deadline.
>
> *Jim:* I know what you mean.

Bob: Is everything up to date with you?

Jim: Well, yes, just about everything.

Bob: Just about?

Jim: I'm having some difficulty getting callbacks on the Foster project.

Bob: Any other delays?

Jim: Well, we may have to push the budget meeting back until Sharon gets the numbers together.

Bob: Do I need to bring her in and work with her on that?

Jim: No, no . . . I can do that.

Bob: Well, then, do you need me to make the phone calls on the Foster thing?

Jim: No, you shouldn't have to do that.

Bob: Who should do it, then?

Jim: Me.

Bob: Listen, be sure to keep me updated on your progress. I don't want to be surprised.

Jim: Sure thing. On the salary thing . . .

Bob: First things first, Jim. You'd better review your performance objectives—after you have everything else under control.

Jim: Yeah, thanks, Bob. I'll let you get back to work.

Bob: Thanks. Any time.

Bob dexterously maneuvered Jim away from the salary issue onto an unrelated topic. He was able to do this because Jim was reacting, not consciously considering his next move. Bob slipped from the topic of a raise to project delays, then dismissed Jim's attempt to return to the subject of a raise as less significant than project concerns. Expert negotiators recognize such diversions and return the interaction to the track they desire. They are versatile in their responses. Let's see how Jim might have altered the course of the negotiation to his favor:

Jim: My review is coming up, and I thought it would be a good time to talk about my salary. I understand that several of my colleagues have had their scales upgraded.

Bob: You know I can't talk about individual personnel issues, Jim. Those are confidential.

Jim: You're absolutely right. And I'm only interested in the level of compensation my work merits.

Bob: Have you gone over your written performance objectives?

Jim: They're tattooed on my forehead. I see them in the mirror when I shave in the morning. Can I annotate a copy for you with a self-assessment we can go over?

Bob: It's great you can find the time to think about those things. It seems like I spend most of mine lately trying to keep people on deadline.

Jim: It's a major focus with me as well. I'm all over the Foster people to get me a response on the project, and I'm breathing down Sharon's neck for those budget numbers. Is there any part of the load I can take off your back?

Bob: I'll think about it. In the meantime, be sure to keep me updated. I don't want to be surprised.

Jim: Sure thing. I need to get back on the phone with some people, but this weekend I'll annotate those performance objectives to help your thinking on a salary increase.

Bob: No promises.

Jim: I understand. Thanks for taking the time on this.

▶ HOW A NEGOTIATOR ASSESSES AND INFLUENCES

When asking questions, the skilled negotiator is attempting to understand many things. The first of these is the type of talk the other side assumes they're engaged in and the patterns that emanate from this type of talk. Only then can he consider whether those need to be altered for him to achieve his goals and how that might be done. People don't simply talk. They engage in types of talk: greetings, discussions, debates, arguments: "Let's have a chat," "Now we're bonding," and "Can we discuss this?" Often they never mention the type of talk but operate on an unstated mutual understanding. In either case, the type of talk allows certain things to be said or done and prohibits others. "Let's have a chat" suggests informality and brevity, perhaps some soul-searching, but tends to exclude long-winded lectures and formal meetings.

When people argue, they can raise their voices and make personal attacks, but if they are debating a topic, such attacks should not occur. Discussions are not lectures, and jokes are not insults. Such definitions influence our verbal and nonverbal choices. Linguists and communication scientists study such categorizing at length; some reading of their work is useful for anyone who wants to negotiate more effectively. For our current purpose, it's sufficient to appreciate that what people say and do during all kinds of interaction depends on how they see what is going on—how they make sense of the interaction in terms of a definition or how they categorize it. Jim might have been more effective in his talk with Bob if he'd begun by saying, "Can we step away from team issues for a moment to talk about a personal one?" If Bob agreed to do so, he would then have been more likely to stay on Jim's subject. If Bob were to go off track anyway, Jim could remind him of their agreed-on focus.

Perhaps communication would be easier if people clearly and honestly articulated the types of interaction they intend to create: "Let's have a friendly discussion," "Do you suppose we could debate this topic objectively?" "Personal attack is not among my intentions" and other such declarations of communication plans do occur—but they're rare. People often just engage, letting the type of talk meander. Rather than launch into conversations this way, skilled negotiators seek to

assess and manage the type of interaction that emerges. If, for example, an altercation is developing and is likely to veer the negotiation onto a destructive path, a skilled negotiator will try to alter the direction by redefining its course. Such redefinition often looks like this:

> *Tom:* I've been very patient—more patient than some have. If you expect more of the same from me, you're wasting your time and mine.
>
> *Fran:* The last thing either of us wants, Tom, is to waste time. You have been patient, and that has been a considerable help in creating a cooperative mood during most of this negotiation.
>
> *Tom:* Cooperation is critical here. It has to be two-sided.
>
> *Fran:* In that spirit of cooperation, then, why don't we discuss where to go from here?

Here Fran has used Tom's words to foster a cooperative framework for subsequent discussions. She could have reacted to Tom's angry, defensive comments but instead chose to redefine the interaction from argument to cooperative exchange.

Negotiation is not a series of back-and-forth comments free of any overarching structure. We learn from an early age that the *how* of talk—the types of language choices we make—are guided by the *what* of talk, that is, the definition or category we place on it. Advancing from the fundamentals to skilled negotiation requires both a sophisticated understanding of the *what* of talk and expertise in the development of constructive talk definitions.

Research and our own observation tell us that a substantial portion of our daily interactions is scripted. We've participated in similar or nearly identical interactions so many times in the past that we know what to say and do without thinking at length. Imagine if each time we had a conversation, it seemed like a brand-new experience to us. We would not be able to identify the category of talk. We would have little sense of what to do in such interactions. We'd be confused—even dumbfounded—and we'd be groping for the right words to say. You've likely experienced such conversations—most of us have—but ideally, the vast preponderance of your interactions are much less enigmatic precisely because you know how to engage in them.

Suppose someone walks briskly by and says, "How are you?" Experience tells you that the person isn't really asking for a detailed description of your health but is simply enacting a brief greeting ritual type of talk. The person therefore expects you to reply, "Fine," or "Great. How are you?" Usually, such a question is asked out of habitual politeness. It's scripted, that is, learned so well that it occurs without conscious thought. So does the reply. A considered, lengthy reply isn't necessary. Suppose, however, that this person stops directly in your path. He looks intently into your eyes and asks, "How are you?" Your options have just been expanded. You're not unwittingly enacting a brief ritual; you're in a greeting discussion type of talk. Sure, you could just say, "I'm fine," and move along, but now you're free to say more—perhaps obligated to do so. You might mention that you're starting to feel tired because you've been overworked lately. If the other

person continues to express interest, you might elaborate further. However, if he replies that he's in a rush himself, you're likely to keep your remarks to a minimum. In both cases, however, if he thinks of himself as polite, he is likely to feel obliged to pause and listen or at least arrange a time when he can be more attentive to you. Those are the rules—implied, not stated.

Scripts like these enable us to function in society by guiding us to select acceptable behaviors. Chaos would reign if people said whatever they were thinking, whenever it came to mind. Imagine the kinds of conversations you'd find yourself in. It wouldn't be pretty. In fact, leaving your home in the morning would be a scary prospect. Since much of what we say and do is scripted, our choices are limited unless we chose to become alienated from society.

What all this means for negotiators is that the amount of guesswork required regarding what the other side might say is reduced once they recognize the type of talk they're engaged in. We know from operating in a given culture, for example, that certain types of initiating behaviors and responses are more likely to occur than others. We know how discussions, arguments, debates, and joking are likely to go, what's allowed and what's not. To the extent that we also know the personalities of people involved in a negotiation, their styles of communication, and other important information about them, our task of predicting their remarks is less onerous. Furthermore, as we become more versatile in communication, able to assess on the spot and to respond with thought instead of by habit, we reduce the capacity of others to accurately predict our action choices. Skilled negotiators are not open books. They manage their actions to affect the choices of their counterparts. They understand how scripts work, and they endeavor to avoid slipping into predictable, dysfunctional ones.

▶ THE UPS AND DOWNS OF INTERACTION

Researchers have taken many approaches to studying patterns of interaction that make people predictable. One approach assesses preferences for types of "moves" made. Some people assert themselves constantly. They tend to use mostly one-up moves (⇑). Others are prone to acquiesce (one-down, ⇓) or to sidestep (one-across, ⇒). If you know that someone is inclined to be assertive, especially if provoked, it is possible to manage interactions with that person.

Michael: You are coming on a bit strong in this planning document, aren't you? ⇑

Jessica: Are we? We were just trying to make a point. ⇓

Michael: Well, you sure did that. ⇑

Jessica: Do you think we overdid it? ⇓

Michael: It isn't what I think that counts. ⇑

Jessica: Did Mr. Jenkins say anything to you about it? ⇓

Michael: He didn't have to. You should have seen his expression. ⇑

Once you are able to detect such inclinations in direction, you are in a better position to manage or direct the other negotiator. Again, it's important to know your own inclinations in conversation so that you do not fall into the rut of predictability. It is also useful to determine whether you and your counterpart are creating a dysfunctional pattern. For example, if you both tend to use one-up statements, your interaction will be competitive. If you both tend to use one-down moves, little is likely to be accomplished. I recall standing in line to buy a pie behind an affectionate couple. Their conversation went like this:

She: What kind of pie would you like? ⇓

He: Why don't you pick this time? ⇓

She: That's OK. You pick. ⇓

He: Isn't it your turn? ⇓

This went on for some time, much to the chagrin of the salesperson and myself. I was about to suggest they buy pumpkin when the salesperson said, "The apple is good today." Unfortunately, this only launched the loving couple into another round of one-down comments: "Would you like apple?" "Well, if you would, that would be fine with me. . . ."

Given a tendency for people to reciprocate in kind, there's something to be said for responding to repetitive one-ups with a one-down. This tends to encourage the person who has been using one-up moves to acquiesce with a one-down move. Similarly, if two people are using one-down moves, a one-up move can spur the negotiation along, as the other party is more likely to reciprocate with some assertions of his or her own.

One-across moves are useful in negotiation because they can buy you time and give you a chance to think about how to proceed. By way of explanation, in Western cultures, the inclination is often to tell rather than to ask questions or to consider an issue in silence. As is the case with radio and television, "dead air" in conversation has become something to be avoided, not encouraged. Actually, however, a wise negotiator will resist the temptation to fill all space with assertions. Sometimes a one-across move, such as silence, a comment like "I see," or a pensive look accompanied by "Hmmm" or "Interesting" can buy time and help break a pattern that is hindering you from accomplishing your objective.

Nothing threatens communication versatility more than unchecked assumptions that elicit limiting scripts. Human beings operate most of the day on inference and judgment rather than fact. We see part of an event and infer other parts without checking those assumptions. Why don't more of us take this important step? It could be our cognitive laziness: We use far less of our brain capacity than we can and should. Negotiation mastery requires extensive cognitive stretching. No amount of memorizing strategies and tactics can make someone a proficient negotiator if they are stuck in scripts born of poor assumptions. The best negotiators are like Sherlock Holmes, dusting the back rooms for prints while others contentedly accept the most obvious—and therefore unreliable—clues. The skilled negotiator knows that every situation is multidimensional and therefore more complex than meets the eye.

Let's look for a moment at how easy it is to form limiting assumptions. Imagine meeting a stranger on a bus trip. This person smiles as you take a seat next to him. He moves his bags to provide more room for your feet and says, "Nice day for a trip." Your first impression would likely be that he is friendly. Research tells us that for every impression, there are associated impressions. The concept "friendly," for example, may be associated in your mind with "kind" and "reliable." What else constitutes a friendly person? Figure 2.2 depicts the assumptions you might make in forming a more extensive impression of the stranger.

In your experience, perhaps friendly people have also been courteous, outgoing, charming, generous, caring, considerate, and trustworthy. In a matter of moments, you can formulate a theory of a stranger's personality and thus a sense of what he or she might do during a bus trip. Let's continue the scenario: After three hours, the bus stops at a rest area. You ask the stranger if he'll keep an eye on your computer. He smiles and places the computer where he can watch it more easily. Usually you wouldn't let your valuable computer out of your sight on a trip, but this man is friendly and therefore has a number of other positive traits as well. When you return to the bus, you find that the stranger is gone. His bags are no longer where they were, and your expensive computer is gone as well. What does this mean for the personality theory you built on assumptions about outwardly friendly people? Figure 2.3 shows how your new theory might look.

This example demonstrates how unreliable assumptions can be. Yet each day, we base most of our actions—in negotiation and in life in general—on inference and judgment, rarely on fact. Expert negotiators know this. They know, too, that there are very few facts in guiding behavior in human interactions. Many of the conclusions we draw are based on our own unchecked assumptions and borrowed ones derived from gossip and hearsay. We operate in a sea of perceptions, which means that the world we live in is largely of our own making. Skilled negotiators know that perceptions can be modified, and they know how to do this. Consider the perceptions shared by many people around the world when President George W. Bush wanted to invade Iraq. Before we go further with this example, notice the word *wanted* in that sentence. Did he actually *want* to invade Iraq, or did he believe that he *must* invade Iraq? The two are very different ascribed motives and

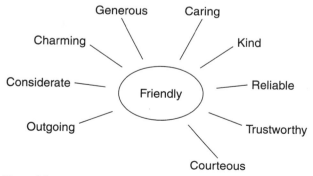

Figure 2.2 How Impressions Are Formed.

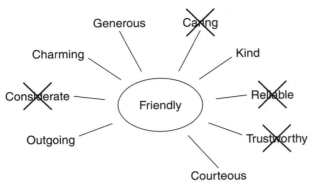

Figure 2.3 How Your New Theory Might Look.

lead to very different perceptions. On September 12, 2002, amid dissent from world leaders and even among his own advisors, President Bush appeared before the United Nations General Assembly and presented his case. Here are a few excerpts from his speech:

> The conduct of the Iraqi regime is a threat to the authority of the United Nations and a threat to peace. Iraq has answered a decade of U.N. demands with a decade of defiance. All the world now faces a test, and the United Nations, a difficult and defining moment. Are Security Council resolutions to be honored and enforced or cast aside without consequence? Will the United Nations serve the purpose of its founding, or will it be irrelevant?

> The United States helped found the United Nations. We want the United Nations to be effective and respectful and successful. We want the resolutions of the world's most important multilateral body to be enforced. And right now those resolutions are being unilaterally subverted by the Iraqi regime. Our partnership of nations can meet the test before us by making clear what we now expect of the Iraqi regime.

> My nation will work with the U.N. Security Council to meet our common challenge. If Iraq's regime defies us again, the world must move deliberately, decisively, to hold Iraq to account. We will work with the U.N. Security Council for the necessary resolutions. But the purposes of the United States should not be doubted. The Security Council resolutions will be enforced—the just demands of peace and security will be met—or action will be unavoidable. And a regime that has lost its legitimacy will also lose its power.

> We must stand up for our security and for the permanent rights and the hopes of mankind. By heritage and by choice, the United States of America will make that stand. And delegates to the United Nations, you have the power to make that stand as well.[14]

In each excerpt, the words he chose either confirmed or modified the assumptions of the U.N. representatives and the world leaders who were watching and listening. Those who thought he planned to order an attack on Iraq to finish what his father had started during Operation Desert Storm may have remained unconvinced that a less self-serving plan existed. Others may have been surprised

and pleased to hear President Bush offer to let the United Nations attempt to stop Saddam Hussein from continuing to violate U.N. sanctions before he would order the U.S. military to do so. The room was awash with perceptions that day, and it was on the basis of these perceptions that world peace might be promoted or destroyed.

All of us act on the basis of assumptions. When assumptions fail to facilitate negotiator goals, we must take time to alter them. *The best negotiators are fully aware of this; they are less concerned with who's right than with who thinks what and why. They are molders of perception, masters of discernment.* Thus they do not begin negotiations with firm statements of position but with questions designed to assess the accuracy of their own assumptions and the nature of the other party's assumptions.

Early on in all my negotiation classes and training sessions, I drive home the crucial role of questions in setting negotiations on a constructive track. Yet most people begin their first role-playing exercises by telling rather than asking. This is especially the case in the United States, where people are often admired for asserting their individuality, demonstrating their competence, and taking the lead. This is fine if the action's purpose is to take a hill in military action or save people from a fire. In negotiation, where the goal is to derive a desired outcome by encouraging the other party to see things at least somewhat your way and to share resources, a strong stance right at the start is often a foolhardy approach. It may feel good, but it is unlikely to help you attain what you want in the end.

▶ IN REVIEW

This chapter has been devoted to ways of thinking about negotiation. These form the foundation for strategies to be covered in subsequent chapters. Because we are taught from an early age to spare other people offensive information and to avoid wearing our hearts on our sleeves, we learn to choose our words carefully in most circumstances. This makes the critical information-gathering aspect of negotiation a challenging process. If all of us, at all times, were to place all our cards on the table, so to speak, there would be little need for interpretation of motive and meaning in negotiation.

Skillful negotiation calls for skillful questioning and constant vigilance in observation. Conditions continually change, and expert negotiators are aware of this. They carefully guard against slipping into dysfunctional, mindless scripts, while utilizing the tendency of most other negotiators to do so, to guide their choices.

Finally, expert negotiators understand how communication works. Like chess players, they think several moves ahead and in terms of how their moves will affect the other side's options. Their word choices and nonverbal gestures increase or decrease the likelihood of the other party's choosing to say or do something that takes the negotiation down a promising path. A number of key choice points must be identified and acted on if the negotiation is to bring about desired outcomes. Of course, this requires study and practice. Negotiation is not a simple process; its mastery is a long-term effort and is never truly complete. There may always be people who are better negotiators than you, but with each day of study and practice, their numbers dwindle.

▶ QUESTIONS

1. Describe in your own words a negotiation-versatile frame of mind and why it is important in negotiation.

2. What is sense-making? How does it apply to negotiation? Describe your own sense-making predispositions. Are you quick to judgment? Consider a recent negotiation in which you participated. How might greater sense-making efforts have influenced the outcome?

3. Observe an interaction between two friends. Analyze it in terms of one-up (⇑), one-down (⇓), and one-across (⇒) comments. How did the use of these types influence the outcome? Repeat this same process in an analysis of one of your own interactions. Do you use more of one type or are you versatile? How does that influence your conversation and negotiation outcomes?

4. Do you formulate assumptions quickly? Do you rely easily on these in predicting what others are likely to say or do? Ask your friends about your tendencies to formulate quick judgments. What did you learn and what might you change in order to become a more effective negotiator?

5. The next time you enter into a discussion, instead of presenting your perspective early on, ask questions of the other person. Report on what you learn from this approach.

CHAPTER ▶ **3**

Preparation and Planning

We move now from the concept of versatility based on a penchant for inquiry to putting it into practice in the initial stages of negotiation. This chapter introduces steps for learning about negotiation counterparts (intelligence gathering) and for formulating strategy. It also emphasizes and illustrates ways that negotiators can present reasoning and stretch beyond simplistic arguments. This kind of flexible thinking prevents negotiation derailment because it prepares the negotiator for the otherwise unexpected. Finally, it looks at how a negotiator's style influences such negotiator flexibility—one's counterpart's as well as one's own.

Most studies of business negotiation have focused on the face-to-face phase, perhaps because it seems the most exciting and challenging part. Yet experts repeatedly advise that the planning of negotiations is crucial to successful negotiation.[1] Nevertheless, time pressures and overconfidence often discourage negotiators from planning appropriately.

These same factors influence us in many new ventures. Let's say you've decided to try your hand at painting for the first time. You could just dive right in. Anyone can put paint to paper or canvas, you might assure yourself. But what if your career, your reputation, or future assignments depended on your success at this endeavor? Wouldn't you want to prepare, to learn about color, line, and texture? The answer depends largely on your inclination to prepare. *Planning inclination* is a social science measure of the degree to which people are prone or motivated to invest time in preparation.[2] You could probably give yourself a score on that dimension right now. If you are "planning inclined," research suggests that your outcomes will be more successful than those of your less preparation-inclined counterparts.

Of course, the inclination to prepare is, by itself, not sufficient. Knowing *what* it takes to prepare is vital. Among the many things a negotiator should know before commencing the interactive phase of negotiation are the following:

- The other parties' needs and interests, to a reasonable extent
- The resources available to the other parties
- The negotiation reputations and styles of the other parties

- The ability and authority of the other parties to make agreements
- Strategies and tactics the other side is likely to use
- A sense of the point at which the other parties are likely to walk away[3]

Although negotiations vary in terms of the amount of preparation required to succeed, these six components provide a useful guideline. The idea is to come up with a big picture of what is likely to happen during the negotiation and how you or your team will respond. Early in a negotiation, it's not always easy to identify what the issues are likely to be later, but advance preparation can provide some useful hints. Consider, for example, the choice of a vendor. If you know how a particular vendor's financial performance compares to that of his competitors, he may be willing to grant discounts. The vendor's staff members are aware not only that you are apprised of the company's weaknesses but also that you've researched the competition and hence understand your options. This is negotiation from a position of strength, enabled by preparation.

A second advantage gained by those who prepare for effective negotiation is a readiness to set the tone and direction of the negotiation. Taking a proactive stance in negotiations is usually the best approach. Why wait for the other party to set the agenda and tone? And in the event they beat you to it, why not be prepared to propose changes likely to bring you greater gains?

I give my students and training session participants a list of steps that are useful during prenegotiation discussions (see Exhibit 3.1). These steps will be covered in detail in subsequent chapters and reviewed at the end of the book. Experience indicates that if you bring this list to prenegotiation meetings and either use it as a guide for your team or review it yourself if you are the only negotiator, your likelihood of success will be enhanced significantly.

James Freund, author of *Smart Negotiating: How to Make Good Deals in the Real World,* refers to the kind of preparation in Exhibit 3.1 as a *negotiation game plan.* Freund proposes, as we discussed in Chapter 2, that we treat negotiation as neither totally competitive nor totally cooperative. Rather, it is a combination, much like ordering from a Chinese restaurant's menu. Competitive bargainers, he explains, can miss the mark by being absorbed in their own positions and thinking too little about the other side. But the more popular, cooperative view of negotiation has shortcomings as well. Here the error in preparation can be focusing too strongly on the other side's wants, needs, and problems, when the focus, Freund believes, should be more on how to influence the other party's thinking and conduct.[4]

Freund recommends conjoining the competitive side of negotiation with the cooperative—in other words, a dual-vantage-point approach to preparation. From the competitive side, the emphasis is on leverage, information, and gaining advantage. From the cooperative side, the emphasis is on problem solving (including solving the other party's problems), rationale development, and creative thinking. This is versatility in action. Freund's composite approach broadens the base from which negotiators can work effectively.

Let's say you've prepared only for a competitive negotiation. Cooperation by the other side may actually throw you off guard and cause you to be too easily satisfied. I can't tell you how many of my students, early in practice negotiations,

▶ *EXHIBIT 3.1*

STEPS IN PREPARING FOR NEGOTIATION

1. Organize your thoughts into primary issues, secondary issues, and clutter issues.
2. Organize primary issues into *ideal outcomes.*
3. For each primary issue and its ideal outcome, develop *contingency plans* and a *BATNA* (best alternative to negotiated agreement).

> IDEAL OUTCOME:
> CONTINGENCY GOAL A:
> CONTINGENCY GOAL B:
> CONTINGENCY GOAL C:
> BATNA:
> (Repeat for each primary issue.)

4. Decide how important maintaining the relationship is to your desired outcomes; this helps determine how much emphasis to put on relational issues.
5. Determine your opening tone (for example, apologetic, determined, higher calling, concerned) and consider how you will maintain that tone—or when to alter it—during the course of the negotiation.
6. Develop *frames* (analogies, metaphors, definitions) to describe your positions on each primary and secondary issue.
7. Decide what you will do in terms of body language to enhance your credibility, emphasize your position, maintain or improve the relationships, establish power, and be persuasive.
8. Decide how you will test your assumptions about your counterparts' *interests* and identify what they *truly* care about.
9. Identify any *common interests* you believe you share—ones that may serve as a bridge across perceived differences.
10. Decide how you will *link* your interests to those of the other side.
11. Determine your *strongest claims* for each of your ideal outcomes and your strongest *data,* especially *objective criteria.*
12. Consider what weaknesses your counterparts might point out and how you will then defend your position.
13. In terms of each ideal outcome, identify what you are willing to concede that the others may want—and what you are definitely unwilling to concede (at least at this point).
14. Decide what you will ask for when you make concessions.
15. Plan what to do or say if something *the others* do or say starts to pull you off track (into clutter issues, placing the blame, focusing on the past rather than the future).
16. Watch out for words that frame the discussion in ways not helpful to your desired outcomes.
17. Plan what kinds of *questions* you might ask of the others if they begin to focus on clutter issues.
18. Consider how you will *involve* them in the development of the solution.
19. Consider which *persuasion strategies* might prove useful.
20. Remember to clarify and secure commitments.

have given away the store because they'd prepared for resistance and instead met cooperation. Others, however, go in expecting cooperation and find themselves facing what they view as irrational resistance. In such cases, they often become fed up with the other side and leave the negotiation with far less than they would have obtained had they prepared for competitive styles of negotiation. If you've prepared only for a cooperative negotiation, you may be similarly caught off guard by the other side's hard-nosed tactics and refusal to seek mutual gain.

The composite approach will prepare you for a greater number of eventualities. As business expert Henry Minzberg has stated, "Setting oneself on a predetermined course into unknown waters is the perfect way to sail straight into an iceberg."[5]

► INTELLIGENCE GATHERING

To prepare adequately for cooperative and competitive eventualities, the skilled negotiator gathers intelligence. Following is a list of various forms of intelligence that should be amassed in the service of effective negotiation. As we've discussed, negotiators must be diligent about ensuring that the information they gather accurately represents their counterpart's true perceptions.

- Interests—mutual and divergent
- Concerns—mutual and divergent
- Emotional issues
- Primary claims
- Evidentiary support—strengths and weaknesses
- Potential avenues around resistance
- Style compatibility considerations

It is widely accepted that an understanding of each party's *key interests* and how they align is crucial. How one achieves this understanding has received less attention. Typically, sophisticated intelligence gathering involves asking strategic questions and observing how they are answered. Most people are not very good liars. Many are uneasy providing only part of the truth. When they are attempting to deceive, their bodies provide clues. Astute intelligence gatherers take notice of these clues. Could information being withheld at this point prove valuable? If this is likely, the next step is to ask questions or disclose information that enables you to test the waters, so to speak.

Robert Redford, actor, director, producer, and founder of the Sundance Institute—an incubator for independent films—described for the *Harvard Business Review (HBR)* the importance of identifying the other side's interests: "I learned that the corporate powers that be aren't going to be interested in the fruits of your labor and passion unless you are adept at understanding their agenda and speaking their language. You must always present yourself more conservatively than you privately feel you are. You can't be forceful, loud, confrontational, or declarative. You have to sell what you have on their terms."[6]

"Selling on their terms" means knowing the other parties' interests, their desires, their deep-seated beliefs, and what they're likely to do. It means under-

standing and appreciating how they communicate, the ways they position their ideas, and their negotiation styles. As Redford learned, if your natural style is at odds with the other negotiator's, strong arguments alone won't suffice to advance your views successfully.

Redford is a consummate businessman who has mastered the extraordinarily difficult businesses of movies and politics. I've read few descriptions of how negotiation works that are as informative and concise in the process as those he provided to *HBR*.

> Well, let's face it—if you're a movie star, you're not likely to be taken seriously. I remember a moment in 1969, when I was asked to speak to a group of 300 bankers in Utah just after I'd purchased the Sundance property. I was nervous and gave a blistering, preaching speech to these bankers about corporate greed and whatnot. At the end, I was greeted with dead silence. As they filed out, the head of the group said, "I appreciate your comments. I just have one question." I was expecting him to say something like "What the hell do you know about banking?" But all he asked was "Did you really jump off that cliff in *Butch Cassidy*?"[7]

Whether right or wrong, eloquent or simple, if your ideas are not phrased in a way that encourages others to listen and learn, they won't do either, not even if you're Robert Redford. So what chance do the rest of us have? Probably a good chance, if we learn, as Redford did, what they care about and how to speak their language. When starting conversations with members of Congress, he focuses on their interests: "For example, you say, 'I know your part of the country,' and start on common ground that isn't political. Once you establish that connection, you can say, 'I understand there are other views, but here's mine.' And then you carefully, intelligently, and rationally lay out your argument, based on a lot of research and absolute control of your information."[8]

Although it's never sufficient simply to use words in a manner the other side will accept, it is crucial to do so. Then you need to back it up with substance, a command of the subject at hand, and persuasive evidence supporting your side, tempered by a true understanding and expressed appreciation of the other negotiator's side.

If you think the other person is deliberately withholding information or deceiving you, making an overt accusation could propel the negotiation in an unproductive direction. Initially, meeting obtuseness with obtuseness is often the best course of action. This approach can be described as "dancing around the issue." Gradually, you dance closer to the core by posing questions of increasing directness or by implying that you know rather more about the issue at hand than the other party may have supposed (so they'd be better off by revealing more to you than by appearing deceitful).

Another strategy for unearthing interests is *apparent self-disclosure*—sharing what appears to be personally held or confidential information, with the aim of eliciting reciprocal disclosure from the other party. Reciprocity is a rule of human behavior; if one person provides something valuable to another, the latter will likely feel at least some obligation to respond in kind. Negotiators may "give away" information specifically in order to elicit a reciprocal response from

their counterpart ("To be perfectly honest, I do have a hidden agenda of sorts. It is . . ."). Because reciprocity is a learned reaction that people often fail to consider carefully, this approach to obtaining valuable information can be more effective than employing direct questions alone.

Another indirect way of eliciting information is to create a hypothetical situation that mirrors the present one. One might, for example, describe a prior negotiation similar to the one at hand, pointing out that the real interests of both parties were never made evident and so prevented them from reaching an agreement. This storytelling approach has other uses as well, but as a way of encouraging others to share information, it can be an effective tool.

More direct approaches involve making statements that indicate one's awareness of hidden agendas or disguised intentions ("There's no hiding the fact that we are both aware . . ." or "I can't help but think that the real issue here is . . .") or asking questions that go to the heart of things ("Would you say the highest priority here is not X but really Y?" or "If you were to list what really matters to you, would you put X first or Y?"). Such probing questions can be posed in nonthreatening ways, as a search for useful information rather than an effort to entrap. We can view questions as being placed along a continuum from "dancing" to "closing in." Your choice of question should depend on factors such as the following:

- How willing the negotiator is to patiently unearth important matters
- The personal styles of the various negotiators
- How delicate the issue at hand is
- Whether relative power is balanced, in your favor, or in your disfavor

In most negotiations, both direct and indirect approaches are used in combination, beginning with indirectness and becoming more direct if the prior approach proves unproductive.

Once the parties' primary interests have been identified, the next step is to separate them along a mutual-to-divergent continuum. Again, perception is key. Interests that appear divergent to one negotiator may seem mutual to another. To the extent that both parties perceive their interests as mutual, either cooperative or integrative negotiation is likely. Where interests appear divergent, then antagonistic, distributive forms of negotiation tend to emerge. It behooves the negotiator who prefers mutual-gain negotiations to discover and show how interests that initially seem disparate are indeed compatible. We'll discuss how this is done when we review the technique of framing. For now, recognize that the process of identifying interests, prioritizing them, and categorizing them is crucial to a strong start.

The same process applies to *concerns*. As each negotiator brings interests and goals to the table, he or she also brings worries—about how things might go awry or how they will then appear to superiors or even whether the negotiation will threaten an interpersonal relationship. Such concerns may be rational or not. One thing is certain: Failure to address others' concerns adequately poses a hazard to successful negotiation.

Related to concerns are *emotions.* Often people are or become emotionally involved with issues or positions at the heart of negotiations. When I spoke with an entrepreneur who was about to sell his company for around $20 million, he said that negotiations had nearly resulted in a deal twice previously but had fallen through largely because he wasn't sure he wanted to sell the company he'd made so successful. This is often referred to as the *endowment effect*—the emotional attachment one has to a key item or idea. Occasionally, I ask my students how much they're willing to pay for a ring I'm wearing. There's always someone who flippantly offers me 50 cents, but most bids are in the hundreds of dollars. Then I tell them that because my husband gave me this ring on our tenth anniversary, I would never part with it at any price. This remark usually sends the bids soaring. When they reach around $25,000, the students say I appear to waver. Of course, I deny doing this! Emotional attachment is as important as any rational argument in negotiation. When emotions are ignored, negotiations are often doomed.

The three key perspective-shaping factors—interests, concerns, and emotions—form an acronym, ICE, that makes a convenient mnemonic device I call the ICE model (see Figure 3.1). Before diving into negotiation, these should be assessed—not assumed. If among your co-negotiator's interests, concerns, and emotions are the factors likely to prove detrimental to desired outcomes, you need to take steps early—and sometimes during the negotiation—to address or reduce their importance.

Once you've identified interests, concerns, and emotions and made efforts to prioritize and address them in a manner conducive to achieving your goals, the next step is to establish some *process guidelines* for the negotiation, including an agenda. Process guidelines include the following:

- Who will start
- Order of topics to be addressed
- Time to be allocated to each topic
- Issues that should *not* be addressed during the negotiation

In short, negotiating *about* the negotiation should take place beforehand to avoid rambling and hazardous diversions. In-person meetings may not be required for this phase. Phone calls, e-mails, and other communications often suffice. Neglect this step, and considerable amounts of time and effort that would otherwise advance the negotiation can be wasted while the parties debate process

Figure 3.1 The ICE Model: Three Key Perspective-Shaping Factors.

▶ *CASE STUDY 3-1*

ACME COMPANY'S NEW MARKET STRATEGY

Roger and Bill have worked together at Acme Company for six years. They are good friends. They've disagreed occasionally, but this has never affected their relationship.

Recently, Roger was promoted to marketing vice president. He has become Bill's boss. While Bill believes that he was equally qualified for the job, he doesn't begrudge Roger his success.

Over the years, Roger and Bill have been quite candid about their opinions of other workers. Bill has been especially vocal in his estimate of a colleague named Liam. According to Bill, Liam has an undeserved superiority complex. He's rude and aggressive to a fault. Roger has always enjoyed listening to Bill's vivid descriptions of Liam's faults. His own view has always been that Liam, though poorly socialized, is a competent worker.

Last week, Roger learned that his first task as marketing head will be an important one. Acme is going after a competitor's market. It will require all the strategic expertise the marketing department can muster. Roger knows that he will need his most talented people to work on this project. It might be difficult, but Bill and Liam will just have to work together. To avoid the appearance of favoritism, Roger has not given anyone the leadership role on the project.

In his characteristic manner, Liam, during the initial planning meeting, took every opportunity to cut Bill off in an effort to advance his own ideas. Some of those ideas were quite good. Roger is impressed with the background research Liam has done and the creative ideas he has generated. If they are to capture this market successfully, Bill and Liam will have to work together even if it means occasionally tolerating Liam's boorish behavior.

At the initial meeting, Bill had all he could manage just avoiding an altercation with Liam. He knew that Roger wanted this project to work. But he felt somewhat betrayed by Roger's convenient lapse of memory concerning Bill's feelings toward Liam. This was only exacerbated by Roger's apparent appreciation of Liam's ideas and disregard of Liam's tactics.

In an effort to make things work, Bill arranged to meet individually with Liam. They discussed the project for several hours and came up with a creative marketing strategy. It could honestly be said that both had contributed equally. Roger was pleased.

This morning, Liam arrived at work early. When Roger came in, Liam presented him with his own revised version of yesterday's plan. Roger assumed that Liam had cleared the revisions with Bill. They were good suggestions. Roger told Liam to go ahead with the revised plan. Later this morning, Bill, Liam, and the marketing staff met to go over the plan. Without warning, Liam announced that revisions had been made and had been okayed by the vice president. Bill was shocked. He arranged a private meeting with Roger.

issues. Furthermore, when such discussions become heated, they may irreparably damage the negotiation.

The next crucial step during the early stages of negotiation is to identify *primary claims*. These are the statements about interests that each negotiator is likely to make. Let's look for a moment at a case and identify the primary claims.

When Bill meets with Roger, what might be his primary claims regarding Liam and his motives? Here are some possibilities:

- "Liam is trying to impress you at my expense."

- "Liam purposely waited until I wasn't around to show you the report so that he could take full credit."

He might also make claims like these:

- "It is impossible for me to work with Liam."
- "Placing Liam in a leadership role undermines our project."

If Roger wants to persuade Bill that a different claim better represents the situation, it would be useful for him to identify the weaknesses in Bill's argument. Stephen Toulmin, expert in the study of human reason, developed a model depicting how arguments are structured.[9] A somewhat simplified form is shown in Figure 3.2.

The *claim* is the conclusion, or position, for which you are arguing. The *data* are the evidence or reasons supporting the claim. Every linkage of data to a claim is supported by what Toulmin terms a *warrant* (similar to a rule). A warrant is a general statement that indicates why the data are supportive of the claim. A warrant may be a chain of logic or a principle. The *backing* is a condition, reason, or justification that supports the warrant. If we take the claim "Liam is trying to impress you at my expense," what might Bill's data for this be? As shown in Figure 3.3, one element could be "He went to you without me, even though we're leading this project together." If he uses that as primary data, the warrant supporting the link between data and claim might be the rule "Fair-minded people avoid going behind the backs of fellow team members." The backing might then be, "Because that's the way things are generally done in business."

Effective negotiation requires dissecting reasoning, both your own and that of the other negotiators. Dissecting your own reasoning allows you to see the weaknesses before they are identified and exploited by your counterpart. If we look again at Bill's claim and the supporting data, there are evident weaknesses. The warrant "People who play fair don't go behind the backs of team members" may be generally true. Roger could, however, dismiss it by claiming that he is more concerned about getting a good report than he is with petty issues of fairness and assigning blame. He might also agree that the rule is generally true but that a spontaneous meeting hardly constitutes going behind someone's back, so

Figure 3.2 Toulmin's Model: How Arguments Are Structured.
Source: S. E. Toulmin, *The Uses of Argument* (New York: Cambridge University Press, 1958).

Figure 3.3 Toulmin's Model: An Example.

the rule does not apply. An alternative approach would be for Roger to say that while the rule applies, he doesn't believe the claim follows. His reasoning here might be that Liam was trying to advance the project for all involved, and although he should think twice next time before neglecting to include Bill, he was not trying to impress the boss; he merely made a mistake. If Roger responds this way, it suggests that Bill may have failed to provide the best data supporting the claim that Liam intended to impress Roger. Better data might include Liam's past behaviors, of which Roger is fully aware, which suggest that he is quite capable of putting his needs above those of others. Bill's claim may be at issue as well. Roger might be less concerned with efforts to impress him than he is with efforts to undermine the project. In fact, he may be flattered by efforts to impress him.

By examining the likely arguments in advance of the negotiation, you can identify weaknesses in reasoning and increase your likelihood of preparing the best claims and supporting data, warrants, and backing. If Bill knows, as suggested, that Roger's primary interest is the advancement of the project, a better claim would be, "What Bill did caused team distrust and undermined the project." His data could then consist of team members' comments to that effect. The warrant follows: "In conditions of distrust, teamwork is compromised." The backing here might be years of experience seeing teams damaged by distrust, Roger's own experience, something Roger said once, or even research on the topic of trust in teams.

There is no one correct claim in this case, but some are sturdier than others and stand up better under attack. Negotiators should lead with their best claims, those least likely to collapse quickly under challenge. The best claims are the ones that the other party is likely to believe and care about. Otherwise, claims tend to fall on deaf ears; they will probably be dismissed no matter how well supported they may be. For example, if Bill leads with a claim about Liams unfair actions, Roger might reply, "Listen, you and I both know Liam's faults, but they aren't the

issue here. You need to get the job done with him—I can't baby-sit." Instead, were Bill to lead by discussing the damage Liam's actions have caused the team, Roger might be more inclined to intervene in some way—at least, perhaps, with a casual warning to Liam. Even more effective might be a claim that rises above any pettiness and focuses strongly on what Roger cares about.

If you were Bill, what would be your strongest claim? How would you lead into the discussion with Roger? What would be your data, warrant, and backing? Are there weaknesses among them? If so, how would you bolster your claim if Roger remarks on one of those weaknesses?

You can use the diagram in Figure 3.4 to select your claim and support it.

A claim likely to get Roger's attention is, "If Liam continues to operate this way, he may misinform you. That's my biggest concern." The data might be business examples in which a "loose cannon" acted impulsively and ruined an important project. The rules might be, "If it happened once, it can happen again" or "Once bitten, twice shy." The backing could be, "Experience is the best teacher."

It's always useful to have backup data as well. In this case, it might be a time when Liam acted similarly and the project suffered. It might be a time when Roger was leading a project and someone acted as Liam is acting now and the results were devastating. Of course, it's important that such data fit the current situation, so that Roger can't respond, "That was an entirely different scenario," or "That person was crazy. Liam isn't crazy."

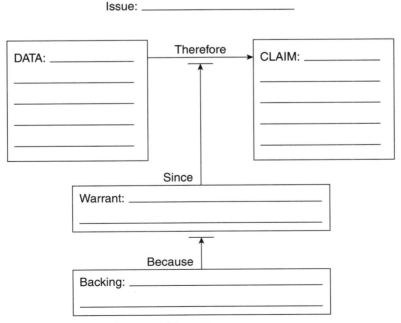

Figure 3.4 Using Toulmin's Model: An Exercise.

The process of selecting and supporting primary claims is essential to successful negotiation. It is a step often overlooked yet one to which negotiators should devote as much time as possible. Advocates and debaters in courtrooms, colleges, congresses, offices, and back rooms everywhere prepare by learning their opponents' arguments and determining where their strengths and weaknesses lie. Likewise, this process is imperative to negotiating effectively.

When selecting claims, you should ask a number of questions:

- Why will my counterparts care about this claim?
- Is this the claim about which they are likely to care most?
- Should I provide reasons why they should care about the claim before I introduce it, concurrently, or after the claim has been made?
- What are my backup claims should this one fail? What is the support for those?
- What is my order of priority for backup claims?
- Have I chosen the strongest data, warrants, and backing for primary and backup claims?
- What are the weaknesses? How will I respond to them?
- Under what circumstances will I discard a claim and move to another?
- Under what circumstances will I persist in advancing a claim and in what manner?
- Even if the reasoning is strong, is it possible that they will dismiss its application to this situation? If that happens, how will I convince them of its relevance?
- What counterclaim are they likely to present? How will I proceed in each case?

Let's look briefly at handling counterclaims. To Bill's claim about the undermining of the team, Roger might respond with a claim of his own: "If this team is so easily undermined, something is very wrong." What should Bill say now that Roger has set the interaction on a different path? If Bill has prepared well, he should have a ready response for this. He might reply, "It's a new team, a very promising team, but its development has now been shaken somewhat." Bill positions the team's disturbance as reasonable, given its "greenness." He might provide data in the form of comments from team members. "One member said he wondered if Liam would take it on himself to implement the changes that will make him look good, rather than the ones the team recommends." The warrant here is, "If one member is unsettled, others are likely unsettled as well." Bill might add that other members had made comments of a similar nature. These extra data both support the claim and make the rule more relevant. Bill could say, "The team is not irreparably damaged, but if this continues, it could be harmful." This addresses Roger's concern while indicating that the team is a good one. It also refocuses the discussion on Liam's actions.

Bill's next claim might involve a solution: "It would help if you let Liam know you want the team to be represented in his next report to you. That's all we're asking." The word *we* positions the proposal as coming not from Bill alone but from the team, thereby reducing the likelihood that Roger will perceive it as a petty proposal serving only one person's interests. Bill asks Roger to "help" rather than totally take over and avoids telling Roger what to say. He leaves Roger much room for personal discretion. He focuses on the primary problem; positions Roger's desired response as supportive of the team; and indicates that if this is done, the team will be able to refocus all its energies on its task. He also implies that this request is somewhat minor, even if quite helpful.

It's very important, when developing claims and their supportive structures, to remain versatile by considering the possible counterclaims that the other party may introduce. No matter how "steel trap" your reasoning, good negotiators can wriggle their way out of responding as you expect. They might dismiss your reasoning as not applicable in this case or propose that in any other situation they'd respond as you chose, but they simply can't this time. They might create delays or present an irrational response to frustrate you and cause you to detour to another position. I mention this because it is insufficient to have strong claims, data, warrants, and backing. Like a traveling salesperson, you must be prepared for rejection. Have other supported claims available, so that if one door closes, you can open another one.

One way to think of this is in terms of a house—let's call it the house of negotiation opportunity. Most people approach a house at the front door, as shown in Figure 3.5. When they receive no answer, they may knock again or simply leave. In this way, a good number of negotiators give up easily. They are the early leavers.

Figure 3.5 The House of Negotiation Opportunity: Trying Only the Front Door.

Astute negotiators are not so easily satisfied. They assume that perhaps someone is in the backyard or doing something that precludes them from hearing their knock at the door. And so they proceed to check that assumption (see Figure 3.6).

The most persistent of negotiators don't even accept a lack of response to a second try or even a third. They believe that there is almost always an entry to an important issue. And so they are likely to conduct an extensive search for that entry (see Figure 3.7). Like any house, negotiation has many possible means of entry. If one claim does not work, even if it appeared at first to be your best, you should consider an alternative. After practicing this approach, you'll learn to spot openings more readily than others do.

To the extent that you've adequately prepared claims in a likely order of presentation and have supported them well, opportunities will be afforded. Negotiators who skip this crucial step must hope that easily seen doors and windows will open to them. That is an approach of weakness, one likely to result in suboptimal negotiation outcomes.

In line with the view that usually there are a number of ways to approach an issue, let's look at Tony Buzan's work on mind maps.[10] Mind mapping is a technique for expanding thought and, in terms of negotiation, for expanding perceived options. When speaking publicly, Buzan often asks people to list the uses of a paper clip. Most people come up with four or five. Then he asks them to list things you *can't* do with a paper clip. Those lists tend to be much longer. Why, Buzan asks? Is it because there are more things you can't do with a paper clip than things you can do? Or is it because by the time the second question is asked, the mind has already had some practice thinking beyond the obvious? It is freed from some of its constraints and therefore comes up with more options. Buzan explains that we use so little of our minds during much of each day that we can derive considerable benefit from stretching it. One way of stretching, a way useful to

Figure 3.6 The House of Negotiation Opportunity: Trying Several Possibilities.

Figure 3.7 The House of Negotiation Opportunity: Trying Every Possibility.

negotiation, is to practice thinking of negotiation choice points in terms of multiple options. Figure 3.8 is a map I developed and then shared with Tony Buzan. It demonstrates the utility of mind maps in negotiation—in this case, when an impasse is anticipated or actually reached.

When preparing for negotiation, it is possible to anticipate potential areas of disagreement. These areas of disagreement may be depicted, as in the mind map in Figure 3.8, as central impasse points from which a number of potential avenues emanate. Skilled negotiators think in such terms. They may or may not draw mind maps, but they do think in terms of multiple options or avenues, and in doing so they journey beyond the obvious ones. Writing your own mind maps on paper has the advantage that you can refer to them during negotiation sessions. You can develop mind maps for each negotiation issue as well. One of Bill's mind maps for approaching Roger might look like that shown in Figure 3.9.

Thinking in terms of multiple options is one of the most challenging aspects of negotiation. Since our minds prefer to do less, we are inclined to zero in on one or two options and leave it at that. Skillful negotiation requires a reluctance to consider only easy or obvious options. Borrowing from Buzan's mind mapping as a practice device can stretch negotiators to think beyond simplistic approaches. The versatile mind-set is an inquisitive one, convinced that behind the rubble of distraction and barriers lie choices that an inexperienced negotiator is likely to have overlooked. Once you start working in this fashion—once you are not easily satisfied—you will be making progress toward expertise in negotiation. Add to your new mind-set the practice of placing on paper or keeping in mind the options available to you at various junctures in negotiation, and you will achieve a considerable advantage even before the negotiation has begun. Figure 3.9

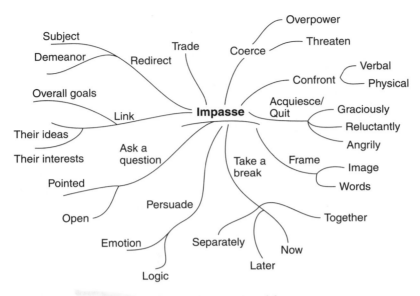

Figure 3.8 Negotiation Mind Map: Opportunity Elaboration.

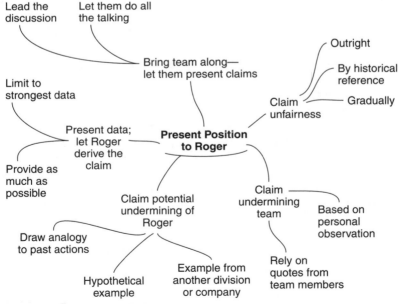

Figure 3.9 Negotiation Mind Map: An Example.

demonstrates how Bill might map his options prior to meeting with Roger. If one fails, he can turn to another.

▶ CHOICE POINT CONTRIVANCE AND RESPONSE

Sometimes there is no obvious path in negotiation, so you have to make one. Skilled negotiators *contrive choice points.* In advance of a negotiating session, they consider what they might say or do to increase the likelihood of opportunities arising that are favorable to their goals. One way to do this is to manage assumptions and categories of talk in such a way that desired types of comments are likely to occur.

When choice points have not been expected or contrived, negotiators must be ready to respond in ways that facilitate their goals. Over time, skilled negotiators learn that certain types of responses tend to work with particular types of choice points. Let's look, for example, at instances of personal attack or blaming. If this kind of situation is likely to arise in a negotiation, experienced negotiators know that. They are rarely blindsided by the unexpected. They ask themselves in advance of the negotiation, or at least at the first sign of impending attack, *How should I respond if an unflattering comment is made about me?* Perhaps the answer to that question is, *I'll focus on the future, not on the past. If they attempt to draw me into placing blame, I'll say, "It would be easy for us to take a tit-for-tat approach here, but it wouldn't move us along to the favorable outcome we both seek."* If that's too wordy or too lofty for you, another option is to say, *"I'm sure neither of us is without regrets, but let's focus on our future rather than our past."*

Consider the following conversation and how the application of the solutions just mentioned might work.

Alan: We need to come to some resolution on how we should proceed from here.

Sam: I agree.

Alan: I don't want a replay of the last meeting, where your team literally usurped the process, totally ignoring the needs of my team.

Sam: I know it seemed that way.

Alan: (angrily) Seemed that way? Who are you kidding? I'm not stupid, Sam. Your people went for the jugular, and you let it happen.

Sam: Does paranoia run in your family?

Alan: I hope you were being funny.

Sam: I don't have to sit here dodging attacks from you. This is a serious situation, and my team is as anxious as yours is to find a good solution.

Alan: I am just letting you know that we will not sit still for the same kind of backstabbing at the next meeting.

Sam: Let's just focus on what we need to do. I don't have time for making you feel good.

This type of interaction is not uncommon in some organizations. There are choice points along the way in this conversation that, if responded to wisely, could lead to a much more positive outcome for both sides. For example, when Sam decides to respond to Alan's anger with a flippant remark about paranoia, he invites further problems. How might he address what Alan said without further alienating him, without accepting blame, without appearing weak, and in a way that puts the interaction on a positive track?

Here are some options:

- "What happened last week was as unacceptable as it was unintentional. It's a part of the past. Shall we move on?"

- "I've spoken with my team, and we all agree that any actions that might cause you to feel that way aren't productive. They'll be avoided, I can assure you that."

- "Things happened on both sides last week that are regrettable. We both know what they are, and I'm sure neither side wants a repeat."

- "We're in this together. We're going to have our differences now and then, as we did last week, but we can get past them, and we should."

The more prepared a negotiator is in terms of knowing the types of choice points likely to occur and how to contrive conducive ones, the better the chances of negotiations going well.

▶ ASSESSING STYLE

Another important form of intelligence gathering in the preparation phase of negotiation involves assessment of style compatibility. Even if you've identified a number of potential avenues for approaching key issues, if your negotiation counterpart's style preference is incompatible with your own, those avenues are likely to be blocked.

Alan Rowe, a colleague at the University of Southern California, and I developed an instrument for assessing your own negotiation style, presented in Exhibit 3.2. Take a few minutes to complete it. For each question, enter an 8 for the response most like you during negotiations, a 4 for the item second most like you, a 2 for the one third most like you, and finally a 1. After you complete each row, there should be only one 8, one 4, one 2, and one 1.

Once you have completed the inventory, add each column. The four numbers at the bottom should sum to 300 if you have filled in the inventory as directed and if you have added correctly. At that point, you are ready to identify your style preferences. If your highest score was in the left-hand column, one of your predominant styles is that of an *Achiever.* Achievers usually go right to the heart of an issue, moving things along quickly. They have little patience for long-winded logic, and they want to win. They avoid concessions whenever possible.

If your highest score was in the second column, you are inclined to be an *Analytical.* This type of negotiator provides a good deal of data and is inclined to walk people through his or her reasoning step by step. Such negotiators speak in

NEGOTIATION STYLE INVENTORY

You must answer all the questions. There are no right or wrong answers. The answers reflect how you see yourself, so respond with what comes first to your mind.

1. When I negotiate, I	focus on my objectives	4	explore workable solutions	8	try to understand their thinking	2	try to avoid arguments	1
2. I explain my ideas best by	being forceful	1	presenting my ideas logically	8	explaining the implication	7	relating my points to theirs	2
3. When I am confronted, I	react strongly to what is said	2	explain my position with facts	8	look for a common ground	4	give in reluctantly	1
4. I describe my expectations	objectively	8	in complete detail	1	enthusiastically	4	amicably	2
5. I get my best deals when I	don't make any concessions	1	utilize my leverage	8	find creative solutions	4	am willing to meet them halfway	2
6. My objective in negotiation is to	achieve my goal	2	convince others to accept my position	8	find the best solution for all	1	look for an acceptable solution	4
7. The way to win an argument is to	be self-confident	4	be logical	8	have novel ideas	3	look for consensus	1
8. I prefer information that	is specific and understandable	4	is complete and persuasive	8	shows a number of options	2	helps achieve rapport	1
9. When I'm not sure what to do, I	take direct action	1	search for possible solutions	4	rely on my intuition	8	seek advice from others	2
10. I dislike	long debates	2	incomplete information	8	highly technical material	1	having arguments	4
11. If I've been rejected, I	persist in my point of view	4	rethink my position	8	relate my ideas to theirs	2	try to salvage the relationship	1
12. If timing is important, I	press for a quick decision	2	rely on critical facts	8	propose a compromise	4	hope to postpone the inevitable	1
13. When I am questioned, I	answer emphatically	2	rely on data for my position	8	respond with a broad question	4	look at how it affects me	1
14. I prefer situations where	I am in control	8	I can utilize my logical ability	2	I can explore new opportunities	4	people are considerate	1
15. I negotiate best when	I use my experience	2	a technical analysis is critical	8	I can explore many alternatives	4	I am in a win-win situation	1
16. When I am the underdog, I	do not show any weakness	2	prepare carefully	8	try to change the situation	4	match my needs with theirs	1
17. When one is antagonistic, I	stand my ground	2	reason things out carefully	4	attempt to rise above the situation	8	look for ways to reduce the tension	1

(continued)

18. If I'm in a losing situation, I	become more determined	consider all my options	look for ways to turn it around	appeal to the others' sense of fairness
19. To achieve mutual gain, I	show a workable solution	clarify everyone's priorities	suggest a mutually beneficial plan	consider both sides of the issue
20. In negotiating, it is important to	know what each party wants	clearly identify the agenda	start by making a positive impression	recognize that each party has needs

Totals: 59 51 80 10

Source: Alan J. Rowe and Kathleen K. Reardon, version 3/27/98.

terms of priorities, and if they make concessions, they tend to make them along those lines.

The *Motivator* scores high in column three. Such negotiators pride themselves on finding clever, novel ways of reaching solutions. They also express enthusiasm in a contagious fashion.

Finally, the *Mediator* is one who scores high in the fourth column. Mediators like to help people find ways to agree. They are inclined to seek compromise or to accommodate so things will work out well for everyone.

Most people have at least two styles on which they score relatively high. The scores may be close together, in which case either style is comfortable, or a substantial number of points may separate them. In this case, the one with the highest score is your *primary style* and the second one is your *backup style*. Occasionally, people score closely on more than two. In some cases, they score closely on three and very low on one. This tells you that you move rather comfortably among the three styles with higher scores but the final one is difficult for you.

As you can see, each style type is potentially in conflict with the other types. An Achiever, for example, could become very annoyed with an Analytical, who provides too much data; with a Motivator, who appears to be a dreamer rather than a doer; or with a Mediator, who seems to be looking for happy endings instead of desired, task-related outcomes. If you are negotiating with someone with entirely or largely different style preferences, there is a good chance that the negotiation will be compromised. If you have a backup style that matches—not in score, but in terms of your own and the other person's comfort in using it—you may be able to bridge your differences by using this style. When styles are at odds, though, and backup styles don't mesh either, the mix isn't conducive to successful negotiation. It's important to know whether you can stretch to communicate with someone whose style differs from yours. If not, perhaps it would be prudent to have a teammate accompany you, one who can stretch or for whom the style in question is a comfortable one. This versatility in coverage is one advantage of team negotiations. When a negotiating team is balanced in terms of the styles that are represented, the person or people whose style best meshes with the counterpart can take the lead, at least when differences arise.

Although it never pays to pigeonhole people, it does pay to draw some useful expectations (be they more or less tentative) from observation. This holds true with negotiation style. We know from research that negotiators who prefer *hard tactics* and are prone to engage in threats, demands, and sanctions do so because they expect that their counterparts will face high costs for noncompliance and so will comply if pressed to do so.[11] Of the four negotiation styles (see Exhibit 3.3), Achiever and Analytical are the types most likely to employ hard tactics. The former may use hard tactics because he or she is intent on moving things along; the latter may do so because the data appear to support his or her perspective. If you scored high on both Achiever and Analytical styles, your likelihood of inclination to use hard tactics is high. If you scored high on Motivator or Mediator styles, you are more likely to use *soft tactics.* Soft tactics emphasize friendliness, create personal liking, build a sense of obligation and reciprocity, and involve indirect approaches to persuasion.[12]

Just as such style categories are useful in determining how you, as a negotiator, are likely to respond in negotiation, they are useful in determining how your

► *EXHIBIT 3.3*

NEGOTIATION STYLES

ANALYZER
Focuses on logic
Makes rational arguments
Relies on data
Prioritizes outcomes

MOTIVATOR
Focuses on creativity
Uses analogies
Fosters collaboration
Encourages imagination

ACHIEVER
Focuses on outcomes
Desires control
Adheres to plans
Seeks compliance

MEDIATOR
Focuses on rapport
Favors consensus
Listens intently
Seeks mutual gain

counterpart is likely to respond to you as well. If you know that she is an Achiever, and a staunch one at that, the likelihood is high that somewhere along the line, she will use hard tactics. It's important to be ready for this or to have someone on your team who is. Similarly, if you know your counterpart to be a strong Motivator or Mediator, soft tactics are likely to predominate. Notice the term *likely*. Planning for negotiation styles provides more of a compass than a map. It indicates the likely direction but does not furnish a complete picture of the terrain. Far better to have a compass than not, but it is wise to keep a watchful eye for flexible negotiators who can stretch or alter their styles.

Style stretching is an important ability. If you haven't already cultivated it, strongly consider doing so. If you scored very low on one of the negotiation styles, you may need extensive practice to adopt that style. Other styles closer to your primary one may come to you more easily. One thing is certain: You won't be a superb negotiator until you become adept at the style types. If the people with whom you work tend to be mostly of a particular style, mastering that style will carry you a long way. Most careers, however, don't afford such stability. So it's important to learn how to communicate with an Achiever if you are a Mediator: how to avoid boring him with your concerns about making people happy and how to phrase ideas so that he'll listen. If you're stuck in a Motivator style, your arguments may be ignored when an Analytical needs data, not dreams, to persuade her.

Is there someone with whom you have difficulty communicating? Think about it: It may be that your difficulty is style rather than issue based. When working with organizations to resolve conflicts among key employees, I've often discovered that their disdain for each other was actually style based. Once they recognized this, they were able to negotiate their differences more effectively. As one senior executive told me, "I'll never be his best friend. But now that I know his style preference is for Mediator and mine is for Achiever, I understand why I get so impatient with him and why he thinks I'm so arrogant. That understanding has allowed us to laugh at ourselves. I might say, 'I imagine you'll want to make some people happy before we move on this.' His reply is something like, 'And you'll want to cut to the chase, damn the torpedoes, full speed ahead!'"

It would be unreasonable to ask every person with whom you negotiate to take the Negotiation Style Inventory before proceeding. However, you should learn to identify style by observing what other negotiators say and do. In the first moments of conversation with another person you can make an initial judgment of his or her primary style or style. For example, while discussing the purpose of an impending negotiation, if your counterpart is an Achiever, you're likely to hear phrases that suggest urgency, directness, discomfort with chitchat, assertiveness in the identification of key issues, and exactness in the proposal of an agenda. An Analytical is more likely to begin by presenting data or information; is more comfortable than the Achiever with using time to develop understanding; persuades, rather than demands or insists; and is likely to propose and reason through an agenda. The Motivator focuses on joint, overarching goals; appreciates efforts to understand each other in service of those goals; persuades with visions rather than what he or she perceives as dry data; and sees agendas serving as useful guidelines

rather than as restrictions on good ideas. Finally, the Mediator cares about mutual gain; casts perspectives in terms of what the other will derive; encourages listening and sharing opinions; and is in no hurry to reach a solution so long as all parties feel that they are making progress.

To repeat, these are generalizations and people often have more than one strong style. Nevertheless, it is possible to gain an impression early in the negotiation and to check that impression along the way. You may also identify more than one style in a person's words and actions, which will give you a better idea of what they are likely to emphasize and expect during negotiation.

Many negotiations fail before they get off the ground because of style differences. Start today to visit other styles. See which ones you are more inclined to use and which ones would be a stretch, if not impossible. Consider why that is so. Envision yourself using a more Analytical approach if you're an Achiever or a Mediator approach if you scored low on that. The more versatility you develop, the better a negotiator you'll become.

One thing a negotiator never wants to be is *predictable.* If you're in a style rut, you're predictable, and that can be the kiss of death. If people know how you'll respond, they can more capably manage your responses in their favor. Sometimes that's a good thing, especially if the outcome is one of mutual gain. In negotiation, however, being managed is often far less preferable than accomplishing at least a good portion of the managing.

Intelligence gathering in negotiation ought not to cease after the first few minutes. Unfortunately, many negotiators try to learn a good deal about their counterparts early on but fail to continue the effort throughout the proceedings. At its best, information gathering is continuous. Assumptions are made and checked regularly. During breaks, team members share their perceptions to produce a more complete and accurate impression (another of the beauties of team negotiation). Solo negotiators should use breaks to make mental and even written notes of their perceptions and to consider how those might inform their next actions.

In the service of intelligence gathering, it's important to notice the types of patterns that you and your negotiation counterparts are inclined to use, as well as the effects on progress that your combined inclinations create. This kind of focus is unusual in negotiation and negotiation training, yet it is extremely valuable. It is one of the skills that separate the novice from the expert. The former goes into negotiation oblivious to how interaction patterns influence the course of negotiation; the latter, fully apprised of such influences, is capable of shifting the course by making a move that encourages reciprocity or at least discourages resistance.

▶ QUESTIONS

1. A. Prepare to engage in a negotiation with a classmate for an item (pen, book, notebook, etc.). Gather intelligence about him/her relevant to the negotiation. What interests, concerns, emotional attachments, style might prove important in formulating an approach? What value does he/she place on the item (e.g., is it the only one of its kind that he/she owns? Does he/she have sufficient discretionary in-

come to buy another? Does he/she seem accommodating? Is there an emotional attachment to the item?)

B. Begin the negotiation based on the information you've gathered. Then discuss with your counterpart the kinds of approaches that worked well and ones he/she believes would have been more effective. What did the latter tell you about your intelligence gathering efforts? Could they have been better? How?

C. Write a brief report including the negotiation focus, information-gathering results, negotiation process description, and what was learned from subsequent discussion.

2. What is the ICE Model? Think about an interaction you had sometime during the past week. Use this model to dissect what occurred. Were interest, concerns, and emotions adequately explored and addressed? If so, how? If not, what should have been done differently?

3. A. Enter into a discussion of a controversial issue with someone in class or with a friend outside of class. After the discussion, write down their primary claim, data, warrant, and backing. Then do the same for your primary claim, data, warrant, and backing. Share these with your counterpart. Does he/she agree with your description of the primary claims and supporting structures?

B. Where are the weaknesses in your counterpart's primary argument? Where are the weaknesses in your primary argument? How might each be altered to strengthen them?

C. Repeat the process in A and B above for one of your counterpart's secondary claims.

4. Review the discussion in this chapter about the Negotiation House of Opportunity. Describe a recent negotiation in which you took part or one you observed. What opportunities did one or more of the negotiators miss that would have brought about a more desirable outcome for them? Why did they miss this opportunity?

5. How do mind maps work as negotiation tools? Think about a topic about which you feel strongly. Consider a type of resistance you might experience in advocating that position to a friend. Place that opposition in the center of the map and create possible pathways branching out from it that might be useful in dealing with the resistance.

6. Administer the Negotiation Style Inventory to someone who negotiates regularly. Before revealing the score, ask the negotiator to tell you which style he/she prefers. Discuss the outcome with him/her and report on the scores and the person' reactions to them. Can this person stretch beyond his/her styles?

7. What is a negotiation choice point? Observe a somewhat contentious interaction between two people. Write down their conversation. Examine it for choice points. Where might one or the other have altered the direction or where did they do so effectively?

4

Prioritizing Issues, Setting and Revising Goals

In Chapter 3, we explored how negotiators identify their own interests and those of their counterparts and how they can translate this knowledge into supported claims. We now turn our attention to prioritizing interests in the service of specific goals. This requires identification of *ideal outcomes*—what, under the circumstances, you'd very much like to achieve—and contingency goals in case the ideal proves to be unattainable.

Once a negotiator has identified, through intelligence gathering, the interests of the other side, as well as his or her own, and has also considered how those interests can or cannot be supported (with data, warrants, and backing), the negotiator is ready to decide which interest is not only a priority but also capable of being advanced and sustained throughout the negotiation. This requires thoughtful rank ordering of desirable outcomes according to research-based predictions.

Assume that you want to find a job that will allow you to rent an apartment on Manhattan's West Side. That is your ideal outcome. As you do research, you realize that employer expectations and competition might make this goal unattainable. In that case, you might decide to alter the initial ideal outcome. Perhaps an apartment in Brooklyn, Queens, Long Island, or New Jersey makes more sense. So your ideal outcome could become your favorite among these. Let's say you choose Brooklyn Heights. It's pricey, but it's your ideal, and you believe that if all goes well in the interviews, it is even attainable. You need contingency goals, though, in case things don't work out. If you like Brooklyn, a less expensive area could be your first contingency goal, followed by a desirable area of Queens, Long Island, or New Jersey. Your prioritization of goals would then look like this:

Ideal Outcome: A home in Brooklyn Heights

Contingency Goal 1: A home in a less expensive area of Brooklyn

Contingency Goal 2: A home in a desirable part of Queens

Contingency Goal 3: A home in a desirable part of New Jersey or Long Island

Your ability to identify these goals as reasonable would have been supported by prior intelligence gathering. Were you to omit that step, you would have risked establishing a pie-in-the-sky ideal outcome and in-the-pits contingency goals. So the identification of goals depends on the quality of your preparation and research phase, described in Chapter 3. This is also the case in negotiation. You need to consider what's possible not only financially and in terms of your skills but also in terms of how the other side's ideal outcomes and likely contingency goals contravene your own. If what the other side clearly wants requires that you not achieve what you desire, you must take this into consideration in establishing ideal and contingency goals. If you are a persuasive negotiator, you may be able to find a way to make your goals and theirs more compatible. If, on the other hand, your counterpart is not likely to be convinced by you, if he or she is stubborn, or if the history of your relationship makes cooperation unlikely, you may need to set somewhat lower ideal and contingency goals.

In Chapter 7, we'll discuss how to set goals for each phase of negotiation—how to take an *if-then approach*. Let's say that you are able to open the negotiation in a cooperative vein. Perhaps you make more progress than seemed possible at the outset. Under those circumstances, you might change your ideal outcome and contingency goals to more ambitious ones. If, instead, you encounter staunch resistance, a lowering of these goals may be in order. This type of *sequential goal setting* allows negotiators to operate with a versatile mind-set. They don't make commitments to goals, though they keep them in mind. As the negotiation unfolds, they form a clearer picture of how much they can reasonably attain, and they adjust their goals accordingly.

In a moment we'll look at a case in which goal development can be handled this way. Before doing so, however, it's important to introduce a form of contingency goal known as a BATNA—the *best alternative to negotiated agreement*.[1] A BATNA answers the question *What will I do if we can't come to an agreement that meets my needs?* If it becomes clear that your ideal outcomes and all contingencies are not attainable, the BATNA is the answer. Skilled negotiators realize that if they have something else they can do if all else fails, all of their eggs are not in one basket. They have an option on which to fall back—and thus they avoid a sense of failure.

When training people to develop BATNAs, I've often witnessed a tendency to blithely say, "Well, if I can't have X, I'll just do something else." Often that something else is a far cry from what they really want—a precipitous drop from the last contingency goal. The best BATNAs are carefully chosen. They are not any old option, nor are they the worst of options. They represent another avenue—and the better that avenue, the more confident a negotiator can be in attempts to attain ideal or contingency goals, because he or she is not desperate. In our relocation example, if you can't live in New York, you could simply say, "I'll just get a job somewhere else." That's fine if you want to do that, but if you really want to live in New York—or at least work there—what would be a preferable BATNA? Perhaps you could live with your New Yorker parents. What's that you say? Not a good idea? OK, then you might consider sharing an apartment with a roommate in one of your preferred New York locations. Is that better? Another

alternative is to borrow money from the bank or from some other source to supplement your income. If that is more desirable than sharing an apartment, it's a better BATNA. A good BATNA is not the worst thing that could happen. It is a reasonable alternative to not reaching one of your more desirable goals. With the "borrow money" BATNA, if you don't get the kind of job offer that will allow you to live in your own apartment in Manhattan or in one of your contingency locations, you still have a reasonable option. Maybe it will turn out to be a temporary option. After a promotion, you could revisit your earlier goals to see if they have become attainable.

Setting a BATNA keeps negotiators from panicking. It is like a safety net. And like a safety net, you don't want to jump easily into it. Endeavor to reach your ideal outcome or a contingency goal, but if things don't go as you hoped or expected, the net will be there. Comforting, isn't it?

To convert theory into practice, let's look at a case and see how ideal outcomes, contingency goals, and BATNAs are identified.

▶ CASE: THE MEMO IN EVERY WOMAN'S DESK

When my article "The Memo in Every Woman's Desk" appeared in the *Harvard Business Review,* it became a controversial case. A young woman intends to send a memo to her CEO. In the draft memo, she expresses her views of why senior women have been leaving the company and why women who work there feel undervalued. After drafting it, she asks a male colleague and friend whether or not she should send the memo to the CEO. Should she send it, or would doing so constitute career suicide? A number of experts responded with their view.[2] But first, here is the memo:

TO: Mr. John Clark, CEO

FROM: Elizabeth C. Ames, Director of Consumer Marketing

I've been working in the marketing department at Vision Software for more than ten years, where I've had my share of challenges and successes. I've enjoyed being part of an interesting and exciting company. Despite my general enthusiasm about the company and my job, however, I was taken aback when I received your memo announcing the resignations of Miriam Blackwell and Susan French, Vision's two most senior women. This is not the first time Vision has lost its highest-ranking women. Just nine months ago, Kathryn Hobbs resigned, and a year before that, it was Susan La Haise. The reasons are surprisingly similar: they wanted to "spend more time with their families" or "explore new career directions."

I can't help but detect a disturbing pattern. Why do such capable, conscientious women who have demonstrated intense commitment to their careers suddenly want to change course or spend more time at home? It's a question I've thought long and hard about.

Despite Vision's policies to hire and promote women and your own efforts to recognize and reward women's contributions, the overall atmosphere in this company is one that slowly erodes a woman's sense of worth and place. I believe that top-level women are leaving Vision Software not because they are drawn to other pursuits but because they are tired of struggling against a climate of female failure. Little things that happen daily—

things many men don't even notice and women can't help but notice—send subtle messages that women are less important, less talented, less likely to make a difference than their male peers.

Let me try to describe what I mean. I'll start with meetings, which are a way of life at Vision and one of the most devaluing experiences for women. Women are often talked over and interrupted; their ideas never seem to be heard. Last week, I attended a meeting with ten men and one other woman. As soon as the woman started her presentation, several side conversations began. Her presentation skills were excellent, but she couldn't seem to get people's attention. When it was time to take questions, one man said dismissively, "We did something like this a couple of years ago, and it didn't work." She explained how her ideas differed, but the explanation fell on deaf ears. When I tried to give her support by expressing interest, I was interrupted.

But it's not just meetings. There are many things that make women feel unwelcome or unimportant. One department holds its biannual retreats at a country club with a "men only" bar. At the end of the sessions, the men typically hang around at the bar and talk, while the women quietly disappear. Needless to say, important information is often shared during those casual conversations.

Almost every formal meeting is followed by a series of informal ones behind closed doors. Women are rarely invited. Nor are they privy to the discussions before the formal meetings. As a result, they are often less likely to know what the boss has on his mind and therefore less prepared to react.

My female colleagues and I are also subjected to a daily barrage of seemingly innocent comments that belittle women. A co-worker of mine recently boasted about how much he respects women, saying, "My wife is the wind beneath my wings. In fact, some people call me Mr. Karen Snyder." The men chuckled; the women didn't. And just last week, a male colleague stood up at 5:30 and jokingly informed a group of us that he would be leaving early: "I have to play mom tonight." Women play mom every night, and it never gets a laugh. In fact, most women try to appear devoid of concern about their families.

Any one of these incidents on its own is a small thing. But together and in repetition, they are quite powerful. The women at Vision fight to get their ideas heard and to crack the informal channels of information. Their energy goes into keeping up, not getting ahead, until they just don't have any more to give.

I can assure you that my observations are shared by many women in the company. I can only speculate that they were shared by Miriam Blackwell and Susan French.

Vision needs men and women if it is to become the preeminent educational software company. We need to send stronger, clearer signals that men are not the only people who matter. And this kind of change can work only if it starts with strong commitment at the top. That's why I'm writing to you. If I can be of help, please let me know.[3]

For use in my classes at the University of Southern California's (USC) Experiential Learning Center, I've developed a case around this memo in which the CEO and Liz meet to discuss it after he has read it. I usually divide my classes in two, with half the class taking Liz's role and the remainder assuming the CEO's role. They then pair off to role-play negotiation in a room where I can see and hear the students through a one-way window and audio system. Before proceeding to negotiate, students set about determining their ideal outcomes, contingency outcomes, and BATNAs for each primary issue. Most of them assume that

the CEO holds all the power; consequently, those playing him are often lulled into a less intensive preparation effort. They fail to realize, as previously discussed, that power is, in most cases, in the eye of the beholder. The skill with which one develops ideal outcomes, contingencies, and BATNAs determines the power level much more than status alone. In other words, the negotiator with only one strong option is in a very vulnerable position compared with one who has identified a number of attainable contingency goals and a strong BATNA. Since negotiation is rarely a process of getting exactly what you want, being prepared with options inspires confidence—and confidence, in the right measure, is a form of power.

Let's look at the types of ideal outcomes, contingencies, and BATNAs that have been set by people using this case for practice to see how their availability bolsters success potential. Those playing Liz have frequently decided that the primary issue is that women at Vision Software feel left out. The players might then decide that their ideal outcome is for the CEO to express concern and take an interest in bringing about change. This is a weak ideal outcome. All the CEO needs to do in this case is to express sympathy and state that he will look into it. I've seen many a deluded Liz walk away content with this outcome. A better ideal outcome would be to seek clear evidence of "strong commitment at the top" and "stronger, clearer signals that men are not the only people who matter." Liz might then have an ideal outcome of the CEO heading a task force to identify issues relevant to the ones presented in the memo. A contingency plan could be to obtain John Clark's support in bringing about change in specific problem areas by assigning a senior vice president to head the task force. Ultimately, after all contingencies, her BATNA might be to go around Clark to the chairman of the board. Here is how this plan would look:

Ideal Outcome: John Clark to head task force

Contingency Goal 1: Senior VP to head task force, with Clark involved

Contingency Goal 2: Senior VP to head task force and report to Clark

BATNA: Go around Clark to the chairman of the board of Vision Software

Liz could tweak this approach by making her contingency plans a bit more specific. What is an expression of concern? What exactly is "support"? The greater the specificity, the higher the likelihood that something concrete will be achieved. For example, she could suggest that at the very least (to show his true support) the CEO would make sure the "men only" bar issue is resolved by changing the hotel where retreats are held. She might consider making her BATNA less adversarial. Instead of approaching the chairman, she might circulate her memo to other Vision women, encouraging them to set up a task force, which would then bring pressure to bear on CEO Clark. This last is a more behind-the-scenes option and therefore a more politically astute approach. Liz's estimation of how Clark is likely to respond should influence expectations of how much she can achieve in one meeting as well as over the long term. Her estimation of her own persuasiveness should enter into this as well.

From the CEO's perspective, the ideal outcome might be to get Liz to go away satisfied so that the issue doesn't become a problem for him. If he is a benevolent CEO, he might want to resolve some of the issues while not giving Liz the impression that he will change the entire company culture on the basis of her observations. His contingency plans might include doing some specific things, such as changing the retreat site. His next contingency may be to do a bit more—perhaps he could also promise to look further into the conditions Liz described in her memo—and his BATNA might be to pass her on to an executive VP who would then handle the issue. His plan would then look like this:

Ideal Outcome: Demonstrate concern

Contingency 1: Change the retreat site

Contingency 2: Promise to look further into the issue

BATNA: Pass her on to an executive VP

Clark, too, could tweak his ideal outcome, contingency, or BATNA. He might decide to be a bit more generous or a bit less. If he believes that Liz is likely to be easily placated, he could offer less—a sympathetic ear might be enough. If he expects that she'll be assertive, he could plan to give more. Were Clark and Liz to pursue the type of intelligence-gathering process described in Chapter 3, they'd each have the kinds of information about each other that helps identify achievable goals. If, for example, Clark knows that Liz is a person not easily satisfied with an Achiever style and not intimidated by power, he may need to do more than show some concern if he wants to get her out of his office and out of his hair. The more each party knows about the other, the more realistic their ideal outcome and contingency goals are likely to be. Trying to establish these in the absence of such information is like flailing about in the dark in search of a door. It's useless and can be dangerous.

Since practice is the only way to become a proficient negotiator, let's look at another scenario and identify key issues, ideal outcomes, contingency plans, and BATNAs for each side. The following describes one side of a case. Take a few minutes to identify key issues, then prioritize them.

▶ TOYS, TOYS, TOYS

MARK—BILL'S BOSS AND CEO OF TOYS, TOYS, TOYS (TTT)

You're about to meet with Bill, your senior vice president of marketing. You've heard via the grapevine that Bill has received a job offer from Charley Harris, your major competitor. You believe that the current vice president of marketing, Jake, could move up and replace Bill—but you'd rather not lose Bill. Jake has been with TTT for only one year. He's still something of an unknown quantity and a little too sure of himself, but you want Bill to mentor him so that he will be successful at TTT.

You have had some doubts concerning Bill's ability to remain in charge of marketing as TTT goes more broadly international, but his ideas have landed important accounts in Germany and France and a very crucial one this past month in the United States. He's creative, easy to work with, and committed, and he has earned the respect of the other team

members, although some have complained that he is occasionally indecisive and that his hesitancy has cost you some accounts. Truth be told, you feel betrayed that he is looking elsewhere—especially at your chief competitor—after you've brought him up the ranks from marketing manager to senior VP over the last five years. If he had problems, he should have spoken to you first before looking outside. However, you're trying to hold those feelings in abeyance to concentrate on keeping Bill with the firm.

You don't mind competing for Bill. Your salary ceiling is $225,000, which is $25,000 more than he is making now. A promotion would not be appropriate at this time, however. Due to company policy, you can't offer him a company car like Charley Harris probably has. You can increase Bill's vacation time from three weeks to four weeks and let him work from home on Fridays. You could probably give him some other small perks if you could just figure out what he really wants. If, however, Bill wants to be an executive VP—or even president—well, in all honesty, you don't think he will perform well at that level.

You're about to meet with him to discuss these options.

Issue 1: Position TTT to go more broadly international

Issue 2: Fill the senior vice president post with a qualified occupant

Your next step is to identify, for each issue, the ideal outcome, contingency plans, and a BATNA. Take a few minutes to do that for the most important issue:

Issue 1:

Ideal Outcome:

Contingency 1:

Contingency 2:

Contingency 3:

BATNA:

Your ideal outcome, contingencies, and BATNA may look something like this:

Ideal Outcome: Bill agrees to stay, and you give him a $25,000 salary increase.

Contingency 1: You add two more weeks of vacation time.

Contingency 2: You offer additional perks.

BATNA: Bill leaves; you promote Jake and give him the training and support he will need.

There are a number of ways to interpret any case, but let's identify the more important major issue, the less pressing issue, and the underlying relevant issue and compare them to the ones you identified (which you may have phrased somewhat differently):

Major Issue: Persuading Bill to stay at TTT

Less Pressing but Important Issue: Bill's confidence level and decision-making ability

Underlying Relevant Issue: A sense of betrayal

As the negotiation progresses, the underlying issue may become the most important one. It may even be the most significant issue right from the start. It's important to be aware of it. In this case, it was explicitly identified and stated; often, however, underlying issues are not readily obvious but are nonetheless important. Let's look at Bill's side of the case.

BILL, SENIOR VICE PRESIDENT OF MARKETING FOR TTT

Charley Harris of Best Toys has made you an attractive offer. You met him at a toy expo two weeks ago. You had no idea that he might offer you a job three days later. He is willing to pay you $250,000, which is $50,000 more than you make now. All moving expenses will be covered, and you'll have three weeks of vacation. He'll also give you a company car and a $10,000 signing bonus.

Despite all of this, you'd like to stay in your current job. You enjoy working for Mark. The accounts you've landed in Germany and France are just beginning to pay off in sales revenues. A recent new account in the United States has been a big coup for TTT, and you would hate to just leave it before it is fully developed, especially under Jake's leadership. Jake is VP of marketing and has been with TTT for only one year. He has potential, but he's still too green and tends to be abrupt. He needs mentoring and training. You must weigh your desire to stay against your worry that as the company expands into more international markets, Bill may decide to hire someone senior to you or even replace you. Also, Harris's offer is attractive and could become even more so with some negotiation.

You believe that Bill is likely to be offended by your consideration of Harris's offer. After all, Best Toys is TTT's biggest competitor. You appreciate how Bill has guided your career over the past five years, but you do have to look out for yourself. There are a lot more people on the scene these days who have solid international marketing experience, and they'd love to have your job. Bill may decide that one of them should lead TTT's international expansion. This thought tends to make you somewhat hesitant to act hastily on deals. You don't want to make any mistakes.

You are going in to Bill's office to tell him of your offer from Harris.

Bill's Major Issue: Doing what's best for my career

Bill's Important but Less Pressing Issue: Desire to stay with the firm

Bill's Underlying Issue that May Prove Relevant: A sense of obligation to Mark

Again, you may have listed issues or versions somewhat differently. Using the ones presented here, however, Bill's initial goal is to convince Mark that the primary issue is one of career progress. This doesn't mean that Bill's sense of obligation or Mark's sense of betrayal won't emerge as issues. However, unless Mark insists on making his sense of betrayal the most important issue, Bill may be able to persuade him that the critical issue in his own decision must be his career. If the betrayal issue cannot be avoided, Bill might address it and then move back to the career advancement issue. The interaction might proceed like this:

Mark: Listen, Bill. I understand your concern about advancement, but threatening to jump ship tells me that all I've done to help you so far means nothing to you.

Bill: You feel betrayed?

Mark: Of course I do.

Bill: Actually, I was anticipating that you might drop me.

Mark: (*surprised*) What?

Bill: You've hinted more than once that my international experience is limited.

Mark: How does that translate into my letting you go?

Bill: I could ask how my interest in career advancement translates into betrayal. To me, it's only natural to look for opportunities, but I wouldn't be here having this discussion if I'd failed to notice what you've done for me in the past.

Mark: If I can assure you that I'm not interested in anyone having your job but you and that I'm willing to discuss with you the actions you need to take to place a promotion on the horizon, would you still consider going with Best Toys?

Bill: If you can bring that horizon a bit closer, Best Toys will drop like a stone from my mind.

Mark: Sounds like a deal to me.

Notice how Bill and Mark prioritized their issues. At first, they seemed at odds. Mark was focused on betrayal, Bill on advancing his career. When Bill explained that he was thinking that Mark might, in a sense, betray him by letting him go, they were on the same emotional plane. They managed to disentangle betrayal from the primary issue of career advancement, which Mark effectively addressed by offering to provide Bill with assurances and opportunities. Neither Mark nor Bill allowed himself to let the betrayal issue take the lead among priorities for long.

The identification and prioritization of relevant issues is extremely important to effective negotiation. A major reason why people become sidetracked in negotiation is that they have failed to identify and prioritize the issues and to identify their ideal outcomes, contingency plans, and BATNAs. Necessarily, the more complex the nature of the negotiation, the more complex this critical step will be. It is worth every ounce of effort expended on it, however. The negotiator who can remain focused has a considerable advantage over a distractible counterpart. Moreover, as negotiators gain experience, they become better able to allow side issues to be discussed without jeopardizing achievement on major issues.

▶ STAYING ON TRACK

Once negotiators have established goals, their next task is to advance them during the actual interactive part of negotiation. Since a good deal of meandering from subject to subject happens in even the most organized of negotiations, this task is

not an easy one. Typically, this problem arises because of a common negotiation error: a failure to separate *relevant claims* from *claim clutter*. This can be done, to some extent, before the negotiation begins by anticipating what kinds of issues irrelevant to the primary goals are likely to arise. If negotiators can identify such likely diversions before negotiation, they can prepare effective ways of responding to them in advance.

When off-the-track topics arise, the wise negotiator avoids anything beyond a cursory discussion. Such topics constitute claim clutter—utterances that accidentally or purposely divert the negotiation from primary issues and their accompanying claims. In the TTT case, Bill's primary issue is job advancement. One accompanying claim is Best Toys' offer of a much better package. Another is that there have been too many hints about inexperience for him to feel secure staying at TTT. If, during the course of the negotiation, Mark brings up negative gossip he's heard about Charley Harris of Best Toys rather than addressing Bill's claims, Mark is engaging in claim clutter, either accidentally or on purpose. The negotiation would also veer off into potential clutter if Mark were to focus on how Bill's departure would leave Mark in a fix (a guilt approach). Unless Bill can redirect the discussion back to his main issues, this kind of meandering could lead to a poor result.

Expert negotiators frequently ask themselves, *Is this topic relevant to the outcome?* Now, an occasional off-the-track discussion may actually be relevant, even if not on topic. If, for example, the clutter topic is of a lighter nature than the primary issues, discussing it for a short time might serve to ease tensions, like the comic relief in dramatic movies and plays that provides the audience with a brief respite before the tension rises again. Such exceptions aside, however, it's important to remain generally on target in negotiation and to avoid allowing too many irrelevant comments to take the interaction away from your desired course. Accomplishing that objective requires conversational management. The following example shows how a subject that could clutter or even derail advancement toward a goal can be addressed without allowing it to become the focus of discussion:

> *Stewart:* I think we're all on the same page here. We've worked through our disagreement regarding the start date of this project. The only other action we need to take before we leave today is to decide who will lead what phase.
>
> *Mitch:* First, let's talk about how much this is going to cost. We seem to be steamrolling ahead here.
>
> *Stewart:* Cost is definitely an issue and one we discussed in terms of range, as you may recall. You're absolutely right that we need to further pin cost down, but we could do that more effectively with the phase leaders in place, as they will take the lead in defining their task and costing it.

In this example, Stewart has avoided insulting Mitch by saying, "That topic is off target" or by dismissing the legitimacy of his request. In fact, Stewart suggests that Mitch is right to raise this topic given its importance, but he then explains

why Mitch's concerns will be more effectively dealt with by staying on the course Stewart has charted. He disagrees with Mitch, but in an agreeable fashion. Here is another way of handling a similar problem:

Sheila: Let's move on to the next item on the agenda.

Phil: What's the rush? We haven't gone over the details yet. How will we know whether we can commit our people to this project if we don't have a good idea of how much time, effort, and resources will be required at each step?

Sheila: There are a lot of specifics to discuss, Phil. Our purpose today, however, is to outline a course of action without totally committing to any specific actions. Tomorrow, we can address your concern regarding specific details. Does that work for you?

Phil: Not really. I want to know what I'm getting into here.

Sheila: We could take five minutes to look at your particular segment and then continue with the outline process.

Phil: That would help.

Sheila: Good. Alicia can let us know when five minutes is up.

Here Sheila's first attempt to stay focused is resisted. It is a good effort, however. She refers to the agreed purpose of outlining rather than discussing specifics and offers to address Phil's concern on the following day. Unfortunately, Phil is adamant. Sheila then suggests a defined time limit for addressing his concern, after which they will return to the original purpose of the meeting. Sometimes diversions of this type become necessary to avoid conflict. By delegating the timekeeping to Alicia, Sheila avoids the possibility of aggravating Phil by checking her watch and closing down the discussion herself.

Savvy negotiators won't sacrifice the course they have laid out merely because someone says something distracting or potentially offensive. They expect resistance and attempts at derailment. Equally important, they realize that words are weak vehicles of meaning that can be replaced with other words that better suit their needs. To demonstrate, consider whether you'd appreciate someone referring to you as stubborn. Probably you wouldn't. If you think about it, though, the same characteristics that constitute stubbornness are those that create an impression of persistence, perseverance, and determination—all positive traits.

At some point during a negotiation, the other party is likely to use a word or phrase at variance with how you would prefer to have the situation described. Accepting this likelihood will help you keep the poise you need to pause, reflect, and redirect the interaction away from the dysfunctions of conflict or diversion. Suppose a negotiator implies that you're trying to trick him. You are at a choice point here. You could retaliate with some choice words about his own intentions. Or you could say something like "I don't deny taking a strategic approach as both of us are doing today, but the main issue at hand here is . . .". Accused of an ulterior motive, you might reply, "Likely both of us have motives that we've not yet expressed. What's important is putting all our needs on the table and crafting a solution that addresses them."

Such topic management becomes more difficult in circumstances of personal attack. Novice negotiators commonly respond to a personal-attack type of diversion with a reciprocated attack. An experienced negotiator is more likely to deflect the attack in the service of staying on topic—for example, by redefining what was intended: "I see what you call a 'power grab' as an attempt at organizing and saving all of us a good deal of time." Should the other side bring up a sensitive issue, the negotiator might say, "That's a sore point for both of us, but it pales in comparison to what we have in common." When entering a negotiation, it's important to have in mind these kinds of recovery strategies for dealing with diversions. Prepare by considering in advance the types of comments and diversions that might take the negotiation onto a destructive path. Develop if-then scenarios: "If they say X, we'll say Y." "If they do P, we'll do Q."

▶ NEGOTIATING ISSUE PRIORITIES

Although you may have done an exceptional job of identifying and prioritizing interests and articulating ideal outcomes, contingencies, and BATNAs for each issue, when negotiation actually gets under way, the other side may reject your views. They may have different priorities. Some of the issues that you feel are important may be irrelevant to them, or vice versa. They may raise issues you've never even considered. What does the effective negotiator do then? Let's look at an example to see how different priorities are negotiated:

> *Ted:* The two most pressing issues here are who is going to take charge of the project at each stage and how much financial assistance should we give to each stage.
>
> *Michelle:* Those are two important issues, but the most pressing one is to avoid mistakes we've made in the past by rushing where we should have taken our time and dragging our feet where we should have expedited things.

Ted is at a choice point here. He could say, "Michelle, that's history. We learned from it; now let's push on." He could also say, "Let's discuss that later, after we've identified the leaders and discussed the finances." To the former, Michelle might reply, "History repeats itself. The last time we pushed on without considering what we learned, the outcome was disastrous." At that point, Ted would realize that she is not likely to give in easily. He could reply, "OK, Michelle, let's take a few minutes to look at the major lessons." If he suggests waiting until after the discussion of leaders and finances, Michelle might respond, "That'll be too late," or "I'm not being pushed aside, Ted. This step is critical."

At each juncture in their interaction, Ted has choices. At the outset, right after Michelle mentions the need to learn from history, he might say, "Why don't we fold that discussion into the selection of leaders? After all, we need to choose leaders based on their ability to comprehend what went wrong in the past. That way, we accomplish two things at once." This *issue folding* allows Ted to keep his primary issue in place while according a high priority to Michelle's key issue. She may, of course, insist that her issue be considered first and exclusively. If she does, Ted might

counter by suggesting that a focus on past faults could derail their meeting but that incorporating it into the discussion—giving it the consideration it deserves while staying on track—addresses both her concerns and those of the team.

The point is, issue prioritization need not become a win-lose situation. Whenever possible, it should be win-win. If Ted has no luck with the folding-in approach, he might say, "I'll make you a deal. We'll talk about what we've learned, but let's do it by project stage. In other words, we'll define the stage, talk about what we've learned, and then decide on the leader. That puts your interest right up front. What do you say?" Here Ted again addresses Michelle's concerns but suggests a way to continue giving his main issues a high priority as well. This is a very important skill in negotiation. Derailment can occur quickly when two sides can't even agree on which issues to discuss.

Figure 4.1 deals with the varying degrees of interest in issues among parties. The solid lines represent high priority, the broken lines represents interest but not high priority, and the dotted lines represent disinterest. If one negotiator assigns high priority to an issue but the other views it as only of interest, the folding-in and trade-off approaches can be used to work out differences. The real difficulty comes when an issue of high priority to one negotiator is irrelevant to the other. Then their work is cut out for them. The task of finding a link between the two topics, or perhaps folding one into the other, is likely to be challenging. If an obvious link fails to come to mind, one negotiator might place primary focus on the issues both sides do agree on. "Since we both think that issue A is the most important, let's begin by working on A and see whether that leads us to the next most important issue." Thus in the service of addressing the most crucial topic, the negotiator postpones agreement on the lesser ones. It's likely that an effective negotiator, while discussing issue A, will identify or develop a segue into issues that he or she also thinks are important.

Some discussion of issues can be initiated before the negotiation by sending the other side a proposed agenda. We'll discuss agendas later in the book, but even when an agenda has been formulated and accepted, negotiators should be ready for a surprise when the other side tries to introduce or impose a new issue.

Issue Prioritization

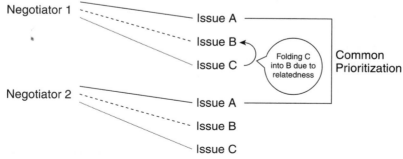

Figure 4.1 Issue Prioritization.

Just saying, "But we have an agenda—we can't change it now," won't necessarily help. If your counterpart considers an issue pressing, you will need to devote some attention to when it will be addressed during the negotiation. The more you learn about the other side's interests, ideal outcomes, contingencies, and BATNAs, the more prepared you are likely to be to handle such impositions.

▶ SETTING PRIORITIES IN TEAMS

It's difficult enough to prioritize issues and set goals as individual negotiators. When negotiation occurs between teams, the task is even more complex. Teams that are cohesive often benefit from improved communication among those members and from shared goals. These same teams, however, can become too insular and resistant to new ideas and novel negotiation techniques. The most effective negotiation teams are those that enjoy cohesiveness yet keep themselves open to new approaches. They may not encourage conflict, but they do not discourage it either. They strike a balance between comfort and discomfort, tried-and-true methods and novel ones. This means that team members are not expected to be clones but are selected whenever possible on the basis of what they bring as individuals, which tasks they'll be able to perform, and how they'll relate to other members. John Adair, in his book *Effective Teambuilding*, refers to these as *task, group,* and *individual* group or team needs.[4] Often these group needs overlap, with part of the task needs fulfilling individual ones and vice versa.

The adept negotiation team works to achieve overlap in group, task, and individual needs. The task dimension involves the accomplishment of goals. The group dimension pertains to relationships among members that allow the task to be accomplished. The individual dimension includes the needs and interests of each person. Sometimes these needs are in harmony, and sometimes they are not. As Abraham Lincoln pointed out, "A house divided against itself cannot stand." A negotiation team with task, group, and individual needs vying for attention cannot be effective. There must be some degree of overlap or a complete acceptance that the task must be given the highest priority.

There are some high-functioning teams that focus exclusively on task. They suppress or dismiss their individual and group relational needs to ensure that the task at hand is accomplished. Jean Lipman-Blumen and Harold Leavitt refer to groups devoted to the task at hand as "hot groups." The hot-group frame of mind is "task obsessed and full of passion," according to Lipman-Blumen and Leavitt. "It is always coupled with a distinctive way of behaving, a style that is intense, sharply focused, and full-bore."[5]

Hot groups may be too hot for some tasks. They are composed of people devoted to the task but not devoted to one another. Lipman-Blumen and Leavitt explain that the task is too eclipsing for the members to develop intimate, empathic relationships. Hot groups are often confrontational, challenging, and critical, with the aim of improving work. These groups ignite organizations and often change them for the better. Despite the benefits of hot groups, however, most negotiations do well with warm groups, which are focused on task but also concerned with relationships. This attests to the importance of relationships to negotiation

success—the importance of mutual support both within the team and across teams. The hot-group member exclusively devoted to task has little time for such considerations and is therefore likely to tread heavily in negotiation. There are times when this is useful, but there are more times when it is dysfunctional. Negotiation teams benefit from a heated interest in task balanced by a strong desire to work together, to respect each member's opinion, and to keep the group relationships intact. It's a tall order. So my advice is to assign a team member the job of ensuring that there is a reasonable balance of attention to task and relationship issues. Be sure, when establishing issue priorities and goals, that people are given a chance to be heard. If there is disagreement, deal with it up front. Otherwise it will fester and cause problems later on. There are ways of doing this in terms of language. Let's say team member Allan is adamant that his prioritization of issues is the best one. It differs from what other team members want. Rather than tell this outlier that he is wrong or that he'll need to accept the majority opinion or leave the team, consider saying something like this: "We've discussed this at some length now, Allan. What would you say to our proceeding with the majority view at this juncture, bearing in mind your suggestion and keeping it as a contingency?" Another option: "Allan, we need to move forward with this, but your advice is serving to keep us versatile. We don't want to become so wedded to one approach that we fail to consider others. In the interest of progress, we should move on, but we'll pause at the end of the next negotiation phase to see if your approach isn't, at that point, the better one."

In both cases, the person moving the team along has kept a door open. Allan's views have not been denied. In fact, they've been described as valuable even if they are not adopted. Most people want their ideas to be valued. Most are willing to proceed if that value is accorded. The suggested approaches balance relational concerns with task concerns and also help avoid later problems—such as Allan's becoming a "loose cannon" and sabotaging the team's efforts.

▶ QUESTIONS

1. Using the examples in this chapter as a guide, identify an ideal job for you, where it would be located, and how much you'd be paid. Then identify contingencies (e.g., less money but the same job and location, or different location but more money). Also, identify a BATNA. List these.

2. What is one of your current short-term goals? What is an ideal outcome? Contingency goals and BATNA? Practice this for two more short-term goals.

3. Think of a goal you'd like to achieve that is or might potentially be blocked by a friend. What are his or her ideal outcomes? Possible contingency goals and BATNAs that are causing him/her to block you? Is there a way for you to link one of your goals with one of his/hers so that what you want is more similar than initially assumed? Try to create a prioritization chart showing the link between at least one of your goals and one of theirs.

4. Using examples in this chapter, analyze an actual conversation or negotiation in terms of how well the participants stayed on track. Do the same for one of your own conversations or negotiations.

Ethical Considerations

Before discussing persuasion, it is important to discuss the issue of ethics in nego-
tiation. Persuasion, after all, suggests getting people to do things they wouldn't do
otherwise. As we'll discuss in Chapter 6, this isn't an accurate perception of per-
suasion. It is true of coercion and manipulation, two other forms of influence. But
persuasion is more typically a process of encouraging people to choose to take an
advocated position or proposed action. It involves choice on the part of the person
being influenced. Nevertheless, persuasion ranges from ethically best or good
practices to ethically suspect practices, even if people aren't being duped (manip-
ulated) or forced to comply (coerced). To avoid slipping toward the ethically sus-
pect end of the persuasion continuum or into manipulation or coercion,
negotiation counterparts need to draw a line that they agree not to cross. This
chapter assists in that effort.

We start with a question: What is ethics? Most of us know it has to do with
behaving in moral ways. Societies typically develop more or less strict guidelines
for behavior. Some go so far as to impose laws that prohibit behaviors considered
abhorrent. For example, the United States has a law prohibiting bribery in busi-
ness—but what this law considers a bribe is viewed in other cultures as the entry
price to doing business, an expected and accepted practice of incurring favor.
Who is right? Many countries have passed legislation prohibiting discrimination,
yet other countries consider, for example, the hiring of women to work along with
men a breach of ethics.

These examples show how difficult it is to develop a set of ethical standards
that doesn't somehow ignore or trample on someone else's set. Equally problem-
atic is the setting of standards to which people are unable to adhere. For example,
should we tell hostage negotiators to never tell a lie? What if lives are at stake?
Should they use delaying tactics—perhaps telling the hostage taker that a heli-
copter and the money he or she requested are being arranged? Philosopher Do-
lores Dooley addresses this question with regard to societies as well. She argues
that some of the lapse in ethics is due to the imposition on people of standards to
which they cannot possibly adhere. Can a starving person be expected not to steal
bread? Perhaps, but he'll die. What Dooley proposes is that ethical standards be
reachable—not so oppressive that people simply give up. She provides a defini-
tion of ethics sufficiently broad to allow for this kind of adaptability to conditions:

"Ethics refers to our beliefs about what comprises a happy life, what makes for a worthwhile society; ethics also includes our beliefs about what behavior contributes to or frustrates the achievement of a worthwhile society. Finally, ethics wonders about what features of character are worth cultivating. These aspects are all interconnected in most ethical systems. Beliefs about what is 'right' and 'wrong' and what kind of people we should become—these only make sense when closely linked to our beliefs about what comprises a 'worthwhile' society."[1]

This definition does not mean we should be forever changing our beliefs as an unmanned boat at sea changes direction without benefit of an anchor. It does mean that ethics is an evolving subject inextricably connected to our definitions of a worthwhile society, not a set of standards that, once defined, must never change. Dooley explains:

> The pervasive assumption has long been that morality is a *completed system of divinely authorized and certain beliefs*. To modify this way of thinking about morality may seem, to many, like a sacrifice of the *security* that certainty brings. While appreciating this concern, I am, nevertheless, reminded of the American philosopher and educationalist, John Dewey, who claimed that a quest for certainty down through the ages has held human societies captive and made morality into a static enterprise. A quest for certainty, Dewey continues, prevented many human communities from taking the daring and innovative steps required to provide a morality that makes a social difference—a morality which could genuinely affect the *quality of human living.*[2]

In short, morality can be too narrowly defined and thus irrelevant to the people it is supposed to guide. It can be too broadly defined and therefore of no use to people because they cannot find its limits. Much has been written of this in regard to the raising of children—the indulgence and absence of rules that has, many believe, created an epidemic of immorality among adolescents. So where does this leave us? Can a set of ethical guidelines be developed that is neither too narrow nor too broad, or must we throw up our hands and say, "It's no use"?

The answer is not an easy one. If it were, the debate over ethics would not have been waged for so long. Our task here, however, is to ask a somewhat specific question and in doing so to perhaps limit the dimensions of the task. That question is this: Can a code of ethics for negotiation be developed, and can that code be maintained throughout the course of most negotiations? I believe a code is possible—not a static one for all negotiations but certainly one that individual negotiators can work with to keep them within a range of good, better, and best practices—one that can be maintained by mutual agreement. The goal of this chapter, then, is to help negotiators devise such ethical guidelines for themselves and their negotiation counterparts that in the short run contribute to positive negotiation outcomes and in the long run contribute to a worthwhile society.

▶ THE STICKY WICKET THAT IS ETHICS

Unscrupulous negotiators can cause considerable harm to others. Lying, cheating, and manipulating are all in a day's work for them. What is worse, they can benefit from books that teach negotiation strategy. To prevent would-be deceivers from

sharpening their skills, one might argue that only the purest, most honorable forms of negotiation should be taught. Indeed, the Greek philosopher Plato believed that common people should not be taught the suspect persuasion tactics that were used by Sophists around 400 B.C. An elitist, Plato believed that teaching people about persuasion would only add to the arsenal of tactics already in the hands of dishonorable men. Plato's student Aristotle was unconvinced by his mentor's argument. If the common people were left in the dark regarding questionable persuasive tactics, he proposed, they would become easy prey for the more scurrilous members of society. Aristotle argued that more is to be gained by teaching people persuasive techniques, so that they will know both when others are attempting to persuade them and how to resist.

Little is to be gained from learning only pure forms of influence in negotiation. To do so leaves one unprepared for the real world. However, much may be gained from a frank examination of what constitutes ethical negotiation. Let's begin with the question of whether an act, in and of itself, is unethical. Before making that determination, the context in which the act occurs must be considered.

During the time I was writing this book, police in England charged a woman with the murder of her husband. She had allegedly killed him after he punched her in the stomach. She was found guilty, but upon appeal, information previously disallowed in the court was revealed—the woman was pregnant with quadruplets at the time of her husband's attack. Was her response therefore self-defense and defense of her unborn children, or was it simply murder? Whatever one's opinion, the additional information about the woman's pregnancy provides contextual input that colors the situation.

Most ethical considerations are similar, in that determining whether an action is right or wrong depends on the available information regarding such issues as who did what first, who had the most power, what provoked the action, and what choices were available to the parties involved. There are few completely right answers to questions of ethics. After all, such answers are derived through human decision-making processes, which are imperfect. Add to this the existence of two types of ethical or moral forms of judgment: public and private. Mary Warnock, in *An Intelligent Person's Guide to Ethics*, attempts to separate these two forms. Public morality has to do with the common good, whereas private morality "rests on feelings of that I must do, or refrain from doing, something, never mind the consequences, or what prudence might dictate."[3] Given the complexity of ethical issues, both private and public, any attempt at crafting a steel-trap definition of morality for all people for all times is an exercise destined to fail. Aristotle grappled with this difficulty. Unlike his predecessor, Plato, he did not believe that a set of objective criteria exists for the determination of morality. Aristotle looked to the institutions in which people function to provide the means whereby people would not simply avoid hurting each other but become and stay good and just. Human good, he argued, requires social cooperation. In other words, people help each other define and do moral things.

Negotiation occurs within social contexts. Some of these contexts encourage moral behavior; others encourage the attainment of goals at any cost; still others are

somewhere in between. Within these contexts, negotiators themselves are inclined or disinclined to what they understand to be ethical behavior. Some have a keen ethical sense, encouraging them to avoid actions that are generally considered questionable or reprehensible. Ethics is always a matter of degree, not absolutes. Actions in question lie somewhere along a continuum of accepted practice. And accepted practices are influenced by what we have come to consider natural. Warnock points to the discomfort many people feel about gene manipulation in the service of saving lives. The reason often given is that such practice is not natural. And yet these same people are often quite accepting of plastic hip joints and surgical interventions. These are quite unnatural as well; the only difference is that they have come to be considered natural and therefore ethical. Most ethical questions are informed by what we have come to accept; in business that can mean a range of behaviors that serve the common good of the company though they may be at odds with the common good of society as a whole.

Professors Raymond Friedman and Debra Shapiro propose that whether a behavior is ethical depends on its context.[4] It is difficult to imagine a negotiation scenario in which context could be ignored when determining where, on the ethical continuum, an action belongs. Friedman and Shapiro use an example similar to one previously cited—negotiating with terrorists for the release of hostages. If lives could be saved through deception, many would consider that deception important to serve the greater good. Or suppose you were negotiating on behalf of a powerless community group that was attempting to block a toxic waste disposal facility in its neighborhood. Would deception be understandable or even acceptable? What if the facility's developer had a prior history of misrepresenting data about the leaching of toxins into public water supplies? Would a positive outcome for the community justify the use of deception in this negotiation?

Answers come hard in situations like these. Just as juries in criminal trials are charged to determine what represents guilt *beyond a reasonable doubt,* negotiators must ask themselves what constitutes misrepresentation, inappropriate concealment of data, misleading shaping of impressions, and other distortions of the truth. On the other hand, is it smart negotiating to inform your counterpart of all your interests? Or of which methods you intend to use to persuade them? Or of all your data and exactly how much you can concede? Of course not. Yet we must find a way to monitor ourselves, to recognize when we're on the verge of crossing the sometimes nearly imperceptible line between ethical and unethical negotiation.

What can we use for a moral compass in the murky terrain of the ethical gray area? There are no clear rights or wrongs; rather, there are varying degrees of consensus on whether certain behaviors are understandable or acceptable, given the conditions in which they take place. Researchers and theorists have attempted to distinguish generally accepted, traditional, competitive bargaining tactics (exaggerating demands, pretending not to be in a hurry, hiding one's bottom line) from more questionable tactics (misrepresenting information, bluffing, exerting influence on an opponent's colleagues).[5] Many scholars argue that when confronted by an unethical opponent, a negotiator has a moral right to self-protection. Again, however, it's a matter of degree. Suppose that the offenders withhold

pivotal information or pretend to have been duped while in actuality obtaining exactly what they want. Many people would consider it well within the realm of justifiable action to respond in kind. On the other hand, if the aggrieved parties responds with lies, empty promises, or outright fraud, consensus would likely judge them to be out of line ethically.[6] They would be considered to have gone too far, even if some degree of retaliation were justified.

How far people will go depends in part on how responsible they feel for ethically questionable behavior (see Exhibit 5.1). According to some psychologists, people tend toward either an internal or an external locus of control. If you have an internal locus of control, you tend to see yourself as a causal agent of what happens to you. However, if you have a predominantly external locus of control, you see outside factors as the predominant cause of negative outcomes in your life. A person with an internal locus of control will be less likely to make excuses if discovered engaging in questionable tactics. He will see those actions as largely products of his own choice. Even the most internally focused person may blame outside conditions if those are sufficiently extreme. Although few negotiations have life-or-death outcomes, in the fever of engagement they may appear to have career-threatening outcomes, which may drive otherwise ethical people to unethical extremes. The financial world relearned as much during the Enron scandal. Day by day, some Enron executives had convinced themselves that their questionable dealings were crucial to their own career or their company's welfare.[7]

Michael Elliott of *Time* magazine pointed out that shortly before the Enron scandal, many observers would have placed its CEO in the "pantheon of American business." Why, Elliott wondered, did otherwise intelligent people allow their

▶ *EXHIBIT 5.1*

HOW COULD THEY HAVE DONE IT?

In the *Wall Street Journal Europe* article "How Could They Have Done It?" Holman Jenkins, Jr. drew on the work of Harvard's Max Bazerman and Northwestern's David Messick to explore how Enron executives could have believed that someone wouldn't one day blow the whistle. The answer may lie less in the desire for profits at any cost than in psychological tendencies. For example, people often believe that they are immune to common risks because they have an exaggerated confidence in their ability to control situations. They overestimate the likelihood that they will experience good future events and underestimate the likelihood of bad ones. And in many cases, people who "have it all" believe they deserve it. They surround themselves with people who agree with them, who also "have it all," and soon there are few messages coming their way that would give them pause.

Bazerman does not believe that business schools can teach people to be ethical. The schools can, however, teach students to remain aware of the systematic errors in thinking that can start a decent person down the slippery slope to unethical decisions.

Sources: H. W. Jenkins Jr., "How Could They Have Done It?" *Wall Street Journal Europe,* Aug. 29, 2002, p. A9; M. Bazerman and D. Messick, *Sloan Management Review,* Jan. 1996.

value systems to take such a turn? A host of "heroes of glamour capitalism" had graced the covers of leading business publications. After Enron and other scandals, many found themselves under a harsher spotlight, their actions and motives questioned. The lesson Elliott draws from Enron is that we should entrust our prosperity to "those with their feet on the ground, not on a pedestal. Even if we built it for them."[8]

The slippery slope of unethical decisions is made even slicker by the general acceptance of a broad range of negotiation behaviors, such as exaggerating demands, pretending not to be in a hurry, asking for more than you really expect to get, and hiding the bottom line. These kinds of tactics are generally accepted in distributive negotiations where mutual gain is not the goal. In this category of what may be called *borderline tactics* are more questionable ones, such as misrepresenting information, bluffing, influencing an opponent's professional network, and encouraging people from the other side to defect to yours. Clearly, these tactics are further down the slippery slope, yet a host of conditions is commonly used to justify their use, including the importance of the issues or outcomes of a negotiation, time pressures, power imbalances, use of similar tactics by the other side, and an attitude of "business is business, so anything goes." In some cultures, it is common practice to take advantage of outsiders, who are viewed with suspicion and distrust. And negotiators who might otherwise refrain from unethical tactics often justify their use in service of the collective good ("If it were just me, I wouldn't do it, but my whole team was going to suffer").

To check how flexible your ethical standards are, let's look at a few situations. See if you have clear answers as to how negotiators should proceed in each of the following circumstances:

- Your company is about to declare bankruptcy. A deal is on the table. If you accept it, you've been told that you must provide an incentive to the chief negotiator. He'll expect a payment of $10,000. Your company stands to receive $25 million if you do this. A lot of jobs are at stake. People are depending on you. What will you do?

- You are a hostage negotiator. Ten people are being held at gunpoint inside a bank. The hostage taker has threatened to kill one of them every ten minutes if you do not promise him that he will go free if he surrenders. Should you lie to him?

- A job promotion could be yours if you appear to be a better candidate than one other person. You know that that this person has some family issues that could prove difficult. His wife is leaving him, and he's been taking medication to help him through it. If you tell the interviewer about this, it just might bump you up to the top of the list. Should you tell?

- You are about to close a deal. Your team leader has promised a delivery date that is unrealistic, if not an outright lie. Should you tell the other side or remain quiet?

If we had a single standard such as "Do unto others what you would have them do unto you" and people could stick to it, the right answers would come into

focus more easily. In negotiation, however, as in much of life, difficult choices arise and pressures exist to pull us away from the abstract ethical answer.

We shouldn't give bribes, lie to people, reveal personal secrets, or allow others to draw us into their lies. This sentence tells us how we should, in the abstract, respond to the four scenarios. Were your responses to those scenarios in accordance with no bribery, no lies, no revealing of secrets, and no going along with lies? Were your responses halfway there? Did you, for example, reject bribery and lying?

With these types of pressures on negotiators, it may be a wonder that so many stay on the best-practices end of the continuum. For some people, the reason is a strong personal morality; for others, a company culture that discourages unethical practices. Even when negotiators are not guided by personal ethics, they may fear being found out, because many people are good at detecting liars and cheats, and most would-be manipulators, bluffers, and cheats are identified rather easily; their body language often gives them away (if other people don't expose them first). This is a deterrent.

Perhaps we can at least say that certain types of behaviors should be avoided. Despite the difficulties inherent in attempting to judge behaviors out of context, a general list of tactics to be avoided could include bluffing, falsification, misrepresentation, deception, and selective disclosure.[9] Each is a form of lying. The difficulty, again, is that some forms of deception are not only considered acceptable but also expected. A study of professional labor negotiators revealed that they expect a certain amount of deception in negotiation. They expect, for example, that opponents will hide information and try to build up false perceptions about their limits and determination. Yet these same negotiators consider some types of deception unacceptable—for example, making overtly inaccurate statements, such as those regarding costs. They may find it acceptable to say, "We cannot pay a penny more for health care" but not acceptable to say, "Adding physical therapy to the benefit package will cost us an additional $100 a year per employee" when it will only add $20 a year. The first statement is a bargaining stance; the second, a falsehood. The first indicates negotiation savvy; the second, deceit. Labor negotiators also expect what is said across a negotiation table to be exaggerated, but they count on more honesty in private discussions.[10]

Because most competitive negotiations involve at least *some* accepted forms of deception, the best advice to negotiators is to rely as much as possible on persuasion rather than manipulation and coercion. Persuasion is not something an individual does *to* another person; it is done *with* that person. It is not always pure, but it relies more on strong evidence and skillful communication than on trickery and force.[11] This is an important rule to bear in mind during negotiations—one that is helpful in sorting out whether a particular tactic is ethical. Is the other person being deprived of choice by deception or threat? If so, the action in question is at least marginally unethical. What a negotiator decides to do about that depends on whether he or she is an ethical person. As Aristotle argued, we can't stop teaching how to persuade and negotiate simply because some people will use what they learn in devious ways. It's important that people understand how to advance their ideas and causes and that they be capable of spotting deception.

Whether you decide to fight fire with fire—that is, deception with deception—is ultimately an individual decision. But such tactics, most experts agree, usually come home to roost. The good news is that skillful negotiators rarely, if ever, need to stoop so low. As they learn to persuade, they rely on that skill to realize their goals and to make the heads of deceptive counterparts spin.

That's all well and good, you may say, but how do these ethical negotiators monitor themselves as well as their counterparts? What self-constraints do they use, especially when the other side is engaging in unethical actions? One option is to develop together (preferably before negotiation starts) a list of behaviors neither of you will slip into. A simple list might include behaviors that are dishonest, disrespectful, irresponsible, bullying, manipulative, or inconsiderate. Sometimes all it takes is a simple mention of this kind of list after introductory remarks and before negotiations get under way: "As every negotiation expert in the world knows, when you're caught up in trying to achieve desired outcomes, it is easy to slip into strategies that are unethical. I'd like to take a moment to agree that we will not allow ourselves to do so, that we will operate on a higher plane, avoiding . . . [list]." If this seems too heavy-handed or awkward, you might say instead, "Let's agree right now to treat each other with dignity; to reject pressures to manipulate, bully, or in any way demonstrate the kind of disrespect that can only damage our short- and long-term goals." Then simply move on. If an infraction occurs, you can return to the agreement and nudge the other side back on track. And they can do the same if you begin to slip.

If your counterparts refuse to accept a set of ethical guidelines, agreement to a general rule might suffice: "We agree, as we hope you do as well, to refrain from misrepresenting our positions in any way and to use mutual regard and respect in all our dealings." If you make this kind of statement early on in the negotiation, it is less likely to be construed as blame. You might introduce this comment or the ones mentioned earlier by saying, "Something we do at our company as a matter of course—and as a reminder to ourselves and to others—is to talk briefly about the limits to which we'll go to achieve the upper hand." Then use the "We agree . . ." statement or provide a short list of unethical actions that will not be used by either side.

If you have had a long-term relationship with a negotiation counterpart, instead of providing a list or making a blanket statement about ethics, you might say, "Let's try today to continue to treat each other with the respect and regard that has made our relationship so strong." It is possible to raise the issue of ethics even during the course of negotiation, if it seems appropriate to do so. Again, blaming isn't the best course of action. Instead, you might say, "We seem to be getting a bit desperate here, slipping into ways of talking and acting toward each other that aren't typical of our relationship." Another approach is to say, "We've established a very productive process here, free of manipulation or coercion. As things get more intense, it may become tempting to do otherwise. I'm sure you agree, that would not serve either of us."

It's important to choose an approach that works for you, that sounds like something you'd say, not something rehearsed. If you want people to treat you in an ethical manner, though, you need to treat them that way yourself. In negotia-

tion, it is often tempting to do otherwise. You need to ask yourself and your team members what makes ethical sense to them. What lines do you refuse to cross? Where are the gray areas—and will you enter them? If you need assistance with this, there are organizations devoted to the understanding and promotion of ethical behavior.[12] Check their Web sites. What you find will give you a launching point from which to consider and discuss among team members the ethical constraints you wish to place on yourselves and your counterparts.

▶ ETHICS AND EMOTION

If, indeed, persuasion is generally more ethical than coercion and manipulation, then forms of persuasion that are devoid of emotion may be even more ethical. It could be argued that persuasion based on reason alone is more honest than persuasion that relies on eliciting an emotional response. Yet reasoning alone is often insufficient to provide a galvanizing force to action. Providing people with extensive reasons for protecting their health may lead to their acceptance of the need but not to the actions that would bring about that protection. In such cases, people must often be provoked to action by some emotional story or image. The same is true in negotiations. Getting people to act on an agreement, for example, may require emotional persuasion. If telling people that they are about to be emotionally provoked inevitably leads to resistance, is it then unethical to proceed with emotional persuasion? This question has been the subject of considerable debate among philosophers and rhetoricians. Richard Whately, the eminent nineteenth-century rhetorician whose work contributed greatly to this area, recognized the dilemma of needing to use emotion to provoke people to action yet being unable to apprise them of the intention to use emotion because that knowledge would lead to resistance or resentment. He wrote, "The mind is sure to revolt from the humiliation of being thus molded and fashioned, in respect to its feelings, at the pleasure of another, and is apt, perversely, to resist the influence of such a discipline."[12] Whately acknowledged that should the person using emotion be perceived as doing so for his or her own special interests, the resistance and resentment will be even greater. Yet he advocated the use of emotion as necessary to get people to take that step—from rationally accepting the need for action to *taking* action.

Where does this bring us in our attempt to grapple with questions of ethics in negotiation? Unlike bluffing, falsifying, misrepresenting, and selectively disclosing, emotion cannot be easily regulated by preagreed guidelines. It simply doesn't make sense to craft a rule that states, for example, "We will at all times remain completely unemotional." It isn't realistic to ask people to be unemotional. People are emotional. If a negotiator's intentions are not self-serving at the expense of the other party, the use of emotion is at least understandable. It is hard to imagine a skilled negotiator whose language is free of emotional expression. The question negotiators must ask themselves, however, is whether they are using such emotion to provoke action that will harm the other party.

I observed a negotiator working for a large technology company attempt to partner with another large technology company in the acquisition of a multimil-

lion-dollar government grant. After he'd received what he considered to be an agreement from that company that they would indeed be working together, he heard that a competitor was attempting to dismantle the agreement. This would mean that the prospective partner might defect and join the competitor, thus closing out any hope of the negotiator's company getting the grant. After hours of rational discussion about what to say to whom, including whether to appear to have even heard of the attempted interception, the negotiator decided to send an e-mail to his prospective partner. The e-mail would not mention any gossip about another company attempting to undermine the agreement. It would not lay out, at length, rational arguments about why the partnership would lead to success. Instead, the negotiator decided to write the following: "Yesterday the members of my team were told of our decision to work together. They were delighted. On a personal level, I want to say that getting to know you has been a pleasure, as is the prospect of working as partners." The negotiator used an emotional appeal to partnership, emerging friendship, and obligation. Was this unethical or at least to-ward the unethical end of the continuum? My response is that it was tactical but not dishonest. An agreement had been reached, the team was indeed delighted, and the negotiator had enjoyed coming to know his counterpart. He'd opted to use emotion to provoke his potential partner to do the right thing—stick with their agreement.

Whenever persuasion comes into the picture, ethical considerations are there as well. Ultimately, as we've said, the decision to keep one's actions at the more ethical end of the continuum is a personal one. The important thing is to be aware that the temptation to move toward the opposite end is ever present. But in the long run—and often in the short—the use of unethical tactics undermines posi-tive relationships and, if discovered, can lead to resentment. The skilled negotia-tor knows that most people are sufficiently intelligent to notice when they are being manipulated. So if private morality does not nudge you toward the ethical in negotiation and public morality escapes you as well, it's wise to bear in mind that habitual use of unethical approaches tends to destroy credibility and make enemies. There is a difference between the use of style, emotion, and effective wording to enhance agreement and provoke desired actions and the manipulation of people into doing what is potentially harmful to them or their cause. The skilled negotiator does not lightly enter into the latter. Even when deciding to fight fire with fire, a negotiator should feel pulled. When manipulation and coer-cion come easily, it is a sure sign that a negotiator has abdicated the responsibility to resist the temptation of unmitigated self-interest.

▶ RESPONDING ON THE SPOT TO UNETHICAL NEGOTIATORS

The flip side of the question of how ethical to be in negotiation is how to handle un-ethical behavior from a counterpart. Even if you both agree, early on in the negoti-ation, to be ethical in your dealings, the other side may decide to deviate from that agreement at some point in the negotiation. It's always wise to be alert to this possi-bility. A word from Machiavelli is instructive on this point: "Any man who tries to be good all the time is bound to come to ruin among the great number who are not

good. Hence a prince who wants to keep his authority must learn how to not be good, and use that knowledge, or refrain from using it, as necessity requires."[13]

Taken too literally, this advice might seem to contradict prior advice regarding ethical conduct in negotiation. Taken in the spirit in which it was likely intended, however, the message is to be alert to the possibility of unethical behavior on the part of others and be prepared to respond effectively to it.

What if you suspect, for example, that your negotiation counterpart is withholding critical information? You could confront him or her with your suspicions. You might say, "I have a feeling that you are not telling me the whole story," or less directly, "Have you shared with me all the details you'd want to have if *you* were making this decision?" Alternatively, you might suggest that were you in your counterpart's shoes, you might be inclined to withhold critical information. Listen to the response. Then you could try what has been called a "chink in the defense" approach, in which the goal is to get the other side to admit to a small or partial lie about something, which you can then use to encourage further disclosures. For example, you might say, "Given that X is not totally true, can you tell me if I have all the facts on Y before we proceed?"

At times it's best to come right out with your suspicions: "I can't help but feel that you are not being completely up-front with me on this." The phrase "completely up-front" sounds less blatantly attacking than the term *dishonest*. It suggests that the other negotiator has been relatively honest—but not completely. Also, the phrase on *this* suggests that this type of behavior pertains to the issue at hand rather than to all of the negotiator's actions. It gives the other side some wiggle room. In the interest of wiggle room, you might say, "I've come to trust you completely, but on this issue I sense some holding back." Again, you're letting the other party know that something is amiss, but making the allegation indirectly gives the other negotiator some face-saving options not available in the face of a direct attack. Another alternative is to treat the behavior in question as clever by saying humorously, "I'm glad you don't own the bank where my money is," or, "If I had your cleverness, I'd be a lot richer." Of course, determining whether to use this type of approach depends on whether the other person is likely to find your comments at least somewhat humorous and complimentary. Most of us like to be thought of as clever in negotiation. Implying or stating that the other side has been so can indeed be a compliment—but with the added advantage of apprising them that you are not oblivious to their tactics.

Sometimes a period of silence, accompanied by a skeptical look, is the best approach. Study the face or faces of the other side. This "make them squirm" approach is useful when you believe that the other side will find it unsettling. It encourages people to provide information they've been hiding or to cease engaging in unethical actions because they feel caught. A simple "Come on now" or the somewhat flippant "Get real" can also prompt a return to ethical negotiation. At other times, it may be necessary to be more explicit: "Two can play this game, but it won't lead to any winners." Those are fighting words in some circles but are occasionally worth the risk. "Each of us is capable of manipulating the other, but that is not our purpose here today" might prove a useful follow-up. Skilled negotiators have a range of options available and choose, based on the nature of the

unethical actions with which they are confronted, whether to be indirect or direct.[14] As a rule, however, it is wise to remember that none of us is perfect and that all people are pulled toward unethical practice at one time or another. As Aristotle observed, it is a rare person who can find the midpoint on questions of behavior. He explained that moral virtue is a mean or midpoint between extremes, adding the following:

> For this reason it is a difficult business to be good; because in any given case it is difficult to find the midpoint—for instance, not everyone can find the centre of a circle; only the man who knows how. So too it is easy to get angry—anyone can do that—or to give and spend money; but to feel or act towards the right person to the right extent at the right time for the right reason in the right way—that is not easy, and it is not everyone that can do it. Hence to do these things well is a rare, laudable and fine achievement.[15]

Aristotle's advice—for those of us not among the rare people who can always find the midpoint—is to "take the next best course." Doing this entails being aware of the errors into which we are liable to fall and then to drag ourselves in the opposite direction, "for we shall arrive at the mean by pressing well away from our failing—just like somebody straightening a warped piece of wood."[16]

As ancient as this advice is, it's still useful for the negotiator. Since it is human nature to stray from best practices, it's wise to tread lightly when confronting others with the error of their ways. When possible, it's best to give the other side wiggle room; a chance to save face, to correct unethical approaches to negotiation without complete disgrace. Of course, the nature of the offense determines the required response to a certain extent, but nailing someone to the wall for having strayed from the mean does not serve a negotiator. Remaining silent and allowing unethical actions to take place is not the answer either. As Aristotle recommended, the answer is, as always, somewhere in the middle. In general, then, the best course of action is to take the high road. Rather than getting down into the mud with an unethical counterpart, consider bringing the negotiation to a higher plane. Operate as if the other negotiator is capable of ethical conduct while making it clear that you are not oblivious to unethical tactics: "This game is beneath us both" or "Is this an act of desperation or of exhaustion? It certainly isn't our normal way of working with each other." Another possibility: "It's tempting here to deceive each other, as if the outcome might benefit the one who does it best, but neither of us will emerge a winner under those circumstances." This implies that you know what is going on and that you even understand why but that together you could rise to a higher plane. Of course, you'll want to keep your eyes open for slips back onto an unethical course. If such slips appear likely, skilled negotiators often pause to negotiate the way they'll negotiate. "I suggest we pause now and then to assess whether we've maintained the type of mutual respect we've both valued" is one way to do this. Involve the other side in an agreement to be ethical and in the maintenance of the agreement (for example, "We appear to be slipping again into self-serving action" or "The track we're now taking isn't in the spirit of mutual regard we'd agreed to maintain").

Managing ethics in negotiation is possible, albeit difficult. Skilled negotiators train themselves to do so. They learn with practice whether to directly deal with unethical behavior or simply let the other side know that they've noticed it and leave it to the offenders to change their ways. They realize, however, that if such management is necessary, they are dealing with someone not to be trusted. A wise negotiator remains ever vigilant.

I spoke with a CEO who told me of a time when his wife saved him from a very bad deal. He was negotiating to place a subsidiary of his company in a foreign country. The person with whom he was dealing was charming and persuasive. His dress was impeccable. Before the CEO was about to close the deal, his wife said to him, "That guy is pulling the wool over your eyes." The CEO was astounded. His wife rarely said anything of this nature about his business partners. She had detected a kind of smoothness in his ways that made her uncomfortable. The CEO decided to check her perceptions. He offered to open the subsidiary if some promises could be made. All of them required steps that would indicate whether he was dealing with an honest person. Within a week, the negotiation was called off. Not long afterward, the CEO received a phone call from the FBI. They wanted to know if he'd come across a certain person in his dealings. That person was the impeccable dresser. The CEO explained that he had just let a deal drop with the man, to which the FBI agent replied, "Good thing, because we've been looking for him for years. He's a fugitive."

Obviously, if we need to talk about ethics—to devote an entire chapter to it—there are unethical people out there. If you are wise in your negotiations, you'll *check the checkered past of your counterparts.* Dress and demeanor are not sufficient indicators of a respectable past. Just ask the FBI.

▶ QUESTIONS

1. Reread the section on the ethics continuum. What is your opinion of what separates ethical and non-ethical actions in negotiation?

2. To what extent do you think business negotiations are expected to be at least somewhat deceptive? In other words, are business dealings by their very nature somewhat unethical? Is it possible for an organization to insist on completely ethical dealings by its employees at all levels?

3. Apply the same questions in number 2 above to government. Are there times when deception, for example, is a good or acceptable thing? Give some historical examples to support your point of view.

4. Go to the library or Internet sources to study a hostage negotiation case. Analyze the negotiator's actions in terms of the discussion of ethics in this chapter.

Report:

1. Read Machiavelli's The Prince. Why did Machiavelli write this advice? Select from the book one form of deception that is benign, one that is strategic and one that is ulterior in nature. Explain why in each case.

2. Read Aristotle's Ethics. Describe several key perspectives that still apply today, and several that do not. In each case explain why, providing examples from current events.

3. Choose a book on the topic of ethics. Describe the author's key perspective. Compare and contrast those with your own experiences in negotiation or with what you read in Chapter Five.

4. Interview an accomplished negotiator on the topic of ethics. What are his/her views regarding a continuum of ethical action in negotiation? Does he/she have any hard and fast rules of negotiation ethics? Describe one of his/her negotiation experiences in which a difficult ethical decision was made. Would you have acted similarly had you been in his/her shoes? Why or why not?

CHAPTER ▶ 6

The Persuasive Opening

Negotiation typically involves convincing the other side to accept outcomes less desirable than those they initially had in mind. Of the three forms of influence already discussed—coercion, manipulation, and persuasion—the last is the one we focus on now. When effectively employed, persuasion moves others from one view or course of action to another, more desirable one—not by force or deception but through compelling arguments or emotional appeals. At its best, persuasion leads to *private acceptance,* whereby the person persuaded chooses to adopt a new view or take a different course of action. Unlike the act of *compliance,* in which the individual "goes along" for a short time, private acceptance involves considering a change and embracing it; it is therefore typically of longer duration. The achievement of private acceptance requires skillful persuasion because people are generally disinclined to change, especially if it involves considerable effort or seems to stand in opposition to their prior beliefs and ways of acting. If, for example, you are trying to convince someone to lose weight or stop smoking, that person must come to their own private acceptance. The person must believe in the change, or he or she is likely to slip back into old ways once the persuader's back is turned. Sometimes the goal of persuasion is simply short-term compliance. "Clean your room," a parent might say to a child, "and I'll give you an ice cream." The child may comply but is unlikely to internalize the need to clean up on a regular basis. The latter will stem only from the child's private acceptance—and as a parent, I can attest to the difficulty inherent in achieving long-term room cleaning. It's not for the meek of heart.

Knowing, then, that successful persuasion is often a challenge, we now focus on the means to achieve it. Chief among the required skills is the ability to organize issues in a manner that is acceptable to the other side while also conducive to reaching your goals.

▶ SETTING THE AGENDA: LEADING WITH STRENGTH

In Chapter 4, we discussed the importance of prioritizing issues and also the goals associated with those interests. Even if you've done your homework and know what your negotiation counterpart considers the key issues and the ideal out-

comes and contingency goals for each, you should go into negotiation with some tangible means of ensuring that you're right. This is where agendas come into the picture.

Agendas stipulate the important issues for negotiators, just as the headlines and positioning of newspaper stories indicate their importance to the reader (or to the political agenda of the newspaper ownership). When a newspaper editor decides to give a story front-page placement, the editor is vesting that story with power, plainly indicating that it is or should be of importance and interest to the reader. Similarly, a negotiation agenda indicates which issues are worth talking about and their order of importance. This second role of agendas is crucial. Some negotiators prefer to deal first with less contentious issues or ones of less importance. Others prefer to jump into the deep end, so to speak—to deal first with difficult or key issues, saving the easier and less important ones for later in the negotiation. There is no right or wrong approach, but there are better and worse ones, depending on what is at stake, characteristics of the negotiators, time pressures, and context considerations, all of which we'll review in this chapter.

Novice negotiators often fail to recognize that setting an agenda is a negotiation in and of itself. It gives you an opportunity to (1) situate issues in a manner conducive to reaching your goals and (2) either trade issue positioning with the other side, to make them feel good, or resist such trading, to demonstrate that you won't be an easy mark in the negotiation to follow. Expert negotiators know which positions they are willing to trade and how to use these trades to arrange desired positions for the issues of importance to them.

Most people know the importance of agendas in negotiation; far fewer know how to develop them strategically. Many novice negotiators consider them a waste of time, a deterrent to getting to the heart of the issue. This is especially the case in cultures where "time is money." Yet agenda setting, like all negotiation moves, should be strategic and based on informed observations regarding which positions and moves the other side is likely to take.

When you're forming an agenda, the first question to ask yourself involves *primary and secondary issues.* We discussed how to identify these in Chapter 4. Many experts suggest beginning an agenda with secondary or even nearly irrelevant issues that are likely to result in early agreement (and thereby establish a positive problem-solving context). This approach often creates an atmosphere of success and cooperation, so it is generally a wise move. A note of caution, however: I've seen negotiators intent on establishing a cooperative, amicable problem-solving context become so captivated by accomplishing it initially that they failed to take steps to secure its continuance. When the mood changed, they felt cheated and became annoyed or angry at having put so much effort into civility only to have it abruptly turn to conflict. Attaining a positive climate early on in no way ensures it will remain so. When more serious, significant issues are raised, emotions may turn—and turn abruptly. Savvy negotiation requires constantly assessing the climate and remaining alert for signals of deterioration in the desired atmosphere. In team negotiation, one member should take charge of watching for such cues. Some amount of conflict may be fine, even helpful, but should the negotiation appear to be veering off on a damaging detour, this team member can

signal the others so that they can take reparative measures. This can help the team maintain a tone and direction of interaction conducive to achieving its goals. Similarly, although digressions to topics outside the agenda are occasionally warranted, an overly flexible agenda can allow a detour to become a derailment.

If negotiators anticipate intense conflict and either are not skillful at handling it or fear that the relationship might be damaged, the *lead with agreement* agenda approach can be very useful. If, however, a negotiator or team is confident in its conflict-handling skills, leading with the most challenging issue—even telling the other side you intend to do so—can sometimes prove successful. The first step in agenda development, therefore, is deciding whether to lead with agreement or with potential disagreement. From there, you may develop two optional agendas—one to use in the event of reasonable success on issue one, another should you achieve less than desired success.

The agenda-setting format would look like this:

Issue 1: _____

If outcome on Issue 1 is *highly cooperative,* Issue 2 will be _____.

If the outcome on Issue 1 is *moderately cooperative,* Issue 2 will be _____.

If outcome on Issue 1 is *uncooperative,* Issue 2 will be _____.

Once you have considered primary and secondary issues and the anticipated level of agreement on each, you should address the *order of critical points.* Here the major task is to identify the issues that the other side is likely to concede and the issues on which they are likely to hold firm. Even if a negotiator decides to open with the most contentious issue, she need *not* lead with the most contentious *aspect* of that issue. If negotiators expect resistance on a point and instead meet less than anticipated, they are likely to be more cooperative (unless they suspect malicious intent). If you present your position in a forthright manner—encouraging trust and leading with an issue about which the other side expects contention but on which you plan to concede—you can expect to meet less resistance. If this occurs on yet a second point, your counterpart may become even less resistant—raising the possibility of greater cooperation on more critical points.

Of course, you should avoid abruptly switching to an uncooperative mode after you have lulled the other side. They probably would feel duped—and might become more defensive or aggressive than they may have been before the cooperative opening phase. *In negotiation, it pays to ease into disagreement and connect it with earlier agreement, rather than to launch into it abruptly.* Connection to agreement can take the form of "We have established a strong base of agreement here, but we both know there are wrinkles of differences that we should iron out before proceeding." Here the differences are positioned or framed as minor in comparison to what the two sides have in common.

Wording is important throughout negotiation, but the early stage is often an especially delicate time. In this stage, much is decided about how "poised for battle" each side must be. Remember how much meaning words carry and how easily another person can derive an entirely different meaning from a word than the

one intended. Good public speakers devote considerable attention and practice to the first few minutes of their remarks. In the opening moments, many impressions are formed—impressions that are often resistant to change. In negotiation as well, such impressions are created, and the words used early in the negotiation can make or break progress. It pays to plan exactly *what* will be said and *how* each issue will be introduced. Practice these introductions in front of people who understand how the other side thinks. They can provide valuable assistance with word selection and help safeguard the negotiation against premature demise. In fact, they are a crucial component of agenda setting. On your copy of the agenda, make note of the words you'll likely use to introduce a new issue. Consider relating it to success on a prior one or to the issue's importance relative to some other key issue.

This brings us to another important consideration. Before the order of issues and points is finalized in written form, consider whether success on any given issue might lead to success on others through a sort of *agenda domino effect*. If the other side concedes in one area, concession on related issues might easily follow. It often pays to *bundle* issues in terms of background logic. Suppose, for example, that Liz, in the memo case in Chapter 4, can convince the CEO that interruptions and disparaging remarks inhibit women's contributions and progress at Vision Software. She might follow up with a connection to the "men only" bar, describing it as equally obstructive. If the CEO abhors obstructiveness in his company, then any issue that can be bundled into that category might reasonably benefit. Skilled negotiators often tentatively bundle topics, especially if they believe that a particular line of reasoning is likely to prove successful and that topics in that bundle can be linked to it. *Especially with issues of primary importance, a topic's presentation order may be profitably determined not only by salience or importance but also by how it links to other important topics.* Either way, negotiators should decide *before* negotiations begin whether to order an agenda by priority alone or to bundle issues. Adept negotiators are capable of doing both. They may order issues according to their importance, but if they make progress on one major issue that might cast a halo effect on another, they are ready to move that related issue to the fore. Such versatility in agenda formulation develops over time, but even the fledgling negotiator can benefit from practice in this area—for instance, by developing a flowchart delineating how issues could be bundled depending on where initial progress is made. Here is an example of issue bundling:

Issue 1: _____

If the outcome on Issue 1 is *highly cooperative,* Issue 2 will be (priority issue topically related).

If the outcome on Issue 1 is *moderately cooperative,* Issue 2 will be (possible move to topically related issue).

If the outcome on Issue 1 is *uncooperative,* Issue 2 will be (topically unrelated issue).

In especially uncooperative or uncollaborative conditions, bundling is unlikely to be useful. Another approach to agenda setting is to purposely "take a

beating" on some issues up front in the hope that the other side will feel inclined to let you win on a subsequent issue ("We'll forgo our interests here for the benefit of the entire negotiation" or "In the interests of progress, and given how strongly you feel about this issues, we will accept your proposal"). This won't work with experienced negotiators knowledgeable about methods for managing reciprocity or with those unconcerned with reciprocity. It is a common approach, however, one you should know about as an option and also in order to avoid succumbing to its purpose when the other side uses it.

Agendas of all types benefit from negotiators' estimating the *issue time allocation*—including at what point to move on from an issue when complete success is unrealized. To some extent, of course, individual allocations depend on the time available for the entire negotiation. If you know that the negotiation is scheduled for two hours and you have four issues to cover—say, two primary and two secondary issues—allow thirty to forty-five minutes for each primary issue. If discussions on the primary issues go well, consider saving the two secondary issues for another time or assign them to team members to work out later—perhaps by phone. Obviously, it's important to allocate time so that negotiators don't become so involved in discussing one topic—as often happens—that they neglect the others. But time allocation should remain somewhat flexible, depending on how significant each issue is in relation to others.

Issue 1: _____ (45 minutes)

If the outcome on Issue 1 is *highly cooperative,* Issue 2 will be
 (priority issue topically related). (45 minutes)

If the outcome on Issue 1 is *moderately cooperative,* Issue 2 will be
 (possible move to topically related issue).

If the outcome on Issue 1 is *uncooperative,* Issue 2 will be
 (topically unrelated issue).

If bundling will not be involved, you could use a simpler designation of time allocation:

Issue 1: _____ (45 minutes)

Issue 2: _____ (45 minutes)

Issue 3: _____ (25 minutes)

Issue 4: _____ (10 minutes or postpone)

How you ultimately set up topic choice within the agenda and time allocations for each is a matter of comfort. You can put them in one agenda list or keep them separate, but be sure to include time allocations, even if they are only estimates. This is especially important if you've decided to place your most important issues later in the negotiation. I've seen many negotiators spend so much time on their minor issues that they failed to even get to discussions of their major ones.

▶ NEGOTIATING THE AGENDA

Once you've decided on your preferred agenda, it's time to share it with the other side before the negotiation begins. Some negotiators, by the way, refuse to do this; they prefer to negotiate the agenda at the beginning of the actual negotiation. There is nothing inherently wrong with this approach of having the two parties propose their agendas and openly discuss their justifications. When the parties are suspicious of each other, it may have a certain appeal. Some negotiators prefer to keep an agenda in mind but share only the first topic or two, leaving the remainder open (or planned only in their own minds). They may believe that this gives them a strategic advantage. Such a *partial agenda-setting approach* is recommended only if the negotiator or team is so skilled at topic management and so time sensitive that few guidelines are needed. Otherwise, any surprise advantage gained by not revealing the full agenda preference is likely to be offset by the possibility of getting off track—or being led there. Among the other risks are spending too much or too little time on a topic, forgetting your plan of action, or having the other side best you by taking the lead on topic prioritization. Your safest approach, particularly if you are not yet highly adept at managing the course of a negotiation or if you're unsure of your skills generally, is to agree on the agenda a week or so in advance of the negotiation.

The *element of surprise* in negotiation is often overrated. People are usually too smart to be susceptible to this tactic. When a negotiation is important to them, they are going to be prepared. Assume that they *will* be. They will have their own desires about the agenda—and probably some hidden motives as well. If you are up front, they are more likely to be, too. That doesn't mean you should share all your thoughts or strategies—it just means letting them know what you expect to cover and in what order. If you initiate the agenda discussion, remember to leave some room for their input. You could title your agenda proposal "Draft Agenda" or "Suggested Agenda," which conveys that you're open to input and reduces the likelihood of a defensive reaction. Provide a brief paragraph that includes some of your reasons for the order of topics you propose and that briefly states why it behooves both sides to adopt this approach. It may be sufficient to offer only a short review of why you have proposed first and second topics, accompanied by an even briefer reference to why the other issues follow. Invite revisions. If you've done a good job of explaining how the agenda suits the needs of both sides, revisions are likely to be minor. If you know in advance that your counterparts are likely to propose revisions, you might indicate that they should feel free to reverse topics one and two or redistribute time allocations in some way. If you take this approach, however, be sure that starting with the other topic (rather than the one you originally proposed) is not likely to put you at a disadvantage. Your overall goal is to be flexible—but not so flexible that you might as well have skipped having an agenda in the first place. Offer some possible changes that are not harmful to your side, and ideally the other side will choose among those instead of making more radical revisions.

If possible, avoid a confrontation over the agenda. Even if you expect a largely distributive negotiation, why start off angry? It doesn't pay. Your *opening*

tone should be nonconfrontational. Avoid—or at least postpone—attempts to appear powerful. Save such displays for a point when firmness will help—not when it may cause irreparable damage. If you distrust your ability to remain calm and poised during the initial phases, write your opening comments at the top of the agenda page as a reminder. Consider as well any comments the other side may make to which you might react negatively. Then practice constructive responses you can make that would keep the negotiation from going astray.

▶ A STRONG OPENING STANCE

With an agenda in place, the next consideration in terms of persuasion is your *opening stance*. This differs from your opening tone. It conveys your initial position or attitude in the negotiation. Sometimes the opening stance must be a firm assertion, though perhaps with some recognition of the validity of the points the other side is likely to advocate. In such circumstances, it's wise to convey how convinced you are of the appropriateness or correctness of your position. Teachers have a saying among themselves: "Don't smile until Christmas." (In other words, don't appear too friendly and cooperative until the students have come to respect you.) In negotiation, this might translate to "Don't smile until they know you're not a pushover."

The foregoing should be taken with a grain of salt, of course. The nature of the opening stance, and all subsequent stances, depends to a certain extent on the stances the other side takes or that you expect them to take. It does little good to open as firm and unrelenting, then stick with that stance even after the other side opens with one of cooperation.

The more extensive your preparation and the more accurate your anticipations of the other side's stances, the better able you'll be to respond with a stance that advances your goals. Again, the interaction of a number of factors informs that choice. It's better to prepare for a variety of eventualities. The best way to determine likely opening stances is to create a series of *if-then scenarios*. "If, as we expect, they open with a firm stand, indicating that they are unlikely to cooperate, then we will respond with an equally strong affirmation of our position. If, however, they open with some indication of a willingness to budge, then we will respond by opening a window for them as well." You then proceed to determine what sort of window of opportunity you'll open for them. It could be a specific concession, a style choice, or allowing them to take the lead. Rather than responding in kind, the following if-then scenario is also an option: "If, as we expect, they open with a firm stand indicating that they are unlikely to cooperate, then we will respond by suggesting that we too considered such a stance, but after evaluation of the potential benefits of this alliance, we're ready to do some trading if they are ready to do some too." This type of approach should be considered before the negotiation begins and, in the case of teams, should be accompanied by designation of a person who will decide during the negotiation which possible approach should be taken. Jostling among yourselves while trying to decide how to respond will lower your credibility and communicate either a lack of preparation or an absence of consensus—both dangerous impressions.

The beginning of any negotiation is all about creating and forming impressions. Persuasion begins even while negotiators are taking their seats and making small talk. People formulate *attributions* that guide their choices for future behavior. In this early phase, few things should be left to chance. It's something like a runner's start at the beginning of a race. If you are awkward off the mark, you will need to devote considerable effort to reaching your optimum rhythm and pace.

Don't forget to consider your emotional stance—body language, gestures, facial expressions. Manage the potential for your emotions to influence those of your counterparts. Have you ever noticed yourself crossing your legs or arms when a companion does so? As part of relating to others, we often mimic their postural moves and gesticulations. Also, in situations in which we are unsure of our emotions, we look to others for feedback. If they respond well to us, we think more positively of ourselves and therefore of the relationship in general. Many of our impressions and reactions are nearly automatic—thus our mood and receptivity to others are often more a function of how we perceive their reactions to us than of any planned, highly cognitive determination. Knowing this, negotiators who attend to how their expressions and actions will affect the other side have a distinct advantage. They can manage impressions and *reactions* more effectively because they are aware of the possibility for emotional contagion—and are therefore introspective about how their eye contact, vocal inflections, and other body language can alter impressions to their advantage or disadvantage. Expert negotiators familiarize themselves with the kinds of impressions they evoke. They take a good hard look at themselves and decide what they may need to alter in expression, dress, and demeanor to elicit reactions advantageous to their goals.

To accomplish this, negotiators must not be oversensitive. They should be willing to learn from others how they are perceived—and to treat those perceptions as useful input. For example, if you are a young-looking female and the other side consists of older males, you could become defensive if they perceive you as inexperienced and thus easily swayed, or you could use that information to shape a strategy. You can determine what initial impressions and actions you should take to alter their impression, or you can decide how the impression suits your needs. Perhaps you don't mind their considering you less of a challenge than you actually are. You may decide that you won't go to great lengths to change their initial opinion, but you also won't let it affect your actions. As time passes, you will reveal your expertise and gradually alter their views. Whatever your actions on issues of how you are perceived, make them thoughtful ones.

▶ THE IMPORTANCE TO THE AGENDA OF FRAMING

Framing is an important persuasion strategy frequently used in negotiation. Framing refers to the manner in which negotiators present options to influence their counterparts' choices.[1] Why will we pay more for a drink in a hotel restaurant than we would for the same drink at a fast-food restaurant? It's the same beverage, yet the hotel's atmosphere is such we accept that drinks must necessarily cost more—and perhaps far more than any cost-based comparison would justify.

The decor is a form of framing, which conveys information that influences how we judge the acceptability of paying more or less for the same item. With the help of others who organize contextual features or information in influential ways, people make decisions during negotiation about available options. Negotiators often frame the options that they want the other side to choose in terms of gains, thus affecting the perceived value or acceptability of those options. They may also frame as likely losses the options that they want to dissuade the other side from choosing.

Early-stage framing involves presenting the negotiation itself and each key issue in ways that elicit desired responses from the other side. For example, a negotiator might propose a frame of cooperation by describing the negotiation as "an opportunity for us to find the common ground we both know exists below surface difficulties" or "a chance for us to make a good working relationship a great one." The placement of an issue within the agenda could be framed in this way: "We propose placing this issue first because it is the foundation on which all other issues rest" or "We could postpone this issue and pretend that it does not exist, but that would be tantamount to mutual deception. We know this is our stumbling block, and we propose moving it out of both our paths." If accepted by the other side, frames of this sort orient subsequent discussion toward cooperation (and imply that hostility is therefore out of bounds).

Erving Goffman described as "focused interaction" situations in which people openly join together to sustain a single common focus of concern. When people play games, for example, they know that certain types of unsporting or must-win displays are unacceptable. After all, it's just a game. When people share a definition of a situation, certain types of actions become required, others prohibited, and still others irrelevant. A frame is placed around the interaction that broadly defines what should and should not be said or done.[2]

I was once part of a negotiation about who would write a book for a nonprofit organization devoted to protecting the rights of children, many of whom remain at risk for far too long after suffering abuse. We met with a publisher known for a passion for books that seek to make a difference in society. It seemed a perfect match. The publisher's method of choice for such books, however, is to locate an expert and have that person tell the story. We wanted to place the expert, a judge passionate about the rights of children, in the limelight, but we wanted the book written by an established writer who'd studied the topic from a number of angles. The discussions stalled. Then a persuasive frame was introduced by the cochair of the organization, a successful movie producer. "If I wanted to do a film about Oscar Wilde, I would search for the best expert on the subject," he said. "Let's say I visit him and find myself immensely impressed. Do I throw up my hands, fall on my sword, and say, 'You're the expert—why don't you make the film?' Why would I do that? He's an Oscar Wilde expert, not a movie producer and director. So why are we discussing having our expert write the book? He's wonderful, but he's not an established writer." This frame gave perspective to our thoughts and direction to subsequent discussions. Both the writer and the expert were willing to do whatever the publisher wanted in order to get the book out and in so doing advance the rights of children. This frame indicated that we might not advance those

rights if we "fell on our swords"—backed away from all our plans and let a formula that worked for some books be adopted for ours. It was a very powerful reaffirmation of our goals.

As a negotiation skill, framing is indispensable both in the presentation of issues and in ongoing discussion of them. When people haven't defined (or haven't had defined for them) what type of interaction they are engaged in, they have trouble determining how to proceed effectively. They operate in a cloud of ambiguity. Moreover, when negotiators do not jointly define a frame, one side will operate according to one set of rules while the other side operates according to another. Fortunately, many everyday interactions are so routine that we have no need to state them explicitly: "We're having a greeting ritual together" or "Now we're about to say good-bye." But in negotiation, those who manage frames can gain considerable advantage. Likewise, disadvantage accrues to those who leave frames to chance, who leave them to the other side to manage, or who simply assume that the other side shares their frame. If we add framing to the agenda formulation process we've developed so far, it looks like this:

Issue 1: _____ (45 minutes)

Frame: _____

If the outcome on Issue 1 is *highly cooperative,* Issue 2 will be
 (priority issue topically related). (45 minutes)

Frame: _____

If the outcome on Issue 1 is *moderately cooperative,* Issue 2 will be
 (possible move to topically related issue).

If the outcome on Issue 1 is *uncooperative,* Issue 2 will be
 (topically unrelated issue).

Issue 3: _____ (25 minutes)

Frame: _____

If Issue 1 is to be connected to Issue 2, a frame can help do this. "Since we agree that X is our first priority, it follows that we must now turn to Y or we'll be putting the cart before the horse." Skillful negotiators know how to establish such frames. They know how to move from one frame to another. They can read the situation and decide if a shift to a new frame can be successfully achieved. In more scientific lingo, linguist Adam Kendon describes such actions in this way: "A participant wishing to change to a new frame may precede any actual change by small maneuvers in the direction of the new position that would, if completed, constitute a position suitable for a different kind of interaction. If the co-participants are willing to follow the participant's lead, they will make complementary moves, rather than moves that would compensate for them and so maintain the status quo."[3]

Kendon cites as an example the way in which people cue each other that a discussion is about to end. One of the participants may step back a little, which could be interpreted as a desire for closure. The other person steps back to acknowledge the closure bid, thus enabling both to enter a closing phase of talk. We often do this kind of thing without really thinking about it, since we've all done

conversational closures so often. Yet many people do not do them *well*. Moreover, many negotiators fail to move dexterously from one type of frame to another. When they are clumsy, their intentions are interpreted negatively, and the negotiation is threatened. It's always advisable to have a few frames in mind for each issue in case one fails to impress.

Frames are important not just in the early stage but also throughout the process of negotiation. Suppose a negotiator begins to suspect that a counterpart is about to become hostile. Research indicates that when negotiators perceive that an opponent is likely to become hostile, they are likely to become hostile themselves *in advance*. Thus if negotiators position themselves as unlikely to attack (perhaps by suggesting a cooperative frame), the other side will be less inclined to assume a hostile approach. Also, when negotiators appear to be defending themselves with punitive tactics (rather than engaging in unprovoked attacks), the other side is likely to avoid overt hostility. Of course, that defense should appear justified. Similarly, when negotiators believe that an otherwise low-power counterpart is nonetheless armed with a punitive capability, they may be less likely to engage in provocation. If a punitive action is framed as defensive—"I had no choice, given what he did"—it is less likely to elicit an attack. Of course, research alone cannot tell us with perfect accuracy when other factors might enter into decisions about punitive action. But research can tell us about tendencies, and such information is important. If negotiators know from experience (and perhaps from study as well) that allowing their actions to be seen as hostile attacks rather than defensive actions is likely to lead to strong retaliation, it behooves them to alter that frame. "I know you have a good deal of power in this negotiation, so I'm inclined to protect my interests" is the kind of statement that may prove useful in preventing the other side from engaging in an all-out attack. It frames the negotiator's action as one born of little choice, prompted by fear of the other side's use of hostile power.

When interviewing for a job, people often prefer not to mention their prior salaries. A prior salary is an *anchor* against which an available offer can be judged, but it's also a frame that may help or hinder success in a job search. A jobseeker fears, often with good reason, that a past salary might frame his or her worth in a way detrimental to obtaining a desired or justifiable salary. If the prior salary was low, it could influence the interviewer to lowball the offer. If the prior salary was higher than the new company's range, the interviewer could consider the jobseeker out of the running.

Framing can take the form of metaphors or images. Let's say two companies are partners in a failing joint venture. They face a decision whether to continue the venture or end it. Imagine that a representative from the protermination team goes up to the whiteboard and draws a picture of a large tree overhanging a cliff (see Figure 6.1). Then he says, "Our joint venture is much like this tree. It hangs precariously over a cliff. One strong gust of wind, and it will likely topple and crash at the bottom." A member of the antitermination team asks for the marker. He steps up to the board and says, "Our joint venture does indeed look like this tree. I agree that on the surface, at least, it is in jeopardy. But we are forgetting one very important aspect of this image." This negotiator then steps forward and draws a series of lines from the base of the tree into the cliff (see Figure 6.2).

Figure 6.1 Tree Metaphor Used as a Frame.

He turns back to the group and says, "This tree, like our joint venture, has deep roots holding it firmly to the ground. No amount of wind can topple it if we continue to nurture those roots, something we haven't done well over the last year. This tree will grow straighter and will thrive for years to come because it is rooted deeply, as our joint venture is rooted in a relationship that goes back decades."

Using a metaphor, both negotiators have framed their positions. The second negotiator did not deny the validity of the precarious tree frame but instead used it to form his own pro–joint venture, persuasive appeal. He *reframed* the issue. The beauty of this action is that it builds on a frame the other side already clearly sees and accepts. In other words, the other side had already done part of his work for him. Had the second negotiator erased the tree diagram and started from scratch

Figure 6.2 Expanding the Tree Metaphor to Reframe the Issue.

with an unrelated frame, he would have been asking the other side to accept an entirely new conceptualization rather than borrowing from one they already accepted.

As with other aspects of negotiation, framing at its best is not done in isolation from other contextual considerations. If, for example, a negotiator knows that the other side's opinion leaders have Achiever negotiation styles, she would be wise to frame her positions in terms of immediate actions and quick benefits. If, however, the leadership is composed primarily of Motivators, she should choose images and words that suggest novel, clever means by which their goals can be achieved. Analyticals are inclined to respond favorably to frames derived from reliable data. Mediators tend to be influenced by frames that show how well a particular course of action will satisfy both sides.

Other sorts of information about the other side's interests and inclinations can prove useful in frame construction. Are they sports oriented? A sports frame could be powerful. Do they enjoy travel? A frame incorporating an image from one of their leader's favorite locales might work wonders. Much depends on the skill with which the frames are introduced. Knowing a counterpart's affinity for Paris, a negotiator might say, "The Parisians once were sure that the Eiffel Tower would be a failure of major proportions. Their negative predictions were premature for reasons they hadn't thought of. Ours might be as well, so let's begin today with open minds." The Eiffel Tower frame could flop if the person to whom you address it likes all things Spanish and disdains all things French. Fairhurst, Cohen and Cahill provide a useful example:

FRAMING OUTSIDE THE BOX

A U.S. Department of Energy facility produced uranium products for defense programs from 1953 to 1989. In 1989, uranium metal production was suspended after a series of controversies concerning off-site contamination. Like many other government-owned, contractor-operated facilities, the site began environmental remediation to deal with its legacy of toxic and radioactive waste. It also undertook a protracted, multiyear closure. Over a seven-year period, one contractor conducted three downsizings, with many more planned to achieve site closure by 2006.

The first downsizing was involuntary, marked by an abrupt dismissal of more than two hundred employees. The construction industry culture of the contractor, where abrupt dismissals were routine, was clearly at odds with the old manufacturing culture of the site and employees' expectations of continued work. The second downsizing was voluntary and marked by the presence of the National Defense Authorization Act for Fiscal Year 1993, Section 3161, in which Congress conferred a windfall of education, health, and cash benefits on the country's Cold War workers at many defense facilities. The voluntary downsizing program was framed as a "positive opportunity" distinguished from the first downsizing. However, employees were also told that if they did not voluntarily leave and take advantage of Section 3161, they would be involuntarily separated. Unexpectedly, so many employees sought to leave the site that many of them had to be turned down.

During the second downsizing, a workforce restructuring manager, Matthew, was brought in to meet with employees. Matthew described the atmosphere when he began meeting employees to tell them their jobs would be terminated and to address their concerns: "Was I nervous? Absolutely. Because these were people who worked at this facility—some of them for twenty-eight years—who were literally within months of retirement,

full retirement, who had just been told, 'Either voluntarily leave the facility or we're going to lay you off.' We had people who had sick children in the hospital, who had wives who were sick, who had husbands who had lost their jobs. It was a very threatening time . . . probably the most gut-wrenching time of my entire life."

Matthew decided that what appeared to be two conflicting or contradictory objectives—the downsizing process and the employees' aspirations for job security—could be transformed into a common cause where all of the actors' objectives could be minimally addressed. Thus Matthew contrived to transform a potential source of conflict into a rallying point. He formulated a managed attrition plan for downsizing and workforce restructuring. Commenting on this new approach and how he presented it to other people, he said,

> Most everybody thinks inside a box. This box is 3161. I don't play computer games, but I saw a game on my son's computer one time called Pong. And there was a ball that just bounced around on the inside here, and it just left streaks and patterns and all that stuff. And I told [the employees being asked to leave], "You understand that this is all 3161, and all your ideas are bouncing against these walls, and these are parameters you built for yourself. . . . Then bounce around on the outside because you got all this room to matriculate if you just look at it that way." And then we began to share some ideas like, for example, separation benefits and those kinds of things. Don't look at these narrow inside walls. Look at what you got outside here. And one of the fellows who is the director for the Department of Energy down there said, "Geez, I didn't realize we could do that." And I said, "Well, I guess I'll ask the obvious question—Did you ask?" 'Well, no." So, "OK, I'm going to tell you, you can do that." Of course we had some Washington officials there, and they said, "Yeah, there's no reason why you can't do that. You just never looked."

The rallying point was a frame from which more favorable interpretations of downsizing followed. Matthew described the rallying point frame:

> If you look at the program we have designed through the managed attrition approach . . . we will pay you [employees] to leave this facility—just simple normal severance, . . . seven thousand dollars. Now the advantage, the trade-off to the employee, is first, you've got about a two-year notification that your job is going away. Here, [speaking of the first downsizing] you were given a sixty-day notification. OK, so you're looking at . . . seven hundred twenty days as opposed to sixty days. Big difference. And if you look at the average employee per ten thousand dollars income, it takes one month to find a job. For a forty thousand dollar employee, they're going to be unemployed for four months. Here, they've got five times the lead to look for work. The trade-off is [that] the employee says, "Well, you know, I'm going to be involuntarily separated. I'm going to get the same benefit. Why would I want to wait?" Well, the difference is now you've got a two-year opportunity to look for work, with us assisting you with retraining opportunities and all kinds of things including [names of universities]. You've got some opportunities to take some skills with you so you can leave employed versus leaving unemployed.

A workable, persuasive frame of greater opportunity was found by taking into account both the employees' and the organization's interests. It offered a new landscape of action. The two-year notification, along with severance and retaining benefits, came to be viewed by many as an opportunity. It saved significant money for the company and also avoided the brain drain (key people leaving) that was threatening the optimal functioning of the organization. All because he thought creatively and positioned resulting options in attractive ways.[4]

A powerful persuasive tool, framing deserves considerable attention at all stages of negotiation. It is imperative to smooth transitions among agenda items, especially in advance of potentially contentious issues. It can be particularly effective and long-lasting when it incorporates a story or image, which often bypass the kind of cognitive resistance that occurs when words alone are used. Pictures, images, and stories can be less threatening than plain speech, especially if they create a neutral representation that is informative to both sides, thus disengaging the parties from their differences. Pictures, as they say, are often worth a thousand words. Stories can be worth a thousand more (see Exhibit 6.1).

▶ SAMPLE FRAMES

Framing takes practice. It's difficult for many people to think in terms of metaphors, stories, images, or creative wording, especially if they've been trained to "get to the point." So I end this chapter with some sample frames to exercise your mind. In time, you may find yourself framing with ease.

- Our situation is much like that of a sailboat without a sail; we can motor about, but we can't go out onto the high seas.
- All of our disagreements have been constructive ones. They've challenged us, sometimes tested us, but they've produced better solutions.
- The United States and Russia, England and France, and Germany and France are all former competitors who became allies. If they could do it, so can we.
- The question before us today is not "Do we want this to work?" but "Are we willing to do what it takes to make it work?"
- Our relationship at the moment is like a healthy plant left too long in a window. It's strong enough to survive and thrive, given half a chance.
- We both know where we want to go, but we keep using a go-kart to cross a highway.

I'll close this chapter with an example that's somewhat indelicate but clearly shows how useful frames can be in creating a shared perspective. After working with some senior executives on framing, I asked them to create their own, based on a case in which two sides had reached an impasse. After we'd discussed several good examples, one of the groups called out to me, "We have a great frame." One executive, suppressing a smile, rose and walked to the front of the room. He drew a large, Y-shaped figure on the whiteboard. "As you can see, we are now at an important decision point," he said, looking at the group with persuasive sincerity. "We can take this road," he continued, pointing to the left side of the Y, "and work toward the profitable collaboration we both desire." He then pointed to the right side of the Y, pausing so we might momentarily consider the positive nature of his demeanor and words. Suddenly his expression changed. He looked directly, chal-

▶ *EXHIBIT 6.1*

FRAMES AND THE FAIRIES

Irish folklore is replete with stories of fairies who mischievously lurk among humans, their lives running parallel to ours. They were considered responsible for many curious events, and although they are not spoken of much in today's Ireland, the effects of stories about them are evident even today in the form of superstitions and in a certain acceptance of the otherwise unexplainable. Rather than simply a means of entertainment, fairy legends were actually persuasive messages about social rules, digestible ways of framing information.

In her book *The Burning of Bridget Cleary,* Angela Bourke explains how stories passed down through generations functioned as arguments about reality, frames of a sort that afforded an understanding of things that would otherwise make little or no sense:

> Viewed as a system of interlocking units of narrative, practice and belief, fairy-legend can be compared to a database: a pre-modern culture's way of storing and retrieving information and knowledge of every kind, from hygiene and childcare to history and geography. Highly charged and memorable images like that of a woman emerging on a white horse from a fairy dwelling are the retrieval codes for a whole complex of stored information about land and landscape, community relations, gender roles, medicine, and work in all aspects: tools, materials and techniques.[5]

Bourke explains the persuasive power of stories as due in part to their application to people's lives, how closely fairies resemble people, and how such stories can be told without lecturing people. They allow advice to be given in a way that allows the adviser to act as if he or she never intended to lecture or even imply but only to tell an interesting story.

Unlike simple words, stories are also enduring. As Walter Benjamin explains in his celebrated essay "The Storyteller," "The value of information does not survive the moment in which it was new. It lives only at that moment; it has to surrender to it completely and explain itself without losing any time. A story is different. It does not expend itself. It preserves and concentrates its strength and is capable of releasing it even after a long time."[6]

Bourke herself writes, "Fairy-legend charts the territory of no-man's land. It carries with it an air of the preposterous, the nod and wink, that allows one thing to be said while another is meant. It permits face-saving lies to be told, and disturbing narratives to be safely detoured into fiction if children are found to be listening, or if the complex web of family relationships means that someone may take offense, or threaten retaliation."[7]

So we see that what today is often viewed as an amusing characteristic of Irish creativity and penchant for entertainment may actually be a wellspring of information framed in ways that allowed advice and crucial information about living in society to be remembered and passed along.

lengingly, at the team representing the other side of the case. "Or you can take this road and just *fork* off on your own!"

The whole group roared. Perhaps you had to be there, but it was a priceless frame, competently delivered, though clearly not for all occasions. It provided a shared picture, as frames are supposed to do—in this case, a memorable one.

► QUESTIONS

1. Define the following:
 Private acceptance
 Compliance
 Order or critical points
 Primary and secondary issues
 Agenda domino effect
 Partial agenda setting
 Opening stance
 If/then scenarios
 Framing
 Reframing
 Anchor

2. Describe in your own words what "leading with agreement" means. Describe a time when you did this effectively in a negotiation (between friends, within your family, in business, etc.).

3. Over the next few days observe people negotiating. Analyze their opening approaches. Which ones worked well? Which ones should have been different and how?

4. Describe at length with dialogue a negotiation you observed or one in which you participated. Was an agenda used—even informally? If so, was it effective? If not, how might an agenda have been employed effectively?

5. The next time you attempt to persuade or negotiate use at least one of the forms of framing described in this chapter. Write about the results. What would you do differently if you had it to do over?

6. Describe two sides of a controversial current event. Develop frames that might be used by each side of the debate to make their arguments more compelling or clear.

Persuasion Strategy Choices

Chapter 6 was devoted to setting up the structure of the negotiation and positioning issues in ways that facilitate further persuasion. Now we'll look at the use of *persuasion strategies* in the course of negotiation. There is an extensive array of persuasion strategies—also commonly referred to as compliance-gaining strategies. Researchers in this area have made many attempts to create an exhaustive taxonomy or list of persuasion strategies. One such list, developed in 1967 by Gerald Marwell and David Schmitt, generated decades of research directed at determining the types of persuasive strategies people use in a variety of situations.[1] Researchers Kathy Kellerman and Tim Cole composed a much longer list of strategies, incorporating many of Marwell and Schmitt's categories. Kellerman and Cole's taxonomy follows in "Strategies and Their Definitions."

People vary widely in their ability to learn and effectively use such an extensive array of strategy choices. Skilled negotiators are aware of the breadth of their options, are apprised of many of those listed by Kellerman and Cole, and are experienced in the application of such strategies. They may have found that certain types of compliance-gaining strategies do not work well in particular corporate cultures, for example, or for particular roles. Doctors persuade other doctors, for example, by using different strategies than those they use with patients and nurses. Teachers may attempt to persuade students in ways very different from those they use to persuade each other.

▶ STRATEGIES AND THEIR DEFINITIONS

Over the years, many researchers have developed taxonomies of compliance-gaining strategies, that is to say, ways of getting people to do things they might not choose to do otherwise. At the University of California, Santa Barbara, Kellerman and Cole undertook the monumental task of integrating strategy definitions across sixty-four conceptually distinct taxonomies. The following material is adapted from the table of these strategies that these researchers developed for their article in the journal *Communication Theory:*[2]

Actor Takes Responsibility: Try to get others to comply by stating your willingness to help them or even work on the request yourself. That is, try to gain their compliance by *offering to do it yourself as a means of getting them to do what you want.*

Altercasting (Negative): Try to get others to comply by pointing out that only a person with negative qualities would not comply.

Altercasting (Positive): Try to get others to comply by pointing out that a good person with positive qualities would comply.

Altruism: Ask them to *give you a hand* out of the goodness of their heart—just do it for you.

Assertion: Forcefully state what you want. Demand (command) them to comply.

Audience Use: Ask them in front of other people as a way to back up your request.

Authority Appeal: Use or rely on a position of power.

Aversive Stimulation: Do things they do not like until they agree to comply. Bother them until they do what you want.

Bargaining: Negotiate a deal where you each do something for the other so that every party gets what it wants.

Benefit (Other): Point out how it helps people other than themselves if they comply.

Benefit (Self): Tell them you personally would benefit if they do what you want.

Benefit (Target): Point out how it helps them if they comply.

Challenge: Challenging, provoking, stimulating, tempting, goading, or galvanizing them to comply.

Compliment: Praise them, their abilities, or their accomplishments to gain their compliance.

Compromise: Make a concession to them so that they will make their concession to you and do what you want.

Cooperation: Be cooperative and collaborate with them; try to gain their compliance by offering to discuss things and work them out together.

Criticize: Attack them on a personal level to get them to do what you want.

Debasement: Act pitiful and pleading. Debasing, demeaning, degrading, devaluing, humiliating, or lowering yourself so as to deprive yourself of esteem or self-worth to get them to do what you want.

Debt: Remind them that they are in debt to you for things you have done for them in the past. Indicate that they owe it to you to do what you want.

Deceit: Try to get others to comply by misleading, lying to, or deceiving them.

Direct Request: Simply ask or state what you want without giving any reasons for them to comply.

Disclaimer (Norms, Rules): Downplay or disavow restrictions and constraints that might prevent them from doing what you want them to do. Point out that otherwise applicable procedures, rules, norms, or expectations should be broken in this instance.

Disclaimer (Other): Downplay or disavow the ability of anyone else to comply with your request. Point out that other people cannot help you or do what is needed.

Disclaimer (Self): Downplay or disavow your reasons for asking. Indicate that (1) you do not want to make a bad impression or have bad intentions, (2) you do not really want to make the request and are doing so reluctantly, or (3) you simply have no choice but to make the request.

Disclaimer (Target): Acknowledge and sympathize with why they may not want to comply. Try to gain their compliance by indicating that (1) you understand and are aware of their reasons, feelings, and abilities and (2) that you are sensitive to their needs and concerns even though you must ask them to do what you want.

Disclaimer (Task): Downplay what you are asking them to do. What you want them to do is not what they think it is and should not pose a problem; it is not awful, arduous, difficult, or dumb.

Disclaimer (Time): Downplay or disavow being busy as a reason to refuse your request. Point out that presently there is—or shortly will be—enough time for them to do what you want.

Duty: They should fulfill obligations, responsibilities, and commitments that they have.

Equity: Being fair, just, and impartial means that they should do what you want.

Esteem (Negative) by Others: If they do not comply, other people will think worse of them.

Esteem (Positive) by Others: If they do what you want, other persons will think better of them.

Esteem (Negative) by Actor: You will think worse of them if they do not comply.

Esteem (Positive) by Actor: You will think better of them if they comply.

Expertise (Negative): Point out that because of the way the world works, unfavorable things will happen if they do not change their behavior.

Expertise (Positive): In the natural course of things, good outcomes will occur if they do what you want.

Hinting: Indicate indirectly what you want, hoping they will figure it out and comply even though you never come out and really say it.

I Want: Try to get others to comply for no reason other than you want them to.

Invoke Norm: Indicate that they would be out of step if they fail to comply; prod them to conform to what others have, do, or desire.

It Is Up to You: Tell them that the decision is theirs to make, and it is up to them.

Logical/Empirical: Make logical arguments. Use reasoning, evidence, facts, and data.

Moral Appeal: Appeal to their moral or ethical standards. Let them know what is right and what is wrong.

My Concern for You: Refer to your regard for, consideration of, interest in, and feelings for them.

Nature of Situation: Be attentive to the situation or circumstances you find yourself in; then gain compliance by taking note of the appropriateness of their behavior to the situation or the appropriateness of your request in the situation.

Negative Affect: Be really negative: Express negative emotions, act very unfriendly, or act displeased to get them to do what you want.

Not Seek Compliance: Make no attempt to get others to do what you want.

Persistence: Persevere (continue) in your attempts.

Personal Expertise: Refer to your credibility. Try to gain their compliance based on your experience, know-how, trustworthiness, and judgment.

Positive Affect: Be really positive: Express positive emotions, act very friendly, and create an appealing impression. Charm them into doing what you want.

Pregiving: Do positive and nice things for them in advance of asking them to do what you want. Give them things they would like and only afterward make your request.

Promise: Offer to give them a reward or something they would like if they do what you want.

Promote Task: Promote the value and worth of what you want them to do. Identify positive qualities of the thing: it is important, meaningful, rewarding, enjoyable, and so on.

Self-Feeling (Negative): State that failure to comply will result in an automatic decrease in their self-worth. They will feel worse about themselves.

Self-Feeling (Positive): State that they will feel better about themselves if they do what you want.

Suggest: Offer suggestions about what you want from them. Subtly propose an idea that indirectly points out and describes what you want them to do.

Surveillance: Indicate your awareness and observation of what they do. Refer to your general vigilance, surveillance, scrutiny, or monitoring of their behavior.

Third Party: Have someone else intervene and ask them for you.

This Is the Way Things Are: Refer to rules, procedures, policies, or customs that require them to comply.

Thought Manipulation: Convince them that the request you are making is really their own idea.

Threat: Say you will punish them if they do not do what you want.

Value Appeal: Point to central and joint beliefs that should guide what they do.

Warning: Alert them to possible negative consequences of their behavior.

Welfare (Others): Tell them how other people would be hurt if they do not do what you want. The welfare of others is at stake.

Why Not? Make them justify why they should not comply. Point out that there are no real grounds for not doing so.

Your Concern for Me: Refer to their regard for, consideration of, interest in, and feelings for you as reasons to comply.

If, at each negotiation choice point, sixty-four strategy types had to be considered, most negotiations would fail by virtue of complexity alone. Communication expert Michael Roloff suggests that people handle such complexity by developing strategy categories that allow simplification of choices.

> For example, a teenager may say to his or her parent, "If you buy me a new car, I *promise* that I won't drive yours anymore."
> The parent replies, "Let me *warn* you, cars are expensive to maintain. After gas and insurance, you won't have any money left."
> The teen counters, "Let's *compromise.* I will buy the gas and you pay for the insurance."[3]

The teenager and parent have categorized their strategies as promise, warning, and compromise. What this suggests, Roloff says, is that people tend not to work with an onerous list of strategies when determining what to say. Rather, they think first of what *type* of strategy they need at the time and then select among specific options with those categories. To make sense of what is being said to them and to help determine their own responses, people also impose categories on the comments of others. Sometimes they do so strategically; that is, in a manner that allows them to respond in a preferred way. Roloff's second example is useful in clarifying how this works:

> Strategic categories may be evident as individuals comment about each other's discourse. The aforementioned teen may say to the parent, "If you don't buy me a car, I will just take yours."
> To which the parent replies, "Don't *threaten* me!"
> The teen then retorts, "Why not? You always *order* me around!"

The discourse of the teen has been placed by the parent into a strategic category called threat, and the teen views the parent's prior discourse as orders.[4]

This kind of category imposition limits the options of the other side unless they notice they are being hemmed in and decide to move in a different direction—perhaps by ignoring or refusing to react to the category. Reactions can be dangerous in negotiation. If, when the other side accuses you of making a threat, you automatically react defensively, you have lost some control by reacting rather than responding. It's easy to see how this can work in a clever negotiator's favor. Armed with the knowledge that the other party tends to react quickly rather than respond thoughtfully, the clever negotiator can lead that party to say or do a number of things that the negotiator may wish them to do. In Roloff's second example, the teenager may actually want to cause a fight to legitimate an indignant storming from the room. This leaves the parent feeling upset, which suits the teenager quite nicely. If the parent decides not to succumb to upset, does not allow the teenager's categorization of her comments to take hold, but instead proceeds with a considered response, the teenager's outburst and retaliatory categorization of the parent's comments is less likely to win the day. It takes an observant parent with steely nerve to step out of such a limiting scenario. The same is true of a teenager wrongfully accused. Should his parent impose the wrong category—for example, "There you go again, trying to start a fight"—a considered response on the teenager's part would be difficult but likely more effective than a reaction. A considered response might be "It may seem that way, but I was actually only disagreeing with you on a small point."

Like the observant parent or teen, skilled negotiators recognize entrapping categories and do not allow them to define their intentions. A warning goes off, so to speak, when they hear what they've said or done categorized in a manner likely to limit their options. They pause, reflect on the type of strategy imputed to them, and then offer a new one. Consider the following conversation:

Susan: I can't accept your proposal. Not at this point, anyway.

Paul: Why such rigidity?

Susan: What you call rigidity is actually caution. I haven't refused your proposal; I've merely indicated that accepting it at the moment isn't possible.

Paul: I worked on it for two weeks and you want to drag out a decision?

Susan: I want to give all the work you did the thoughtful consideration it deserves, rather than slip into premature judgment that won't serve either of us.

Susan relabels her actions in a manner less threatening to Paul. The actions he categorizes as rigidity, she calls caution. What he considers to be dragging out a decision, she redefines as deserved, thoughtful consideration. Listen to skilled negotiators and you'll hear this kind of relabeling or reframing. They don't overdo it, but they do take notice when labels threaten to harm their efforts, and they quickly shorten the shelf life of such labels. I use the expression "shelf life" intentionally. The longer a dangerous label is allowed to exist as the accepted definition

of what has transpired, the more momentum and credibility it gains. When possible, it's best to nip it in the bud, as exemplified in the following conversation:

Fred: You're expecting too much. (*Attack*)

Al: What do you mean? (*Inquiry*)

Fred: You want this project finished in record time, but I can't drop my other obligations to suit your schedule. (*Attack elaboration*)

Al: That's why I chose you for this, Fred—your sense of responsibility. I'm not surprised that you're in demand. What kind of flexibility do you need? Maybe we aren't as far apart on this issue as it seems. (*Compliment, reframe, inquiry*)

Al doesn't allow himself to become ensnared in a dysfunctional exchange of personal attacks. He responds to an attack with a question, buying himself time and gaining some information in the process. He then thinks of how to relabel what Fred says as more indicative of agreement than disagreement. He bypasses the attack and instead compliments Fred. This is a marvelous skill and one worth considerable practice. As discussed in Chapter 1, the way things are said is extremely important in negotiation. Skillful negotiation requires an experimental approach, trying first one way of saying something and then, if need be, another. This approach avoids reaction traps. Research has shown that the offensive or defensive stances taken by negotiators are often the result of reactions to strategic choices made by the other side.

▶ THE ACE MODEL

Skillful negotiators may also avoid having to consider the use of sixty-four or more persuasive strategies by categorizing them in terms of their type of appeal.[5] When people use reasoning rather than emotion to attempt persuasion, research indicates, they draw on three types of appeals, using one or a combination. The three appeal types are *appropriateness, consistency,* and *effectiveness*, which form the acronym ACE.

Appropriateness appeals involve the application of social pressure. Say you ask someone to accompany you to a school reunion. He declines because he has far too much work to get done. You might say, "All our friends will be there. You have to go." That's an appropriateness appeal. If your friend is not easily swayed by social pressure, you might appeal to consistency. *Consistency appeals* pertain to what a person like himself (or like the type of person he aspires to be) would do. "It's not like you, a party animal, to miss this reunion" is a consistency appeal. It attempts to influence by appealing to some positive self-image. *Effectiveness appeals* relate to actions that will help bring about a result the person desires. In terms of the reunion, you might say to your friend, "If you take a break now and go to the reunion, it will stimulate you and recharge your mental batteries. You'll do better work when you return."

The ACE model is a handy, hip-pocket technique for selecting a promising persuasive appeal. Young people are often more influenced by appropriateness considerations. They want to be liked and admired by others. Consistency appeals

to work best with people are more individualistic; who have "minds of their own," so to speak. They're more concerned with their own self-perceptions and remaining consistent with those than they are with others' opinions. Effectiveness appeals work best when the larger issue is less personal, more focused on attaining the desired result. Sometimes the desired result is to look good to others; in such cases, appropriateness and effectiveness appeals to work side by side. At other times, being consistent with one's self-concept is the desired outcome, so consistency and effectiveness appeals work together.

The three concerns can also be at odds. In some issues involving ethics, a peer group may want you to act one way, but your conscience or perception of self is inconsistent with that action. In large crowds, on the other hand, people may feel relieved of consistency concerns. In a mass of people, their own identity becomes less important than being part of something with friends or admired others.

To use the ACE approach effectively, a negotiator must apprise herself of the other side's focal interests. How likely are they to be swayed by others' opinions? Are they strong-willed individualists, guided by their own values and rules? Would they be willing to put aside others' opinions and self-consistency to achieve a desired goal? Determining the answers to these and similar questions can enable negotiators to select the most promising type of appeal.

Most of the strategies listed by Kellerman and Cole may be categorized as appropriateness, consistency, or effectiveness strategies. For example, "Audience Use," "Benefit (Other)," "Debt," "Invoke Norm," "Moral Appeal," and "Pregiving" are appropriateness strategies. Consistency strategies include "Altercasting" (positive and negative), "Altruism," and "Thought Manipulation." Effectiveness appeals are ones like "Benefit (Target)," "Expertise" (positive and negative), "Personal Expertise," "Promise," "Self-Feeling" (positive and negative), "Threat," and "Warning."

The expert negotiator brings to a higher level of consciousness the processes people use in selecting among persuasion strategies. We've discussed two methods—selection based on categorization (promise, threat, pressuring, and so on) and selection based on appeal type (appropriateness, consistency, effectiveness). Most of us do this without much thought—many with little thought at all, reacting rather than responding to comments by counterparts. The more skillful communicators and negotiators attend more closely at choice points in interaction. They consider whether, for example, labeling someone's comment a threat is going to advance their goals. If cooperation is what they seek, then such labeling is likely to be counterproductive. If, however, they wish to upset the other person with the hope of later offering a solution to the upset, the threat label might prove useful.

Similarly, effective negotiators think about whether a person is more likely to be influenced by an appeal to what others think or do (appropriateness), with what is in line with his or her self-image (consistency), or with what will achieve task goals (effectiveness). Even negotiators who have never heard of the ACE model engage in this kind of mindfulness—to use Ellen Langer's term, a *higher-level thinking* that enables them to manage negotiations to their advantage. The following example, taken from a book I wrote on persuasion, demonstrates how

appropriateness, consistency, and effectiveness concerns can affect someone's reasoning and therefore the resulting conclusions:

> A recent dispute in a Los Angeles County city over whether to block certain roads to through traffic demonstrates how people can be torn among appropriateness, consistency, and effectiveness issues. An active member of the community visited her neighbors to determine how they intended to vote. One neighbor, Elaine, who had recently moved to the area, had not yet decided how to vote on the issue of closing off streets. Her husband was convinced that doing so would reduce traffic and thereby make the neighborhood safer for children. He argued that the proposed street closings would cut down traffic and lessen pollution and thus benefit the neighborhood as a whole. Elaine was inclined to agree with her husband until the community activist arrived at her door. The activist complained that closing off streets was an attempt by a small group of vocal people to exclude the rest of society and create an elite neighborhood. She considered it against her liberal principles to keep people from driving down public streets and a burden to have to weave one's way through one's own neighborhood. She pointed out that none of the people proposing the street modification had clearly indicated the benefits to the neighborhood as a whole. Moreover, she said, most of the neighbors on Elaine's street were opposed to the modifications.[6]

In the example so far, the activist neighbor, in her efforts to persuade, has used three types of appeals: (1) *inconsistency* of blocking off public traffic with liberal views (the neighbor assumes or has reason to believe that Elaine identifies with such views), (2) *appropriateness* of agreeing with "most of the neighbors," and (3) *ineffectiveness* of believing people who hadn't even presented a good case for the modifications. This triple-barreled approach could have easily backfired if Elaine were to find fault with one of the appeals (for example, if she doesn't really care what other neighbors think). It is typically better to lead with one or two strong appeals based on gathered information about the individual you're attempting to persuade. Let's return to our example to see what happened.

"Elaine found herself torn among concerns for the safety of her children (appropriateness concerns for a mother and effectiveness considerations as well), and her desire to do what would be best for the neighborhood (effectiveness) while still maintaining the sense that she is the type of person who makes up her own mind (consistency)."

"Obviously, Elaine is not the type of person who leaps to decisions. As a person who considers alternatives, she found herself enmeshed in a conflict among appropriateness, consistency, and effectiveness considerations."

Elaine's neighbor had effectively created ambiguity, which no doubt expanded Elaine's options beyond her possible knee-jerk acceptance of her husband's view. She may have even moved sufficiently far from that view to increase the likelihood of Elaine's voting against the blocking off of the streets. We don't know exactly which of the sixty-four types of compliance-gaining strategies the neighbor used to make her appropriateness, consistency, and effectiveness appeals, but they must have been ones that were acceptable to Elaine, given her re-

sulting concerns and disinclination to adopt her husband's view without more thought on the matter. Elaine's new consideration derived from the tendency of all people to more or less accept certain types of appeals to their reason. Since people do use appropriateness, consistency, and effectiveness considerations in their decisions about issues, it is easy to see how these three criteria can also be used by persuaders to encourage one form of behavior over another. Effective persuaders are like detectives. They attempt to locate criteria that carry the most weight with the people they wish to influence. They then formulate strategies to show how their recommended behavior favorably responds to those considerations. In other words, in Elaine's case, the neighbor might have known of Elaine's liberal leanings. Appealing to consistency with these was then a reasonable course of action. She may have then decided to use a positive or negative self-feeling strategy ("You'll feel good about yourself if you comply" or "You'll feel badly about yourself if you don't comply") or a value strategy ("People like us value these kinds of freedoms"). Since the consistency appeal went well—seemed to get Elaine's attention, anyway—she then moved on to effectiveness appeals, perhaps using a logical/empirical compliance-gaining strategy ("There are no facts to support the other side's views"). Seeing that this approach made an impact on Elaine, she then appealed to appropriateness concerns by indicating that most other neighbors were opposed to the street closures (self-esteem compliance appeal: "Others will think more of you if you agree with them").

This is how being aware of the types of appeals that are likely to work in a given situation helps a negotiator select among specific compliance strategies in a manner that facilitates persuasion. Obviously, this is not for the faint of heart. It takes a level of attention most people are unwilling to devote to the persuasion dimension of negotiation. But it is one of the talents that sets the more skillful negotiator apart from the less skilled.

▶ INTRODUCE FIRST OR EXPLAIN LATER?

Once you know the persuasion approaches available to you, you face two questions: Should you launch right into these approaches without any introduction? And will you need to offer some postappeal explanation? Compliance-gaining strategies often require a buildup at the front end or an explanation at the back end. To lessen the likelihood of resistance, experienced negotiators may use introductions to segue into promises, requests, or other strategic moves—or they may provide an immediate subsequent explanation. If you make a strong promise early in a negotiation, for example, people are likely to become skeptical of you. (*Why is she offering this now? Is she worried, desperate, or trying to dupe us in some way?*) Making a request too early in a negotiation can also cause a negative reaction, unless you accompany it with a very good reason. Robert Sanders and Kristine Fitch hold that "the social meaning of a single 'message' depends on the meaning relations it has with other components of a larger whole."[7] No message occurs in isolation, and the effectiveness of a strategy often depends on the talk leading up to or after its use. IBM chief executive Lou Gerstner once championed a program of idea sharing that was intended (among other things) to amelio-

rate the effects of status in situations in which a subordinate needed to differ with ideas expressed by a superior. Gerstner introduced the concept of "straight talk" at Big Blue. Employees were expected to use more direct forms of communication in place of the obfuscating techniques of hint and innuendo often used by subordinates in their efforts to influence superiors. As one IBM executive told me, "Even the most junior IBM employee can preface a comment by saying, 'In the interest of straight talk,' and everyone—up to the most senior person present—will listen." This prefacing allowed ideas and arguments to flow more easily at IBM and, when straight talk was working, gave junior people a chance to speak their minds with impunity.

In the absence of ready-made lead-ins like the reference to "straight talk," negotiators can couch their remarks in ways likely to make their ideas more palatable. As a simple example, Sanders and Fitch cite a woman whose supervisor asks her to serve coffee to both him and her male peers. In some cultures, where men aren't expected to know how to make coffee, this request wouldn't be considered insulting. A woman in such a culture might consider the request reasonable and see her compliance as an act of consideration rather than implying a lower professional status. In the United States, however, the boss would be much more likely to take considerable pains to explain his request. He might say, "We all make coffee, Ann, but yours is the best. If you make the coffee today, we'll buy you lunch." He may still be skating on thin ice. Coffeemaking, like the taking of meeting notes, has become a delicate issue in male-female work relations. Were the boss to say, "Bill here baked cookies for us and Frank went to the store for donuts, all in the hope of bribing you to make your famous coffee," he'd have a much better chance of success.

Compliance gaining is often an incremental process, not simply one of applying a strategy in isolation. Sanders and Fitch identified two basic forms of compliance-gaining episodes: *progressive* and *regressive*. In the progressive form, the persuader leads up to the request with a "presolicitation sequence that unearths or deflects sources of resistance." In the regressive form, the persuader follows a direct request with explanations for the request and inducements for compliance.[8] We need more research in this area to indicate with confidence when a progressive approach is superior to a regressive one and vice versa. Clearly, though, negotiators do think in these terms. They consider whether they should lead up to a request or demand—or first make the request or demand and then, if resistance occurs, explain their reasoning. Negotiators have preferences linked to their styles. To save time and get right to the point, Achievers may be more likely than Mediators to take a regressive approach. Motivators may find that prefacing a request with encouragement and attractive images works better for them, while Analyticals may be inclined to lead with data.

▶ IDENTIFYING AND PLANNING FOR OBSTACLES

In line with couching your actions in explanatory frameworks is the task of identifying *obstacles* to persuasion before they occur and using this knowledge to help select strategies. Astute negotiators adapt their requests in anticipation of obstacles they expect to encounter.

It is useful for negotiators to consider how they might respond to delays, for example. Will they be taken as inappropriate actions on the part of the other negotiator or understood as resulting from an absence of authority to comply? A skilled negotiator will ask herself whether a delay is organizationally or culturally based, and therefore understandable, rather than an aggravating reason for anger and conflict.

Is a lengthy or even long-winded statement by the other side necessarily a delaying tactic? It may simply be a matter of a personal style, indicating a tendency to explore many options. If the speaker is a woman, remember that longer explanations are more common in female speech and don't necessarily indicate intentional obfuscation or delay.[9] In both cases, of course, generalizations have their shortcomings. But used with restraint, generalizations can help in identifying or at least questioning the actuality of (and reasons for) what otherwise might be seen as obstacles.

Although the research in this area is still in its infancy, it can help us identify and label types of obstacles. Exhibit 7.1 is a chart of potential obstacles developed by Danette Ifert and Michael Roloff.[10] Skilled negotiators anticipate objections,

▶ *EXHIBIT 7.1*

POTENTIAL OBSTACLES

Obstacle	*Definition and Examples*
Inadequate resources	Conveys that the skills or resources requested are of poor quality: "My sweater is dirty." "I have only $50." "I'm not a very good mechanic."
Possession	Indicates that he or she does not have the requested resources: "I wasn't in class yesterday to get notes." "I don't have the money right now." "I left my jacket at my sister's house in Arizona."
Imposition	Indicates that granting the request would impose on prior plans: "I'm going out tonight." "I need to pay my other debts first." "I'm too busy to do that."
Inappropriateness	Indicates that the request violates a rule or is socially inappropriate (also includes obstacles in which the speaker indicates that there is no need for a request): "I think it's unfair for you to ask." "Mind your own business." "The music's not that loud."
Source responsibility	Indicates that it is the requester's responsibility to take care of the problem: "You need to do it yourself." "Do it yourself." "That's not our problem."

Obstacle	*Definition and Examples*
No incentive	Conveys that he or she has no incentive to grant the request: "Why should I do that?" "There's no reason to do that." "What's in it for me?"
Recalcitrance	He or she does not want to grant the request and provides no other reason: "You can't borrow my car." "I don't want to change." "I won't do that."
Postpone	Does not fully comply but agrees to future compliance: "I'll pay you back next week." "I'll turn down the music after this song." "I'll do it later."
State of mind	Refuses due to an emotion or mental state: "I'm too angry to do that." "I'm too stressed to do that." "I'm too tired."

Source: D. E. Ifert and M. E. Roloff, "Understanding Obstacles Preventing Compliance: Conceptualization and Classification," *Communication Research*, 1998, *25*, 137.

protestations, excuses, postponements, and other obstacles to progress. They prepare responses in advance of the obstacle to avoid being derailed from progress toward their goals. Exhibit 7.2 presents possible responses to some of the obstacles in Exhibit 7.1.

▶ *EXHIBIT 7.2*

SAMPLE RESPONSES TO OBSTACLES

Possession obstacle: "I can't pay that much. I just don't have it."

Response: "What can you pay at this point?"

Imposition obstacle: "That's not going to work for me. My schedule is packed."

Response: "Is there any day that is lighter than others when you might at least try doing X?"

Inappropriateness obstacle: "This is too much to ask."

Response: "If that's the issue, what things might I do, in your estimation, to even things out?"

Source responsibility obstacle: "This is not our problem."

Response: "Perhaps not obviously so. The main problem may be ours, but the ramifications of how we handle it significantly affect you."

Recalcitrance obstacle: "The answer is no. That's final."

Response: "I don't blame you. I'd be likely to respond the same way. Do you think there is another time when some portion of what I'm asking might be feasible?"

Anticipating persuasion obstacles is crucial to successful negotiation. It is not something that should be done only before or at the beginning of the negotiation. It must be ongoing. Obstacles emerge throughout negotiation. They are often provoked by conditions that may be unclear early in the negotiation process. It pays to (1) watch for cues that anticipated or new obstacles are emerging, (2) pause at that point, (3) identify the source of the obstacles, and (4) redirect the process before they loom large. Skilled negotiators aren't obsessed with obstacles (if they were, they'd likely become immobilized). They are aware that they may occur and that many can be avoided or managed given adequate knowledge of their source.

▶ COMMUNICATION MEDIA AS FACILITATOR OR OBSTACLE

The choice of a vehicle for conveying information between negotiators has important implications for progress, and so we discuss it here as a potential obstacle. The richness of a communication medium is defined by its ability to handle multiple information cues simultaneously, to facilitate feedback, and to allow personal relationships.[11] New technologies afford multiple options for communication throughout negotiations. As exciting as new technologies tend to be, using them in negotiation without considering the impact they might have on the quality of communication is risky. It's temptingly easy to just jot off an e-mail to a negotiation counterpart; however, using that medium to try to deal with issues on which there is disagreement or a high potential for disagreement can cause considerable damage to a negotiation and a relationship.

Before deciding on a medium of communication, negotiators should determine the significance of the issue as well as the importance of nonverbal cues in conveying and receiving messages. As a general rule, the more significant the issue, the more negotiators should rely on communication media that allow verbal and visual interaction. In fact, it is quite possible for negotiators to take offense at the use of telephone or e-mail in the handling of delicate or weighty issues. As we'll discuss in Chapter 10, this is even more likely to occur across cultures in which one person's preference for computer-facilitated communication, for example, might be countered by another's disdain. Cultures in which the pace of life is fast are more inclined to appreciate technologies that allow for quick responses. In cultures where relationships are more important than speed of resolution, negotiators are more likely to prefer face-to-face interactions, especially when dealing with difficult issues.

Research does indicate that richer forms of media encourage collaborative behavior between negotiators.[12] Face-to-face and videoconference communications afford more cues for interpretation of messages than telephone, fax, and e-mail. In general, the more distributive the negotiation is likely to be or the more distributive it becomes, the more important it is to have as many cues for interpretations as possible. It is difficult to recognize deception in the absence of nonverbal cues. When nonverbal expression is not available, it is difficult to express feelings and to recover an interaction that's heading down a path that could damage relationships or goals.

Useful as these generalizations are, the choice of a communication medium, like the majority of important negotiation decisions, should be based on an understanding of one's own communication skills and those of the other side. If you know that someone is "terrible on the phone," avoid serious discussion using that medium. If, on the other hand, your negotiation counterpart is highly reliant on e-mail and is more likely to respond if you use that medium, this critical information should enter into your consideration.

Wharton professor G. Richard Shell, in his studies of the effects of electronic communication on negotiations, found that competitive people negotiate better face-to-face, whereas cooperative people find they can become bolder if they use e-mail.[13] Before deciding whether your negotiation counterpart fits one or the other of these profiles, however, you'd be wise to observe the person during the course of negotiation. If you try electronic communication and it appears to be problematic, consider a change. The key is to remain versatile.

One clear benefit of electronic forms of interaction such as e-mail is built-in memory. E-mails can be printed and saved in a file. If you are forgetful or are dealing with a negotiator who is, either by nature or strategically, having a record of understandings and agreements can prove useful. If the record is waved in your counterpart's face too often or brashly, however, discomfort with your obvious distrust have a detrimental effect. On the other hand, should your counterparts be highly deserving of your distrust, letting them know that you are keeping a record may prevent them from easily denying the existence of prior agreements. It's advisable to use e-mail to confirm agreements when there might be some future slippage by your counterpart away from what was agreed, when the passage of time might dim both your memories, or when there are multiple issues and therefore much opportunity for confusion. Some negotiators even tell their counterparts after a negotiation (or a segment of negotiation) that they will be sending a confirming e-mail to ensure clarity of their agreement. They might say, "I will draft a description of what I believe we've agreed to here today. You can then check it to be sure I've interpreted your position correctly." In this fashion, the medium facilitates clarity and thereby reduces the likelihood of misunderstanding and conflict.

▶ CREDIBILITY AND EVIDENCE

Having identified potential obstacles, the next consideration for persuasion is whether the other side is going to believe you know what you're talking about. So we turn here to issues of credibility and evidence. The Toulmin model we examined in Chapter 3 demonstrated the importance of data in advancing any claim. What constitutes persuasive data? For starters, Fisher and Ury, in their book *Getting to Yes*, recommend the use of *objective criteria* to support critical assertions. By objective criteria, they mean information that informs a choice but is also independent of the will of either side.[14] This approach can be highly productive if both sides want to negotiate in a principled way based on fair, objective standards. For example, Fisher and Ury point out, if your car is demolished in an accident, there are a number of criteria you and the insurance company may turn to when

determining fair remuneration. The original cost of the car less reasonable depreciation; the value according to one of the industry pricing guides, such as the *Kelley Blue Book;* the actual replacement cost; and the amount a court might award—those are some of the normal or standard objective criteria used in such cases. If you enter talks with the insurance company without knowing any of those things, you place yourself at a distinct disadvantage.

It's best to enter a negotiation with objective criteria in hand for each issue likely to be discussed. Be sure it's criteria that the other side is likely to consider credible and practical. As important as this step is to successful negotiation, it is often overlooked or given cursory attention. Yet the side that is better prepared with persuasive, objective criteria usually garners far better results than the side that argues in terms of "who's right or wrong" or what they'd like to get. Negotiation success depends strongly on persuasiveness, and use of objective criteria is one very important means of achieving this.

The standard for objective criteria is higher nowadays because so many credible Internet-based information sources (such as corporate, government, and nonprofit sites, search engines, and such databases as LexisNexis) afford us a wealth of information. There is no excuse for coming to negotiations without strong evidence for your claims. There are a number of sources for evidence, among them the following:

- Research support
- Comparison
- Expert opinion
- Expert affiliation or support
- Experience
- Analogies
- Examples
- A new twist

Note, however, that it never pays to drown the other side in evidence. Determining how much persuasive backing is too much is something of an art. A rule of thumb is to present only your strongest evidence. If you add weaker evidence, your counterparts may focus their attacks on that and thereby weaken your argument. Timing of evidence is crucial, as is attending to nonverbal cues of acceptance or rejection. When preparing for negotiation preparation, ask yourself what type of evidence should be presented, in what quantity it should be presented, and when each piece of evidence should be introduced.

▶ SUBJECTIVE CRITERIA

Subjective criteria are also important; if presented in a compelling manner, they can be more effective than their accredited cousins, objective criteria. Not infrequently, when people understand the objective criteria (and even believe that

such would guide them in most circumstances), they nonetheless choose to reject them. Their *emotional reactions* to a certain issue may be so strong, or their history of past wounds so great, that objectivity is beside the point. They simply want to make themselves feel better. This is one situation among many when subjective criteria are of prime importance.

Madeline Albright, former U.S. secretary of state, once gave evidence in a tribunal focusing on war crimes in the Balkans.[15] Asked a number of questions, she responded with objective material supporting her assertions. Then she was asked to describe her own personal experiences. Albright related that she had seen, at first hand, Yugoslavians and Serbs intermarry and live happily together. Without excessive emotional display, her personal observations lent credibility to her position. Here was an official, known for both her erudition and her penchant for objectivity, providing subjective evaluations in a very formal situation. This kind of performance reminds us that emotion is not the antithesis of logic; in many cases, it is a powerful persuasive partner. Indeed, people often distrust what they see as cold-blooded, high-level research that fails to truly address their own experiences. In such circumstances, melding carefully considered subjective experience with objective criteria forges a more compelling argument.

After Vice President Al Gore lost the presidential election to George W. Bush in 2000, many analysts argued that his greatest mistake was trying to win solely on the issues while neglecting to let Americans warm to him as a person. In a highly controversial outcome, Gore led in the popular vote yet lost the electoral college. The controversial aftermath doesn't change the fact that Gore—a friendly, caring man, according to reliable accounts—failed to reach enough voters on an emotional level to ensure victory. Bush, despite an Ivy League background and considerable wealth, came across as more of a warm, friendly, even common man than Gore. Objectively speaking, Gore was more experienced in national and international politics, more intellectually oriented, and arguably more intelligent. Such objective criteria fell short of convincing enough voters in the states critical to the electoral college tally to carry the day for Gore.

Even business negotiations are not free of emotional issues. A food industry entrepreneur who recently sold his company told me that he'd planned to sell it a year earlier for $7 million. Indeed, he'd come very close to closing the deal but then decided against selling. He had found it too difficult to let go of a firm that he and his brothers had started, and a certain emotional pull made him keep the business going. In negotiation literature, the deep emotional attachment a negotiator feels toward an issue or item under discussion has been termed the *endowment effect*.[16]

A year after the first deal fell through, the would-be buyer again made an attempt to buy the firm. This time, the entrepreneur spoke to the buyer of the difficulty he had parting with something he'd built and of his plans to further the company's success. After months of discussions, the buyer finally made an offer even the emotionally attached seller could not refuse. The final purchase price was $15 million, more than twice the amount the entrepreneur had nearly accepted a year earlier.

▶ A MATTER OF TRUST

We've devoted considerable attention to how people reason—and from that, how they might be persuaded. But much of persuasion is about feelings as well. Much that is achieved in negotiation relates to the level of trust each party has vis-à-vis the other. Trust is often the result of subjective rather than objective considerations. In her book *The Mind and Heart of the Negotiator,* Leigh Thompson describes several threats to trust.[17] The first is a *breach of trust* or *defection,* in which one or both parties violate a trust that has been built between them. By way of example, in 2002, North Korea reopened its Yongbyon nuclear power plant and announced that it would restart a laboratory suspected of producing ingredients required for a nuclear bomb. North Korean leader Kim Jong-il expelled U.N. nuclear watchdog inspectors. The move, said the *Times* of London, was North Korea's attempt to pressure the United States into direct diplomatic talks, but U.S. officials refused to negotiate in response to "threats or broken commitments." A strained relationship became even more tense as the United States interpreted North Korea's actions as breaches of trust (shaky as such trust might have been) and refused to come to the negotiating table. This failure of trust came at a precarious time as, poised for war on Iraq, the United States was forced by North Korea's actions to divide its focus. Moreover, its international support was further weakened in a time of crisis.

Another threat to trust described by Thompson is *miscommunication.* As we've discussed, people see the world according to their own biases. They interpret words differently and misread nonverbal actions. Miscommunication occurs frequently in human interaction, and the expert negotiator remains ever vigilant. Mood can affect how people receive information; fatigue and emotional reactions cause people to misinterpret the words and actions of others. Effective negotiation requires both attending to these factors and being willing to postpone or interrupt discussions of important issues in order to deal with the emotions or conditions that are causing comments to be misconstrued. Stepping back and acting as a *balcony observer* of one's own communication can aid the effort to avoid miscommunication.

Thompson also includes *dispositional attributions* among threats to trust. These call into question a person's character and intentions by citing them (arrogance, greed, and the like) as a cause of behavior or incident. This amounts to name-calling. Naturally, people try to account for the behavior of others, especially if such behavior seems threatening. We formulate attributions based on our experience and our interpretation of the situation at hand. If someone fails to return a greeting as you walk past, you might explain this behavior by assuming one of a number of things: The person is rude; you did something to offend the person; the person didn't hear you; the person was lost in thought. The nature of your attribution depends on your mood, your prior experience with this person, and your relationship with the person. People often allow *idiosyncrasy credits* for persons with whom they have good relationships or whom they admire.[18] Idiosyncrasy credits allow the other person to do things that ordinarily would lead to negative attributions of the person's behavior, but (say, because of friendship or admiration) the person "gets a pass" thanks to attributions that let the person off

the hook. When negotiating, it's wise to remember that much behavior is based on attributions, and many of those are biased.

Poor pie expansion threatens trust because those who engage in it are narrow in their thinking and cause the other side to feel uncomfortably restrained. This is why, as Thompson explains, negotiators need to be skilled in expanding the pie. I listened recently to my ten- and eleven-year-old children talk with their friends about what games they might play. Each child wanted to play the game he or she would be most likely to win. Each time a child suggested a game, the others rejected the idea. Interrupting, I asked them whether if they'd considered that games aren't just for winning but also for the fun of playing them. If you want to enjoy yourselves, I continued, shouldn't you pick the game that is most fun instead of the one you're most likely to win? My argument met with some degree of skepticism, but one of the older children said, "Yeah, let's just pick one and play." Unfortunately, they found this solution unsatisfactory. Again, I stuck my nose in and suggested that they negotiate. My son (who is good at this) recommended that they play each of the games in turn, which would give several children a chance to win. Ultimately, they invented a new game in which none of them had a clear advantage. They expanded the pie and ran off together, excited at the new possibilities.

Egocentrism, the fifth threat to trust on Thompson's list, presents a significant roadblock to successful negotiation. Egocentrism is the tendency to view one's own preferences and actions as good and worthy—and the other side's as less so. Egocentric people can't venture outside the narrow confines of their own psychological world. They see things solely from their own vantage points, and they often consider others' ways and views to be not only foreign but inferior. As we've already discussed at some length, it takes a fair amount of understanding and respect for the other side's viewpoints to engender trust in negotiation.

Finally, a poor *reputation,* even when based on rumor or hearsay, can threaten trust. However, better negotiators are wary of sources in such matters and often prefer to obtain such information firsthand. They listen critically to information and opinions about others, preferring to discover for themselves whether the information should be treated as accurate. Nonetheless, the importance of valuing, nurturing, and protecting one's reputation is obvious.

Some other threats to trust include unreliability, inconsistency, lies, ambiguity, excessive control, and insincerity. Trust is a fragile thing; its maintenance is essential to most successful negotiations. The more important the development of a long-term relationship is to a negotiation, the more important it is to establish and maintain trust. It's important for negotiators to consider specifically both in advance and throughout the negotiation how trust can be established and maintained.

► THE IMPORTANCE OF MAINTAINING FACE

In addition to trust concerns, another reason for attention to emotion in the study of negotiation has to do with what Erving Goffman terms *face.* This is "the positive social value a person effectively claims for himself by the line others assume he has taken during a particular encounter."[19] *Facework* refers to communication

that supports or challenges a particular line. Since no one wants to be seen as a loser—or to appear to have been duped or forced to take a particular line of action—negotiation is often characterized by enhanced concern for face. Face is not a fixed psychological state but rather a social condition that can be damaged or lost in the course of negotiation. A kind of social order is created and maintained when negotiators act in ways that show concern for the face of their counterparts. When face concerns are overlooked or ignored, this social order is threatened.

Whenever possible, negotiators should try to maintain the other side's face. A negotiator will commonly refuse to continue if he anticipates a threat to face. He may attempt to manipulate the topics of discussion in order to avoid such threat. If a negotiator appears to be undertaking such diversionary moves, it typically behooves the other side to engage in what's called *corrective facework*—actions to help restore his perception that social order will rule and he won't be embarrassed. Good negotiators can provide accounts for mistakes, misstatements, or misunderstandings that originate with the other side ("Your country's experiences with invasions naturally cause you to be cautious. My country would be the same under similar circumstances"). By imposing a frame on a counterpart's action—perhaps even if the person has become angry or insulting—both the counterpart's face and the negotiation can be saved. Helpful types of accounts in these situations include the following:

- Admissions of fault or shared fault
- Denials of intention to harm
- Acts of omission rather than commission
- Blaming slippage on lack of sleep or misunderstanding

If a negotiator is in a state of fear for face, it's unlikely that he or she will be able to move sensibly toward an effective outcome. When a negotiation is threatened by loss of face, one or more of the above techniques can help get it back on track.

Whenever substantive negotiation takes place, the negotiation of face is going on as well. To ignore the latter is to destine a negotiation to failure. Certainly, there are variations in a negotiator's degree of concern about his or her face. Some people remain on pins and needles about their face throughout a negotiation; others are less concerned. I'd like to say that older or more experienced negotiators are less concerned about face, but anecdotal evidence suggests otherwise. It's important for negotiators to gauge the level of concern harbored by the other side—as well as the extent to which their own concern affects or might affect a negotiation.

There are times when negotiators actually use the fear of losing face as a strategy. The strategies of positive and negative esteem on Kellerman and Cole's list are of this type. They state or imply that if you do not go along with what a persuader recommends, you will not be thought highly of by others and may even be rejected by them. Negotiators using this tactic may, for example, suggest that if a particular course of action is not taken by the other side, they might look bad to important others. This type of approach is risky and not for the inexperienced. As a tactic, it's best reserved for last resorts. Even a hint of potential loss of face can cause a negotiation to spin off in unproductive directions.

Research has shown that lower-status individuals are particularly susceptible to face threats because the same breach committed by them is typically of less concern than it would be to a higher-status individual.[20] Persons with higher status have often learned ways of getting around their affronts that are not available to those of lower status. In many organizations, it is considered an error of judgment—if not an expression of weakness—for a higher-status person to appear concerned about damage to his or her self-concept. Higher-status individuals are expected to remain above such concerns, confident in themselves and, when necessary, able to account for their mistakes in ways that understate their significance. In other words, they know how to make excuses that don't sound like excuses or take other actions that minimize the damage and therefore do not threaten their position.

Some years back, the president of a leading forest products corporation made a misstatement about personnel policy in the impending downsizing of a major factory. When the president's erroneous statement appeared in the company newspaper, rather than apologize or issue a correction, a savvy human resource executive simply changed the stated policy to be consistent with the president's remarks, thus essentially erasing the error. As a young professor, I observed that my less informed, less experienced, and less accepted colleagues would excuse their tardiness with such statements as "The traffic was awful" or "My children were wreaking havoc this morning." The more experienced and well-ensconced professors were more likely to hint at having been involved in an important research phone conversation or having been summoned by some high-ranking university official. Their excuses actually enhanced their standing. If you excuse yourself at great length, it suggests that you lack confidence, which is not good either in negotiation or for career development. Of course, there are times when excuses must be made and even made at length. But a wise negotiator will make that determination carefully.

Sometimes silence is the best response. Far too many people refuse to let any problem lie for a bit. Instead, they feel they must pick it apart and solve it. Always consider *sitting on an issue* for at least a short period before responding. If you are attempting to purchase a product or trying to agree on the wording of a contract and the other side is dragging their feet, it's unwise to appear desperate. If you sense that they need your business as much, or nearly as much, as you need theirs, wait to respond. They are likely to wonder why you haven't jumped. Let them wonder. If you think that a complete lack of response from you is likely to cause undesirable tension, respond in brief: "Thank you for your update. I will get back to you in a day or two." This approach demonstrates that you are not anxious or perturbed but rather considering your alternatives.

Responding with silence, delay, or a brief message can be useful when the other side seems to believe they have more power than you do. This tactic can serve as a power equalizer if they take your reply (or absence thereof) as an indication that you don't feel compelled to make a deal. When you believe that someone else is playing a power game with delays, it's useful to consider other options—or other clients. Reduce your reliance on this party, and it will show in your demeanor.

▶ QUESTIONS

1. Using what you've learned in this chapter, analyze a conversation in which persuasion strategies are used. Reproduce the conversation as you recall it and based on what you've learned, suggest how one or both of the participants might have improved their outcomes.

2. Review the Kellerman and Cole strategies. Which ones are you averse to using when persuading, and which ones do you find quite useful?

3. Describe how the ACE model can be used to assist a negotiator in selecting among strategy types.

4. Review the chart of Sample Ways to Respond to Obstacles. Describe obstacles you've confronted in negotiation, how you responded or reacted and how you might respond were you in those same situations again.

5. Describe a debate that has received considerable news coverage. Select a position and describe the types of objective criteria you would use to advance that position. Give specific examples.

6. Interview an experienced negotiator. Ask him or her about the use of objective and subjective criteria. When is one better than the other? Describe two negotiations, one in which s/he relied on objective criteria, and one in which subjective criteria was crucial.

7. Using an historical example, describe how trust advanced one of the negotiator's goals or how the lack of it lead to diminished negotiation outcomes. In the latter case, what could have been done differently?

8. Have you ever caused someone to lose "face" in the course of a negotiation? How? What was said? How might you have achieved your goals while also maintaining the "face" of your counterpart?

The Role of Power

Although a command of persuasion certainly positions negotiators at a level more advanced than that of their less fortunate counterparts, certain aspects of the negotiation context impinge on the selection of available persuasion approaches. We now turn to one of the most important of these: the balance of power. We'll look at not only how power influences the choices of negotiators and hence their outcomes but also how power can be crafted by negotiators to offset what might otherwise be an imbalance to their detriment.

There are a number of relatively static indicators of power. Among them are rank, gender, age, reputation, status (including socioeconomic), intelligence, reputation (as a "player" or for negotiation expertise), appearance, and even physical size. The more powerful a person perceives himself to be, the less likely he is to listen to and follow the recommendations of people with less power.[1] Furthermore, persons who perceive themselves at a power disadvantage in negotiation tend to monitor their actions more carefully. In many cases, this inhibits choice and renders some negotiators impotent. Yet ironically, this same caution may provide certain advantages. It never pays to be too confident of one's power position in negotiation. After all, most power advantages, even status, can be diminished. Communication expert Klaus Krippendorf explains that people often become trapped by their perceptions of power balances—perceptions that could change if they would realize that power is not an object but something that is defined relationally.[2] As such, power is negotiable. Linguist Robin Lakoff wrote, "Language is the initiator and interpreter of power relations."[3] That is a liberating view, as it suggests that by using language effectively—as advocated throughout this book—you can become the arbiter of your own power. If you also develop the attitude that power is more often acquired than it is ascribed, crafted rather than endemic, you will have the components necessary to tip negotiation power balances in your favor.

When I have a waiting list for a course, usually I welcome hopefuls to attend classes for a few weeks in case an opening becomes available. Some never show, while others attend for a week or so and then disappear. Invariably, a few students remain tenacious. They attend for several weeks, usually asking me after class if they've advanced sufficiently on the waiting list. Eventually, the persistent and po-

lite ones get to me. I start to respect their tenacity and patience. Perhaps I feel somewhat obligated as well—after all, they have taken my advice. So I do everything I can to squeeze them in, even if it means going over the assigned course limit. Essentially, these students have increased their power by demonstrating qualities that I admire. If I lacked a sense of obligation, their approach would be ineffective. Politely but firmly, I'd send them on their way. But the more savvy students recognize (or find out) that I'm unlikely to do that, and so they persist and eventually win a place in the class.

If they had learned from students in a prior class that staying power eventually wins me over, that would be fine with me because it would mean that they'd done their "homework." That appeals to me more than the persuasive efforts of students who tell me that they are university sports heroes and that their coach will call me if I fail to admit them.

Few things are more frustrating than trying to negotiate with people who are obsessed with power. "I'll do X if you do Y," they say, childishly. *Don't call us, we'll call you,* they often imply. They make you wait on the phone or outside their office when it's patently obvious that no important person or issue is holding them up. Their primary assessment in a negotiation is whether they have come out on top. Actually, these people aren't good negotiators; they're bullies. Sometimes they win, but not because of skill.

Skilled negotiators work with power but do not focus on it exclusively. They concentrate on well-articulated outcomes. They make people feel good (but not awestruck) about being with them. In the words of Henry David Thoreau,

> Rather than love, than money, than fame, give me truth. I sat at a table where were rich food and wine in abundance, and obsequious attendance, but sincerity and truth were not; and I went away hungry from the inhospitable board. The hospitality was as cold as the ices. I thought that there was no need of ice to freeze them. They talked to me of the age of the wine and the fame of the vintage; but I thought of an older, a newer, and purer wine, of a more glorious vintage, which they had not got, and could not buy. The style, the house and grounds and "entertainment" pass for nothing with me. I called on the king, but he made me wait in his hall, and conducted himself like a man incapacitated for hospitality. There was a man in my neighborhood who lived in a hollow tree. His manners were truly regal. I should have done better had I called on him.[4]

Skillful negotiation isn't about sending the other side away unfulfilled or longing for better treatment. There is no talent to that and little long-term reward. For skilled negotiators, heavy-handed use of power is a device of last resort. Authority is not half so valuable as respect. A senior executive of a Los Angeles–based defense company once told me, "I've seen supervisors with authoritative power alone get only what they ask for from people. Consequently, they have to expend much more energy to accomplish their work because they have to think of every move their people will make. Supervisors with respect find that people offer to do more and take on more responsibility, which in turn lightens the management load."

Respect is crucial to negotiation. If the other side regards you as a fair and worthy counterpart or opponent (and if they too are fair people), the outcome of negotiation is likely to be positive for both parties. However, if they're not fair minded or if they are operating under duress, it may be necessary to win respect based on ability to gain advantage. "The only thing these guys understand is power" is a common phrase in business in reference to such situations. It's no fun to work in those situations, and it's equally joyless to negotiate with such "guys."

There are times when power is clearly defined. People in the inner circle of most companies have such power. The CEO of a company typically has more power, in a sense, than the people who work for him or her. The negotiator who has resources clearly desired by the other side (who "holds the cards," so to speak) has power. When there is some degree of ambiguity as to who holds the most important resources, however, power can be negotiated. In most cases, reality and perception collide. It is not enough to believe that you have more or less power. The key is to discover what matters to those on the other side and then to shape their perceptions of you and your resources in ways that cause them to consider you powerful.

I once negotiated with a man who was convinced that my knowledge of negotiation made me more powerful. As we proceeded, I realized that whenever we approached a final agreement, he would come up with some new thing that I should provide or concede as part of the deal. I found his habit not just annoying but also puzzling—at least until he obliquely revealed his wish to show his colleagues how he had obtained some very impressive outcomes despite my expertise. In his view, his face was in jeopardy. That realization allowed me to provide him with resources that made his outcomes admirable, while not going so far as to undermine my own goals. This frame opened up options and extricated us from a pattern that was proving dysfunctional. Had my own goal been only to exert power and demonstrate my advantage, surely both of us would have walked away dissatisfied.

If someone possesses more power, you might argue, shouldn't that person win? Why, with supposedly greater power, would a person choose not to win? The answer relates to the subtle but important distinction between views of power as *owned* or power as *crafted*. I. William Zartman and Jeffrey Rubin describe the view of owned power as follows:

> The concept as stated is unable to distinguish between an agent that prevails against no resistance (power) and one that prevails by a hair with tremendous effort. Or if it can make that distinction, as between net and applied power, it has no one criterion by which to evaluate—let alone measure—the competing applications. It tells who wins but does not tell the score! Or again, if the target decides to give in, for its own moral or tactical reasons (such as to buy a counter-concession from the agent), does that mean that the agent has power, whereas it has none if the target is willing or able to hold that same amount of effort in check?[5]

In other words, if a very powerful (in real terms) negotiator decides not to crush the other party or to even allow the opponents impressive gains, does it

mean that the negotiator is not powerful? Of course not. It only means that the negotiator opted not to exert available power in such a way as to severely limit the other party's outcomes. In this way, not only is power partially perception, but also the use of power is optional, so it can't be gauged merely by looking at each side's respective gains. Indeed, many times when skilled negotiators withhold the use of power, they create a sense that they have more power than they may actually possess. Much like the stereotypical gentle giant, a very powerful negotiator can decide not to use power purely because she and others know she can and that's sufficient.

The perception of power can be as attractive as power itself. A Hollywood producer explained to a class of mine that in order to encourage a star like, say, Brad Pitt to appear in one of his films, he would first try to interest another star, such as Julia Roberts. Even if Roberts had not agreed to appear in the film, if the producer managed to arrange a meeting with her, he could then call Pitt's agent and reveal that Roberts had expressed interest and would be meeting with him. Quite often this perceived power over resources will cause the other actor or agent to look at the script more closely and then schedule a meeting with the producer. Thus a producer who appears to have one star in his or her camp (even if not firmly so) has the power to attract others.

Let's now examine a number of other important rules for the use of power in negotiation.

- Establish credibility.
- Do your research.
- Don't have all the answers.
- Don't quibble over the small stuff.
- Create dependence.
- Use the power of who you know.
- Don't appear overbearing.
- Use time strategically.
- Choose the context carefully.
- Use threat only as a last resort.
- Don't play the same power hand twice.
- Remain flexible.
- Familiarize yourself with the political landscape.
- Don't go into negotiation alone.
- Don't let yourself become flustered.
- Find the soft spot.

The first rule pertains to ensuring that those on the other side know why they should listen to you—essentially, by conveying what type of power you have, be it by possessing more knowledge about something than the other side has or by having simply garnered more accolades. All of us have limited attention spans. We

listen to those we deem worth the effort. Therefore credibility, as discussed in Chapter 7, is a very important aspect of negotiator persuasion. We now look at credibility as a source of power as well.

▶ ESTABLISH CREDIBILITY

This rule could easily be misconstrued to mean that you should build yourself up in the eyes of others. When people try to build themselves up, however, others often feel the need to push them down. If you are to be built up, it should be either by others who say favorable things about you or by letting your reputation precede you. Let a team member introduce you. Alternately, in advance of negotiations, provide the other side with a biographical sketch that describes your accomplishments or those of the team members. Keep it short, to avoid making them feel defensively inferior (unless they've given you long autobiographical sketches of their own). If they already know you, your best opportunity to increase your credibility will come from how organized and prepared you appear, since those attributes suggest competence. Taking out notes when appropriate, demonstrating a good recall and understanding of where any prior negotiation left off, suggesting an agenda—these all contribute to credibility, an important form of power.

Credibility is indispensable in cross-cultural negotiation. The Japanese, to cite just one example, want to know the status of each participant. They are less amenable than Americans are, for instance, to negotiating who is in power. For the Japanese, status is much more ascribed than acquired. To the extent that your title indicates status, your power is enhanced in that culture. Note well, though, that as the world shrinks in terms of accessibility and shared knowledge, such generalizations must increasingly be taken on advisement. It is best to learn, before going into a negotiation, what the other side is likely to view as indicators of credibility. Then be sure to take the time to demonstrate that you possess such qualities.

▶ DO YOUR RESEARCH

"He sure knows his stuff" is one of the highest compliments a negotiator can receive. Negotiations are won and lost daily on the basis of background information or lack thereof. These days, when people are often rewarded at work solely for what business experts Jeffrey Pfeffer and Robert Sutton call *smart talk* (sounding confident, articulate, or eloquent), skilled negotiators nevertheless recognize the difference between such talk and substantial support for ideas.[6] Their ears are alert to bluster, which is often evidenced by making things unnecessarily complex or abstract or by excessive criticism and negativism. They see past the smoke screen of feigned expertise, looking for substantial support. If you are up against a person with such skills, you'll need more than smart talk to advance your agenda.

Although you can, to a certain extent, develop expertise power on a given issue by doing such things as frequently visiting relevant Internet sites, you're more likely to acquire such power by keeping yourself open to information from unfamiliar sources. Jean Lipman-Blumen, coauthor with Harold Leavitt of *Hot*

Groups, says future leaders (and effective negotiators, I might add) will be those "who want to be where meaning might emerge, the people who refuse to drink continuously from the same information well."[7] The more well read you are, the more curious about subjects related to your area of expertise, the more prepared you will be to introduce into negotiation information with which the other side may not be as familiar. If you present this information in a constructive rather than disruptive manner and with an attitude of helpfulness rather than arrogance, the other side is likely to be impressed. Those negotiators who are busy attempting to trip up the other side often overlook this method of power development.

An added benefit of knowing your stuff is the confidence that usually follows from such awareness. Research on source credibility over many decades has clearly shown that confidence and conviction are crucial to gaining acceptance for one's ideas—especially if the audience or negotiation counterparts are not of the same mind as the source.[8] Negotiators who've done their homework bring a high degree of confidence to the table. When you neglect your homework and merely focus on maneuvers, the typical result is lowered outcomes. Remember, whenever the other side concedes an issue, they must be able to convince themselves and demonstrate to others that they had very good reasons for doing so—that the evidence was compelling. Never, therefore, enter a negotiation without impressive evidence for your primary and secondary claims. Otherwise, you will go in virtually powerless.

▶ DON'T HAVE ALL THE ANSWERS

Although it's important to do research and to know negotiation issues inside out, it isn't wise to flaunt your expertise. Too many negotiators think they need to (1) be right, (2) be seen as right, and (3) make others feel that they must therefore be wrong. This is a shortsighted approach. Most people are at least partially insecure, and even those who aren't certainly don't wish to be looked down on. It's counterproductive to enter a negotiation in which your outcomes depend to any extent on the goodwill of the other side, only to make others feel you don't respect them. Contrary to common wisdom, the best negotiators endeavor to help the other side remain confident that no matter what the issues of disagreement and no matter how heated the battle may become, they respect the other party's accomplishments and position and are always interested in what they have to say.

Accord respect to the other side, unless and until they force you to do otherwise. Even then, if you can take the high ground while letting them know that you will not be walked on, that is the better course. This can be a tall order, especially for people who find it difficult to "walk in another's shoes." The inability to do so may result in mistaking a brutal and uncivil approach for power when such behavior often really masks desperation and ignorance. Power comes from being in control. Control is often gained (or regained) by keeping the other party content to remain at the negotiation table with you. You can always say *something* good to or about other people, their interests, or their possessions. The best negotiators identify these avenues of compliment, even when abhorrence for the another person is welling up inside them.

The more skilled the negotiator, the more extensive his or her repertoire of what I'll call *esteem-reviving* comments. These are useful when the other side appears to have taken offense to prior statements or actions. "If you don't mind, let's back up here to see if I've misstated my intentions." From here, the negotiator might reframe earlier comments or provide an overarching frame, such as "If I seemed abrasive a few moments ago, be assured that it was only due to my determination to make this work—which is a sentiment I know we share" or "I may have spoken too quickly a moment ago. Let me rephrase what I said earlier." Comments of this nature reposition what has been said.

Some negotiators see such statements as revealing weakness. But used sparingly, they are actually expressions of strength. They demonstrate a level of confidence that allows for occasional admission of error. More important, they can get a negotiation back on track, which is power—in a soft sense, perhaps, but power nonetheless.

▶ DON'T QUIBBLE OVER THE SMALL STUFF

Many a negotiator has lost an entire deal by pushing too hard for minor gains. If you've done your homework, you know what matters most to you, what is desired but not crucial, and what you wouldn't mind having but can easily live without. If you haven't, you can lose track of what matters and focus your effort on obtaining prizes that seem petty to the other side. Engaging in "salami tactics" (that is, trying to "slice off" a few more concessions toward the end of a negotiation) elicits distrust. So does pushing for items that the other side has clearly indicated are unavailable after they have already given you what they perceive to be a considerable amount.

At some point, quibbling creates bad will, but that point is not always easily identified. To avoid seeming petty, it may be wise to bundle a smaller item with others into one package. Or you could state that the item is less important than those already negotiated but you still have a few questions about it. Then choose your questions wisely.

Let's say you're negotiating an employment offer. If you've studied the organization and have spoken with people who work there, you should be ready to ask intelligent questions. You might say, "I've heard that new hires occasionally receive a signing bonus. Perhaps we can look at that, now that the larger issues have been settled." This places your request in context as something not unusual (and therefore not a sign of greed on your part) and, while of interest, of lesser importance than what has already been achieved. If the prospective employer responds, "We used to give signing bonuses, but we are moving away from that," you need to decide whether it's in your best interests to pursue the issue or move on. You might move on to a request that your research indicates the company is better positioned to address: "Could we talk about an alternative, such as moving and travel expenses from where I live, since I'm coming quite a distance?" You'll need to know what is typically part of the package so that you don't ask for something that will be provided as a matter of course. If you believe that the person you're speaking with cannot authorize such a concession on his or her own, say, "I don't need

an answer right now. I'd be glad to call you tomorrow." If the firm really wants to hire you, it is likely to come up with something.

▶ CREATE DEPENDENCE

When I first joined the Marshall School of Business, I taught in an area little esteemed by those who would one day determine whether I would be promoted. I published in leading communication journals, but they were foreign to many business professors. I had strong teacher ratings and that was helpful, but it wasn't enough. I knew I would never gain promotion and tenure by remaining something of an enigma. Yet my insisting that journals in my field were just as good as those respected by finance professors or my complaining that promotion criteria were skewed and unfair would not have helped. What I needed to do was raise my value to the Marshall School. I was determined to publish in the *Harvard Business Review* and other leading business journals, to obtain grants, to write interesting and useful books that received valued publicity, and to develop a course in negotiation. This last became one of the school's most in-demand courses. It also pulled in students from all areas of the business school and beyond. I became, in the dean's words, a "cash cow."

These moves were directed at creating value for my work, and they succeeded. I don't remember consciously saying to myself, "I will now go about creating power." I merely compared what was valued at the time in business schools with what I was doing. Senior colleagues were helpful here. They shared with me the views of the people in charge and provided valuable advice and support. I continued to do my research, teaching, and publishing in communication, but with considerable focus on ways that were valuable to a business school and thus would make all the difference in terms of promotion. This also allowed me to continue research in more tangential areas because those "in power" were satisfied with the main thrust of my work.

I remember well two occasions when colleagues of mine were up for promotion. They believed that promotion was dependent on one's ability to demonstrate impressive productivity. Rarely is promotion a matter of demonstration. It is a matter of persuasion. You have to know what the decision makers value—not what you value or what they used to value but what they value now. Connecting your work to those criteria is critical to making a case for promotion. If an organization doesn't publish clear guidelines regarding criteria for promotion, track down speeches or records of public comments by people in decision-making positions that indicate what gets noticed and rewarded. Make the connection between your work and those indicators, being sure to quote from the source when you do so. Sometimes power comes from knowing what is supposed to be valued and reminding the people who are in a position to affect your career.

Another way to create power, akin to creating dependence, involves causing people to feel good about being with you. Many a job has gone to the candidate who accomplished this, rather than to the one who deserved it solely on merit. What makes people feel good about being with certain others? They may feel more secure, their sense of status or importance may increase, or it may just be

pleasant to be around them. Even honest, skilled negotiators learn comfort-eliciting phrases, expressions, and gestures. If they sense that a counterpart's face is threatened by a mistake or unfortunate occurrence, they will reassure with such statements as these:

- "The exact same thing happened to me not long ago."
- "Let's not dwell on this one instance. Let's concentrate on all the positive steps we've made, largely due to your leadership."
- "Certainly, this issue is an obstacle, but you've gotten us out of jams before, and I'm confident you'll do it again."

The key is not to indulge in excessive flattery. Reassurance is the objective, and achieving it requires neither obsequiousness nor insincere compliments but rather recognition of positive contributions the other side has made.

Henry Kissinger managed to survive many a battle in the Nixon White House not because he got along well with Nixon, not because he was the best diplomat or negotiator, but, as author Robert Greene explains, because he entrenched himself in so many areas of the political structure. He became so valuable to so many departments that letting him go would have led to upset and confusion. He also became valuable by making allies in many places. Greene argues that this form of power doesn't enable as much freedom as comes from being so capable that those in power must keep you around, but it isn't a bad second.[9]

This kind of dependence power is called *centrality*. It accrues from occupying central positions in important networks. When senior people depend on central ones to gather information or make needed connections, the power of the central ones is enhanced. The following equation illustrates the relationship between power and dependence:

$$\text{Power A,B} = \text{Dependence B,A}$$

The power of person A over B is, according to this equation, equal to the dependence of person B on A.[10] Based on this view of power, a negotiator would do well to make sure that the other side depends on him or her for some valued resource. The resource may be information, or ideas on how to make the other side look good to its boss at the end of the negotiation, or it might be simple respect.

During preparation, skilled negotiators consider how such reliance can be created. They ask themselves, *What do I have that the other side might want?* In the early stages of negotiation, they listen carefully for cues to help answer this question. They search for the *potential domain of dependence* and consider ways to emphasize their ability to respond to it. In this way, they add value to their position and help tip the balance in their favor.

▶ USE THE POWER OF WHO YOU KNOW

"It's not what you know but who you know" is an old saw that many of us learn early in life. Yet as a form of power, it's all too often ignored, perhaps because using someone else's power to bolster your own may seem somehow unethical.

Shouldn't negotiation be about fair play, after all? When it is, connections aren't likely to be needed. More often, however, negotiations *are* about power. Dependence relations, who has the marbles, connections, even beauty—since research shows that people pay more attention to attractive others—are all commonly used forms of power. If what a negotiator has to offer is insufficient or if the other side holds—or appears to hold—all the major marbles, connections can go a long way toward leveling the playing field.

Connections may be squandered if negotiators don't understand when or how to use them. They may *drop names* awkwardly and prematurely. "I was with the senior vice president the other day, and he told me . . ." may be an effective call on authority if the person with whom you're negotiating is being obstinate. But the person may consider it too heavy-handed if he perceives it as bullying— or if he dislikes the senior vice president. Before citing the support of another esteemed party, it's important to discern whether that person is highly regarded by the other side. (You also want to be sure that you indeed have their support. The other side may well check on that.) And you want to phrase your name dropping in a way that avoids the suggestion of contrived intimidation. A good negotiator tends to be subtle when implying connections, waiting, for instance, until the subject under discussion relates either to the topic for which you have the connection's support or to the connection personally. "Before last week, I saw that issue differently. But some things Bill Adams told me over lunch have caused me changed my view." Here the negotiator doesn't suggest that Adams is strongly on his side, but he creates the impression that without any knowledge that the negotiation now taking place would occur, the negotiator and Adams happened to discuss the topic now under consideration. The novice might be more likely to say something like "Knowing we were going to meet, I went to see Bill Adams last week." Such an approach typically makes the other side feel trapped, and that is not good. After all, people who feel cornered become defensive, and that rarely helps bring about a positive outcome.

▶ DON'T APPEAR OVERBEARING

In negotiation, power does not accrue to the person who has the right answers— or even the best ones. Indeed, people often respond better to those whom they believe to have some faults. Act like you have all the right answers, and others will often do what they can to hinder you from achieving your goals. On the other hand, if you share credit, involve others so that they have a proprietary interest in making solutions work, demonstrate competence (not arrogance), and allow others to take the lead now and then, the chances of negotiation success are increased.

Following are the kinds of statements that expert negotiators often use to reassure that their counterparts that they are not hogging credit or being overbearing:

"Now I see where you're going with that idea, Ted. It's a good one."

"I hadn't thought of it that way."

"How would we do X if we implement the idea you're proposing?"

"You're a step ahead of me on this one, Evelyn."

"That's more in your area of expertise than mine, so I'd like to hear more."

"What you're saying here is certainly better than what I'd proposed earlier. It also has the advantage of X while also meeting our concern about Y."

Not only do such statements, sincerely spoken, help the other side feel good about working with you, but they also tend to encourage reciprocity. Thus a degree of humility is a form of power. You may well need to remain firm on some issues, but there are always ones on which you can allow others to take the lead.

► USE TIME STRATEGICALLY

Timing is crucial in negotiation. Yet the strategic use of time is a talent in short supply, especially in Western cultures, in which we have convinced ourselves that time is money and so ought not to be wasted. Indeed, time can mean money in negotiation, but only when it's used wisely.

It's important to pace proposals in a manner that fits the circumstances and the other side's expectations. When there is confusion about this, it's often helpful to discuss timing expectations early in the negotiation. Keep in mind that people are generally resistant to change. Even good ideas need adequate support. Most people in the United States want some kind of health care reform. In 1993 and 1994, President Bill Clinton, with First Lady Hillary Rodham Clinton leading the charge, tried to enact sweeping health care reform. Most health care providers and insurers were opposed to the Clinton plan. Convinced that the plan was a good one for the country, Clinton pushed on. The timing wasn't right for the vast amount of change being advocated. The plan died without even coming up for a vote in Congress. Many experts argue that this failure to pace change contributed in large measure to Republican victories in the 1994 congressional elections.

The same error was made by Republican Congressman Newt Gingrich, elected Speaker of the House in January 1995. He pushed for what became known as the Contract with America. It included drastic reforms involving term limits, tax and welfare reform, a strong national defense, and a smaller federal government. Gingrich was extremely successful in gaining Republican congressional support. Where he ran into difficulty was in expecting the public and elected representatives to make the recommended changes rapidly. Leadership experts Ronald Heifetz and Marty Linsky explain, "Gingrich failed to appreciate that no matter how much enthusiasm the public felt for the contract as an idea, in reality people needed more time to get their heads around so many deep and important changes. Gingrich didn't seem to consider how best to pace the work."[11]

Heifetz and Linsky argue that had Gingrich parceled out the change, spreading the agenda over a long period of time, people would have been able to assess the value of the new versus the loss of the familiar in a step-by-step process. Gingrich's insistence on enacting the entire agenda right away frightened people. This impatience, coupled with his being held responsible by many for the govern-

ment's closing down in late 1995, brought Gingrich in a short time from the apex of his career into a downward spiral. Clinton regrouped, made some dramatic midcourse corrections, and won reelection in 1996. Gingrich lost the post of Speaker of the House after the 1998 election.

When determining how to pace the introduction and disposition of issues, experienced negotiators read between the lines. They observe how the other side deals with issues. Do they present a number of them at once? Do they look for agreement in general, or do they press for firm agreement on specific points? Put differently, do they seem more interested in cultivating a workable plan in a gradual manner, or do they appear prone to either-or solutions? Expert negotiating requires taking the time to answer questions like these. It also requires the kind of flexibility we've discussed previously. A change of course may be in order at any point in negotiation. Observant negotiators know when such points have been reached, largely because they're on the lookout for them.

Many of us are used to speedy negotiations: getting the issues on the table and pressing for results on the main ones. Occasionally pulling back, however, and giving the other side an impression that you are not so much interested in a quick decision as in a good one can be a very compelling strategy. It conveys confidence and allays doubts that you might be under pressure (or even, God forbid, desperate), and that in itself can be a considerable advantage.

▶ CHOOSE THE CONTEXT CAREFULLY

When I discussed a particularly successful negotiation with an expert in community-police relations, she said that one of the most important considerations in planning a negotiation is *context.* "The food, the room, the temperature, lighting, and seating are all critical to a positive outcome. When people really don't want to be there, you don't want to give them any additional reasons for not cooperating. We've found that when people are upset, they need access to snacks all during long meetings and excellent food at mealtimes." The environment of negotiation is a powerful facilitator or inhibitor of negotiation success.

Malcolm Gladwell, in his best-selling book *The Tipping Point,* writes of the power of context. He describes the 1984 New York subway showdown between four youths and Bernard Goetz—an unexpected vigilante who, it seemed, just snapped. He drew his gun and shot four youths who'd apparently been provoking and harassing him. Were Goetz's actions those of a criminal mind, a person destined by genetic structure to shoot his gun that day? Gladwell examines that theory but also the very compelling power-of-context perspective. This perspective explains the Goetz event as a product of surroundings:

> The Power of Context says that the showdown on the subway between Bernie Goetz and those four youths had very little to do, in the end, with the tangled psychological pathology of Goetz, and very little as well to do with the background and poverty of the four youths who accosted him, and everything to do with the message sent by the graffiti on the walls and the disorder at the turnstiles. The Power of Context says you don't have to solve the big problems to solve crime. You can prevent crimes just

by scrubbing off graffiti and arresting fare-beaters: crime epidemics have Tipping Points every bit as simple and straightforward as syphilis in Baltimore or a fashion trend like Hush Puppies.[12]

Whether you side with psychological destiny or the power of context in explaining the actions of Bernard Goetz, it is difficult to ignore the influence of environment on the outcomes of human interaction. Whatever traits and inclinations negotiators bring to the table, the way in which the negotiators employ these depends, in large part, on the context in which they find themselves. Our tendency as human beings to make assumptions about people—to credit our limited observations with the power of absolute prediction—is misguided at best. We fail to notice how sensitive animals are to their surroundings and how much information they derive from this sensitivity. We think ourselves different from them. And yet we are not so different. Perhaps our cognitive processing overrides such information, but that does not mean we haven't taken it in. Richard Petty and John Cacioppo wrote of two levels of cognitive processing: central and peripheral. It is erroneous to assume that central processing of information is always the more influential. We take in far more than we bring to the fore of our consciousness, and that information can be very powerful.[13]

This means that negotiators need to consider the context of their interactions. Will all participants be comfortable? Is that what we want? What food options should we provide? What seating makes the most sense in terms of leveling the playing field or facilitating our goals? What color scheme is in the room? How foreign will the environment feel to the other side and to us? These are only some of the questions negotiators should ask themselves before settling on a location for talks. Should we sit across from each other or next to each other? Are there unsettling elements of the context that might pose a problem—such as the lack of a smoking room or access to a large area or outside venue for breaks? All of these considerations affect the power of negotiators. The best arguments in the world cannot completely eradicate the power of context. It's best to be sure that it is on your side.

▶ USE THREAT ONLY AS A LAST RESORT

The best uses of power are not the heavy-handed ones. Research indicates that negotiators who more frequently use cooperative strategies have higher joint gains than those who don't and that those who more frequently use such competitive strategies as demands and threats fail to achieve optimal outcomes.[14] Threat is the act of a desperate negotiator, and desperation is an impression you should not want to convey.

When you resort to threat, you are no longer negotiating; rather, you are engaging in coercion, which is a very different form of influence. Negotiation is aimed at trading concessions to obtain desired outcomes—ideally, for both sides. Coercion is one-sided and shortsighted, in that gains are only likely to obtain as long as you are applying the coercive force. Of course, there are times when one side of a dispute is influenced only by force. Those who rely heavily on the use of force abhor weakness

in others and take advantage of it. Your dealings with them will never qualify as actual negotiation unless and until they can be brought to the table with a willingness to make concessions. Until that point is achieved, dealing with them is likely to be a matter of chest pounding and "my dog is bigger than your dog" volleys. Sometimes that's all that can be done, but we should be clear that the process involved is not negotiation. Once threat enters the dialogue (unless it is well veiled), negotiation begins to give way to altercation. In such a dispute, even if one side proves to be the weaker one and gives up its claim of greater strength, future dealings between the same parties are unlikely to be cooperative.

Where reason does not work, where the people involved are clearly used to compelling others to do their bidding, *veiled threat* may become necessary. A veiled threat is subtle and deniable. Sometimes it takes the form of a simple reference to a powerful acquaintance or ally whom the other side does not wish to offend. "I was speaking to Tyrone the other day about just this matter. He told me you'd see things this way as well." As always, timing plays a role here, too. If a veiled threat is made too early, the other side may well expect the entire negotiation to play out that way. If it comes too late, the other side may have already become firmly wedded to a course of action. In most cases, you should use a veiled threat when decisions are still being made, when an impasse appears to be developing but before it occurs. Obviously, it's a challenge to make this kind of judgment call properly, and many negotiators fail at it. Unfortunately, both practice and some repertoire of ways to make veiled threats are necessary. If you're negotiating with a superior who is resisting something important to you, you might say, "We could go together to speak with Amanda [his superior] to see what she thinks," or, "Since this move could be controversial, would you go with me to Amanda's office so we can get her opinion?" Some bosses find such suggestions offensive, and with good reason. They suggest that you're considering circumventing them with an appeal to a higher authority, which may well make them look bad. One pronounced risk to this approach is that your boss might go straight to Amanda himself and attempt to create such an unfavorable impression of you or your request that it undermines your approach. If you use this tactic, be sure that together you can see the other party (and thus make good on your veiled threat) right away.

A veiled threat can take the form of a question: "How will it look to our constituencies if we don't do X?" or "If we take this approach and it fails, what will John say?" If John's opinion is important, and the other side fears that you'll inform him of your opposition to an approach that subsequently fails, this can work. A more direct veiled threat is, "If this goes wrong, do you envision both of us explaining this to John? I don't want to be put in that position." Using the ACE model, veiled threats can take the form of appeals to appropriateness (what others will think), consistency (how an action will violate positive self-perceptions), or effectiveness (the negative outcomes likely to occur). Presenting the other side with a hypothetical scenario can be useful. "Let's say we go down this road. We take what you insist is the best approach, and we discover that our competitor uses the approach I've just described. I don't know whether I could justify continuing this venture."

Veiled threats are common in negotiation. The skilled negotiator uses them sparingly, to redirect the course of discussion or to prompt reconsideration of an undesirable action plan. The less personal the veiled threat, the better. To use a dental analogy, you don't want to hit a nerve when you merely intended to contour the tooth.

▶ DON'T PLAY THE SAME POWER HAND TWICE

If you resort to the same tactic more than once in a negotiation, be sure you know what you're doing. Because one sign of an effective negotiator is an extensive repertoire of strategies and tactics, you don't want such repetition construed as your desperation due to a limited number of options available to you. The other side will surely attempt to take advantage of that kind of action. They'll see you as predictable and therefore more easy to win over.

Robert Greene describes the hazard of such predictability:

> Do not imagine that to create an air of mystery you have to be grand and awe-inspiring. Mystery that is woven into your day-to-day demeanor and is subtle, has that much more power to fascinate and attract attention. Remember: Most people are upfront, can be read like an open book, take little care to control their words or image, and are hopelessly predictable. By simply holding back, keeping silent, occasionally uttering ambiguous phrases, deliberately appearing inconsistent, and acting odd in the subtlest of ways, you will emanate an aura of mystery. The people around you will then magnify that aura by constantly trying to interpret you.[15]

Contrived mystery works best for people held in high esteem—especially people whose reputation has them so intelligent that they are expected to be difficult to understand. If your reputation does not precede you (in a highly positive sense), you won't want to take such mystery too far. But the important point to remember is that anything that makes you easy to read—or your actions easy to predict—reduces your power. Repeated use of the same strategies is one such indicator.

▶ REMAIN FLEXIBLE

Rules guide our word choices, but those rules are not immutable laws. They are bendable rules, and they are often learned differently by different people.[16] We know that women often speak differently than men[17] and that various types of relationships call for different forms of interaction. Language communities often develop through communication technology, in a manner similar to the development of speech communities among people in close physical proximity. Organizational culture can influence the types of words used, styles of usage, length of conversations, accepted channels of interaction, and the norms for who can talk freely with whom. Speech habits develop over time as groups of people develop something of a shared understanding of how things should be said. Once people move beyond their speech communities, they must learn to rethink what they say, how they say it, and to whom.

The foregoing has important implications for us, since negotiation requires considerable attention to the fit or mismatch of our communication scripts with those of the other side. We would laugh at a scene of two negotiators speaking two different languages because they'd just be talking past each other. Yet even when negotiators are speaking the same language, they talk past each other when one engages in a script that the other does not understand or for which the listener makes an interpretation unintended by the speaker.

As sensemakers, we must constantly reevaluate the effectiveness of our choices. Negotiation is a process of constant discovery, not a set of static strategies. Some moves are intended only to derive a response from the other side that helps us gather more information. At other times, we take informed actions but in the hope, rather than the knowledge, that they are the correct ones. Subsequent reactions or responses indicate to us how correct they actually are. To the extent that negotiators can gather information, experiment a little, and continue to learn, we improve our chances of choosing actions beneficial to our causes. At no time, however, can we be completely sure that a certain choice will secure a desired outcome, because we are never completely in charge of the people or events surrounding us.

This view of negotiation underscores the importance of creative thinking in the process. Constant learning and relearning, experimentation, and a blend of caution and risk in our selection of a course of action and the words and nonverbal expressions we use to employ—these are vital ingredients in successful negotiation. Power, in this sense, resides in being flexible and taking an inquisitive approach to negotiation.

▶ FAMILIARIZE YOURSELF WITH THE POLITICAL LANDSCAPE

Since before Aristotle's time, scholars have wrestled with the relationships of language, politics, and power. Negotiation involves at least two people attempting to influence each other through the use of language. As we've discussed, they essentially cocreate a working reality, agreeing and disagreeing on interpretations of past, present, and future events. Their attempts at formulating interpretations are influenced by political contexts, which are constructed from the use of favored forms of language and, in turn, constrain language choices. More succinctly put, in families, social gatherings, work groups, and organizations, there are ways of talking that are acceptable and influential and other ways that are unacceptable and ineffective. Negotiators who fail to recognize and heed the constraints of the political sphere in which they are operating doom their efforts to failure.

When formulating a negotiation strategy, you should consider four types of political environments, of which you or the other side may be operating in one or more. The first is the *minimally politicized arena*. In this type of environment, power is possessed by those who are truthful and who demonstrate an abiding regard for not only their own outcomes but those of others as well. In a minimally politicized arena, what you see is largely what you get. A sense of camaraderie prevails, along with an absence of in-groups and out-groups. One person's gain is rarely viewed as another's loss. Rules may be occasionally bent and small favors granted, but people tend to treat each other with regard.

The *moderately politicized arena* is characterized by a greater acceptance of behind-the-scenes tactics. Most rules, however, are formally sanctioned, and deviousness is discouraged. Moderately politicized groups and organizations tolerate, rather than encourage, pockets of political activity so long as the goals of the group are facilitated. In such arenas, on the one hand, rules for the greater good are supposed to be followed, but in a somewhat contradictory manner, those same rules are sometimes flouted to advance shared interests. Power accrues to the person who does not appear to be flouting the rules, who works largely within them, and whose comments indicate a respect for rules—but whose actions and manner or speech get things done.

The *highly politicized arena* is one in which conflict is frequent and often pervasive. Formally sanctioned rules are invoked when convenient, rather than being applied consistently. In-groups and out-groups are clearly defined. Many topics are taboo because the people running things don't want them discussed. *Who* you know is more important than *what* you know. Unless you are a political master, such groups are highly stressful. Power goes to those whose tactics bring about desired outcomes, even if formal rules must be broken and behind-the-scenes arrangements must be made. Negotiators from such organizations are more often crafty than outright manipulative, but manipulation is not forbidden so long as it is deniable.

Finally, the *pathologically politicized arena* is characterized by frequent, often long-lasting conflict. Most goals are achieved by going around the rules. Distrust is high, and people spend a good deal of time watching their backs. Such groups and organizations tend to be en route to self-destruction. They often manage to maintain an image of strength for some time, however, before finally imploding. Power in such arenas goes to those who are manipulative and controlling. Members admire language that demonstrates a clear focus on achieving goals, no matter the human cost. Information is massaged. Here business is truly business, and people are expendable in the service of goal achievement.

Clearly, these arenas are quite different, and the people who inhabit them communicate differently as well. Although it isn't necessary for negotiators from a minimally political environment to become like those from a pathological environment in order to negotiate with them, it is necessary to know the difference. Otherwise, negotiators risk communicating ineffectively, and when dealing in highly and pathologically politicized arenas, they risk being managed or manipulated.

▶ DON'T GO INTO NEGOTIATION ALONE

You may be the only negotiator, but that doesn't mean you must be out there with no background support. To advance an idea in negotiation, it should have supporters who are either present at the table or whom you can mention. People are sometimes skeptical of the ideas of one person but comfortable with those that have backers, especially when the backers are highly regarded, powerful people. Many a great idea has fallen by the wayside because its owner took it on the road without adequate evidence of its appeal. Friends in high places are an important

component of evidentiary support. When preparing arguments to support a claim, consider whose backing would enhance its appeal. If you can't obtain that person's support directly, consider how you might demonstrate its similarity or compatibility with ideas that person had previously introduced or supported. If you know that a particular group admires an organization's founder or historical figure, for example, you might explain what that person would think were he present today. This strategy of lining up the support of people admired by the other side to help you convince them of the value of your proposal is often called *getting your ducks in a row*. This can be especially important for less experienced negotiators, whose ideas, when subjected to critical scrutiny, might wither without adequate, credible backing.

Even the most expert of negotiators is cautious when it comes to going the distance alone. They are like what Harvard professor Joseph Badaracco describes as quiet leaders.[18] They know that there are two types of unknowns to deal with in most situations. Some are the known unknowns: significant variables that could go one way or another. Effective leaders and effective negotiators plan as best they can for these variables. Then there are the more challenging unknowns—the unknown unknowns. These cannot be anticipated or planned for; they simply emerge when you least expect them. If a negotiator is on his own, he must manage all the known unknowns *and* the unknown unknowns. That's a tall order.

Look at most sports heroes, and you'll find a support system behind them. Lance Armstrong didn't win the Tour de France multiple times without the support of his teammates. Team members might block the wind by riding in front for a while, carry the key rider's water and food, or pace him and simply be there for moral support. Negotiation teams, at their best, work this way. The best negotiators are realists about how much they can detect and respond to effectively on their own. When they need help, they ask for it.

▶ DON'T LET YOURSELF BECOME FLUSTERED

Negotiation is an ever-changing game. Hard-won credibility may be lost at an awkward moment. Let someone else's reputation unnerve you, and it will be both evident and used to your disadvantage. There's nothing wrong with some nervousness, especially early on in the negotiation. Indeed, it indicates that you're not overconfident and that you're trying to remain on top of things. If you've done your homework, there should be few complete surprises. Should something unexpected occur, take a break. Go away for a while, assess the incident, and then return and ask questions. Avoid becoming defensive or appearing troubled. Asking questions can provide a useful respite and has the added advantage of eliciting information, which you can use to recalibrate and reformulate your sensemaking process.

Skilled negotiators know what to say when they do become unsettled, and they often rely on framing: "That is an interesting twist on things" or "You've obviously done your homework, but let's also consider . . .". Maintaining a steady power balance in negotiation requires the ability to deal with the unexpected, to

sustain an impact without collapsing. Making the effort to remain unflustered in the face of difficulty and calmly taking the time to reframe difficult situations in a favorable manner will pay worthwhile dividends over the course of the talks.

Keep your cool. In fact, start negotiations with determination to do so. If you lose your temper, be sure it's because you believe it's useful to do so. The best negotiators are cool under fire. The more prepared you are, the more you expect surprises and refuse to be thrown by them, the more successful you'll be as a negotiator.

Life is full of twists and turns, unexpected bends in the road. Negotiation is no different. If you can't handle them, you don't belong on the road.

▶ FIND THE SOFT SPOT

I've never met a person who didn't have a concern or insecurity, but I have met many people who acted as if they didn't have one. Most of us don't wear our heart on our sleeve, but that does not mean we're without one. Skilled negotiators encourage people to open up to them or "reach them where they live." They may disclose something about themselves that seems private or personal. This expression of trust often elicits a reciprocal disclosure of information from the other side. For example, mentioning that you have children when you know they do or that you've fought an illness similar to one they've had or that you've shared a career struggle in some way can have such an effect. A bond forms when something personal is shared, and it often opens a door to more sharing. Timing is crucial, of course; it's inadvisable to "open up" too early.

The goal is to discover whether what negotiators claim is the most important issue to them is really so or whether it is something else. That something else may be as simple as leaving the table with enough concessions to suggest that they have negotiated successfully. Their most salient need could be a desire to impress others, or it may be feeling powerful or developing a sense of teamwork or comradeship. Whatever it is, make sure you don't mistake your interests for theirs. Be patient and probing, and you may discover that you are in a position of great power simply because you can fulfill an unspoken personal need that the other side desperately harbors.

▶ QUESTIONS

1. What factors contribute to a perception of power? In what ways may perceived power be increased in the absence of actual power?

2. Compare and contrast the concepts of power, threat, and coercion. When might the uses of threat or coercion be appropriate? Provide examples. How effective would threat or coercion be in such circumstances?

3. How do flexibility and predictability relate to power? Provide examples from your own experience.

4. Discuss the characteristics of the various levels of politicization in an organization.

5. Interview a businessperson. Ask him or her to consider the four types of political arenas and to describe which bests describes his or her organization and why.

6. Have you ever lined up the ducks before attempting to negotiate? Describe how you did this. If you haven't used this strategy find an example from history that shows how it works.

7. We all have "soft spots." Describe how they work in negotiation to the advantage of those who take the time to locate them.

When the Discussion
Gets Stalled or Heated

Before we move into a discussion of conflict, it's important to return to our earlier discussion of the interdependence of negotiators. Conflict is often viewed as a distributive, or win-lose, form of negotiation. This gives the impression that once conflict has begun, the negotiation is in jeopardy for at least one, if not both, of the parties. Yet conflict is a normal, even expected part of negotiation. Any important negotiation has an emotional aspect. To approach the subject in any other way places negotiators at a disadvantage. They are likely to be unsettled or derailed by the emergence of unexpected conflict. Communication expert Donald Ellis explains, "Negative emotions and their expression are an integral part of the daily fabric of life and something that is routinely negotiated in society. Except on talk shows and call-in radio, incivility is typically expressed in subtle ways, although its impact is significant. We rarely tolerate blatant offensive and derogatory language. We are a society quite aware of extreme incivility (hate) and try to marginalize it by enacting laws and memorializing aspects of history that have messages of peace and cooperation."[1]

Coupled with the general tendency of most societies to celebrate cooperation and to understate and even hide the more normal state of periodic conflict, in these societies there is also a preference for appearing rational rather than emotional. Emotionality suggests a loss of control. This view is especially prevalent in business, where phrases like "business is business" and "time is money" indicate disregard for what is often viewed as emotional distraction. Novice negotiators tend to run roughshod over others' emotional expressions, preferring instead to dwell on what they think of as the primary and rational topic. Yet often emotion *is* the main topic. Consider the public debate over how to redevelop the World Trade Center site. Were this treated as a pure business decision, few would accept the final determination. Moreover, were victims' families, New Yorkers, and Americans in general ignored, any purely rational solution would certainly have fallen short. When interested parties are not fairly represented in the negotiation of emotional issues, the result is an exclusive rather than inclusive solution. In the

interest of speedy decision making, emotions are excluded from the negotiations or briefly attended to and then forgotten. This has been termed a *fast-slow approach* to conflict. Negotiation parties rush to reach an agreement, having ignored important constituencies, and then the agreement faces extreme difficulties in the implementation phase. By contrast, in a *slow-fast approach* to conflict, negotiations are conducted as slowly as necessary to ensure that the final agreement is responsive to major constituents. This then permits greater speed in implementation.[2] Exhibit 9.1 illustrates two cases that exemplify the efficacy of each of these approaches.

▶ *EXHIBIT 9.1*

FAST-SLOW OR SLOW-FAST APPROACHES TO CONFLICT RESOLUTION: A CASE OF PROS AND CONS

The *fast-slow approach* was exemplified when in the November 1995 negotiations in Dayton, Ohio, Bosnian leaders endured intensive pressure from their U.S. hosts. Both the U.S. agenda—which included, in significant part, a strong White House desire for demonstrable negotiating successes in Bosnia, the Middle East, and Northern Ireland—and the domestic constituencies of the Bosnian parties placed a premium on reaching an agreement. These conjoined motivations, coupled with the extreme urgency of ending a vicious and devastating war, meant that the three Bosnian leaders and their delegates at Dayton felt intense pressure not to leave the site without a signed result on paper.

The resulting Dayton Peace Accords were acclaimed as the framework for a comprehensive settlement of the conflict in Bosnia. But in the rush to reach an agreement, many details had to be overlooked. Long-term planning was sacrificed for the sake of short-term results: the insistence on a fast result at the negotiation stage simply piled up problems, which remained to obstruct and delay the implementation of the Accords. On the other hand, this use of the fast-slow approach stopped the war and the killing, which was a great achievement. Clearly, the fast-slow and slow-fast approaches each have advantages and disadvantages. The two approaches are not mutually exclusive; rather they need to be balanced as much as possible.

In some important ways, the South African constitutional negotiations of the early 1990s serve as a successful example of the *slow-fast approach*. The negotiation process was at times painstakingly slow, not least because of the wide range of participating groups and factions as well as the complexity of the issues. Undoubtedly, an outcome could have been designed much more rapidly between just the major participants—the government and the African National Congress—and by leaving certain aspects for later resolution. But the seemingly interminable talking between so many parties and the variety of issues addressed, which made the negotiation stage so slow, paid considerable rewards in the implementation phase, when the multilateral nature of the talks made the subsequent "sell" much faster and avoided breakdowns that could have resulted from "constituency lag" between leaders and their supporters.

Source: P. Harris and B. Reilly (eds.), *Democracy and Deep-Rooted Conflict: Options for Negotiators* (Stockholm, Sweden: International IDEA, 1998).

Another alternative is a *slow-slow approach* to resolving conflict, in which time is taken to consider, select, and apply solutions. However, having the time to take this approach is a rare luxury. "Indeed, most frequent pressure is for a fast-fast approach, the worse possible scenario, where there is no time to do justice to any aspect of the conflict management process."[3] Skilled negotiators avoid becoming so ruled by time pressures that they must overlook or dismiss the opinions of key constituencies. They do not allow themselves to become so obsessed with rapidly attaining their goals that they fail to deal with obstacles on the way. They understand that although a train may be destined for Chicago, if the track is blocked, the destination hardly matters. What does matter is fixing the track or, by using switches, carefully detouring without endangering the train. A small diversion may occasionally be necessary to avoid an immovable obstacle. Working through conflict may be such a diversion, or it may even be a necessary part of the route. It will cause a derailment only if the negotiators panic or allow themselves to forget their roles as managers of choice. A *manager of conflict* in negotiation expects and accepts disruption. A *dictator of conflict* in negotiation does not. Astute negotiators are not dictators, so conflict is something from which they learn rather than something they avoid entirely.

While conflict is a normal and sometimes necessary part of negotiation, there are indeed dysfunctional levels of conflict. As Donald Ellis suggests, incivility is on the increase. Individuals are increasingly becoming self-contained units with clearly identifiable boundaries. The more rigid the boundaries become, the more incivility ensues. Add to this the distancing effects of the information society in which, Ellis says, we spend about three thousand hours a year on media compared with two thousand hours sleeping and eighteen hundred hours working. As a result, "we are approaching the end of our communication capabilities, and carrying on additional discourse is increasingly difficult"—and, I might add, increasingly agitating. "This media situation creates conditions of exclusivity rather than inclusivity."[4]

In an environment characterized by increasing incivility, the more successful negotiations are likely to become a haven from, rather than an extension of, such incivility. The "us versus them" mentality so common today sets our experience of the world on edge. The negotiator who knows how to move away from that edge and provide a comfort zone for exchange has a distinct advantage. This is where communication management comes into play and keen observations of context and relationship prove their value. If, for example, the relationship is an inflammatory one, plagued by past arguments and vicious attacks, efforts must be made to keep the level of conflict in check. If the relationship has historically enjoyed considerable compatibility, a period of conflict need not be devastating. It may even clear the air. When conflict does seem excessive or misplaced, you may be able to reduce it by framing it as "an expected part of how we interact but not the entire definition of our relationship" or as "an indication of the passion we both share for this subject." In the case of a compatible relationship, you can frame a conflict constructively as "a healthy indication that we can disagree without becoming completely disagreeable" or "an important diversion in our otherwise highly cooperative relationship" or as "quite natural, given how much both of us want this project to work."

The skilled negotiator recognizes that because unspoken rules exist for how emotions should be expressed, we all suppress or disguise a considerable portion of our emotions. It is therefore the negotiator's first task in such matters to tease out important emotions—to bring them to the surface, where the negotiator can make sense of them and deal with them effectively. The second task is to defuse or redirect such emotions in goal-enhancing ways. Emotions are elicited by perceptions, which are subject to interpretation. As discussed throughout this book, negotiation invariably involves some management of interpretation for the other side, as well as for oneself. Effective negotiation is not a matter of keeping the lid on things but of offering interpretations of ongoing, past, or future events so as to elicit goal-constructive actions.

▶ AT THE EARLY SIGNS OF CONFLICT

Given that conflict is normal in relationships and even healthy at times, the most constructive way to view conflict is as a signal to reconsider a current approach. Sudden outbursts of anger or expressions of disappointment may suggest that a reconsideration of tactics is in order. When body language and manners of speech signal that tempers are on the rise, the best approach is *conflict prevention.* Halt the negotiation and say something like "I don't claim to be a psychic, but there seems to be some discomfort or tension in the air. Is there something I said that is causing that?" If you wish to be less direct, you might say, "Listen, it's natural in negotiations like this for us to have differences in opinion and sometimes discomfort with the process. Maybe we should stop for a few minutes to see if we're both satisfied with where we are." Another option is to suggest, "To ensure that we're on the right track, would you mind taking a few minutes for each of us to play devil's advocate and identify any faults or problems with the process and direction to date?"

Far too many negotiators allow bad feelings to fester. Either they don't detect them or they decide to ignore them. Both strategies are usually wrong. There are times when conditions are not right for addressing a heated issue: People may be tired—perhaps they have been at the negotiation table for too long—or the other side is not in a mood likely to lead to a positive outcome. Under such circumstances, it is advisable to postpone discussion until circumstances are more amenable to cooperation. Otherwise, it's best to address the conflict in some fashion or redirect the negotiation in a manner likely to bring about positive reactions from the other side.

The *PURRR procedure* is one conflict-reducing method to keep in mind during negotiation.[5] The procedure was developed as a means of reading between the lines in conversation, especially in politically sensitive situations:

The PURRR Procedure for Checking Assumptions

1. *Pause* the next time you're about to formulate a judgment about a person based on something he or she has said or done.

2. Make sure you *understand* (on the content and relationship levels) what the person meant by his or her words or actions, especially if hinting is involved.

3. *Reflect* briefly on the information you're using to form this judgment. Ask for more information if needed.

4. *Reinterpret* what just happened by applying an alternate favorable explanation to the one you first considered (for example, this is not personal but more a function of confusion or fatigue).

5. *Redirect* the conversation onto a path that better serves your goals.

The PURRR acronym suggests the image of a cat. And like a cat about to exit its pet door in the morning, the person following the PURRR procedure doesn't just dart outside before checking the terrain. The following example exemplifies this:

Let's suppose your usually easygoing boss is in a foul mood. He approaches you and angrily says, "I need that report tomorrow. No excuses." You weren't going to be late with the report. In fact, you never are. You are at a choice point. Do you get defensive? That depends on whether you've formulated an impression of him that begs a reaction rather than a response. You could say, "What's gotten into you today?" or "How'd I get in the line of fire?" But both of these call greater attention to the negative emotional component of the interaction. If you pause and realize that this is out of character, that he may be under a lot of pressure and that you just happen to be in the wrong place, other options become available. You might say, "I'll have it on your desk first thing in the morning." This response bypasses the relational (angry at you) component and focuses instead on the content of what he said (timely delivery of the report). It also does not engage him in an angry conflict at a point in time when he is acting out of character.[6]

The ability to see past a person's annoying or anger-provoking action to the conditions provoking it is a high-level negotiation skill. It allows a negotiator to bypass the natural inclination to retaliate against someone who has caused offense and to focus instead on saving the negotiation. It gives the other side a chance to be more cooperative because they are not confronted with having to defend themselves while in a bad mood.

▶ HOW TO RESPOND TO POTENTIAL OR REAL CONFLICT

The following are some *conflict reduction tips* for situations, such as the one just described, when you're confronted with potential or actual conflict. Of course, there are times when a negotiator must confront the situation directly and even times when he or she must rightly accuse the other of inappropriate words or actions, ones not conducive to productive negotiation. We'll discuss those types of situations later in the chapter. In general, though, these tips are good to keep in mind.

- Maintain an even strain.
- Ask clarification questions.
- Rather than be contentious, delay with process.

- Make headway on less contentious issues, returning to others later.
- Reposition or frame the problem in positive or mutual-gain terms.
- Frame differences as natural under the circumstances—defuse angst.
- Link something they believe or value to what you also believe or value.
- Emphasize what has been accomplished over what has not.
- Encapsulate conflict issues to avoid infection of other issues.
- Avoid pushing on petty issues or ones that will resolve themselves later on.
- If style is involved, meet them halfway.

▶ WHEN AN IMPASSE IS REACHED

When these constructive approaches are not welcomed by your counterpart or when you have sufficient evidence that the infraction was purposeful and intended to harm you or the negotiation, you face an *impasse situation*. We'll look at specific instances later in the chapter; the following are some general ways to handle an impasse.

- Take a break to strategize.
- Pose to both parties the cost consequences if agreement is not reached.
- Reconsider the amount that might be accomplished at this meeting.
- Visibly lower your dependence on them or raise their dependence on you.
- Break the problem into parts—fractionate it.
- If the impasse is on substance, focus on process—how to proceed from here.
- If the impasse is on process as well, try the shared text approach.
- Keep power in your pocket: a lawyer behind the scenes, advising; a name to drop; a party that may need to be brought into the negotiation; consequences that may obtain on other issues if agreement on this one is not made.
- Don't walk without leaving a door open.

▶ CONFLICT AS A CUE FOR CHANGE

We've discussed the fact that emotions can signal the need for preventive measures, that the most skilled of negotiators see emotional expressions as signals of needed change. In the midst of negotiation, when conflict is already under way, a change of approach may also make all the difference. Communication scholar Linda Putnam proposes, "Emotions cast routine patterns into disarray and create space for new forms of action. Thus, emotions can signal shift-points, punctuation, or crisis moments that help negotiators transform issues, interests, positions, and relationships."[7] Emotions therefore serve as cues to negotiators that more

might be going on than meets the eye. They stretch the sensemaking abilities of negotiators, which may be why many would just as soon keep everything on a rational plane. Cognitive stretching is hard work. Yet it is necessary work, because human beings are only partly rational—and experts often argue that the rational part isn't the larger part.

It's imperative, therefore, for negotiators to know how to read and manage emotions. They must keep in mind that words are, as we've discussed, weak vehicles of meaning and that people will often choose the wrong ones to express their thoughts. They may speak in ways that are unintentionally annoying or insulting. This is when competent negotiators ask themselves, *Should I be doing something different here?* They seek additional information to help them make sense of their counterparts' expressions. They may ask them, "Did you mean to imply that I haven't done my share?" or "When you used that term, was your meaning X or Y?" These kinds of questions can prevent a negotiation from spiraling out of control. If the other side replies in an undesirable way—for example, "I don't think you have done your share" or "I meant X even though you may not want to hear that"—at least a dialogue has begun. If both sides then explore these emotions with some degree of mutual objectivity, often both sides benefit.

Let's look at a conversation in which emotional expression signals a need to reconsider how to proceed. Paul and Craig have been working for some time on a project. Paul represents their company's marketing division; Craig, the company's finance division. Craig wants to spend less on the project than Paul believes is required to do it right.

Paul: We've put a lot into this project.

Craig: Are you implying that we haven't?

Paul: I'm stating a fact. Your people spend most of their time cutting the project budget.

Craig: Speaking of fact, your group seems to think money grows on trees.

Paul: At least we are focused on getting the job done right.

Craig: Frankly, I'm tired of your complaints. If you want more money, why don't you simply ask?

Paul: What do you think I've been doing for the last three days?

Craig: This isn't going to work.

Had Paul or Craig considered that their conflict might be more a signal for needed change than an indication of vast differences of perspectives or goals, there is a good chance that the outcome would have been improved. Craig was at a *choice point* right after Paul's first comment. He could have said, "You have indeed, and we appreciate it" or "We have as well, so we both have a vested interest in making this work." The focus is on compatible interests rather than differences. He could then ask Paul for a specific budget request and data to support it so that he might bring that to his people. He'd then be dealing with something tangible rather than vague accusations.

There are choice points throughout this conversation. After Paul says, "I'm stating a fact," Craig could reply, "I hadn't realized you were seeing things that way. It certainly hasn't been our intention to create an obstacle. Let's take a closer look at our budget to see if it is realistic." Craig may not need to make any additions to what's been given if his review of past provisions allows Paul to see that the budget is quite extensive, compared to those of other projects. Effective negotiation requires this kind of flexibility at choice points. It requires avoidance of tit-for-tat when what is needed is a compliment, an explanation, an exploration, an apology, or an expression of appreciation.

A useful strategy for reducing conflict is *giving them the chance to do the right thing.* If the other side is engaging in actions that are ethically questionable, for example, rather than play "Gotcha!" with them, why not hint that you recognize what they've done and then see if they take steps to right the wrong? The following conversation demonstrates how this is done.

Cynthia: We're not able to provide the raise you requested. We've reviewed your work, and while it's quite good in several ways, others have surpassed you in their improvement, including attendance at seminars.

Jack: Was attendance at seminars required or recommended at my meeting with you last August?

Cynthia: No. But it's understood that self-improvement is respected and rewarded here.

Jack: I have a list of self-improvements I've made in the areas you listed last August. If we could take few minutes to go through these, that would be helpful.

Cynthia: Fine. But the raise decisions have been made.

Jack: I understand. If we go one by one here, I'm sure you'll see that I've worked very hard to advance in the areas listed. It's my understanding from the Human Resources lecture we had a few months back that raises depend on doing what has been recommended in performance reviews. You may recall that in January you mentioned that I'd improved significantly in those areas. Furthermore, it may help for you to know that I've been receiving coaching at my own expense. Perhaps that is sufficiently similar to seminars and could be figured into my raise calculation.

Cynthia: I didn't know about the coaching.

Jack: I now realize it would have been helpful to you had I mentioned it.

Cynthia: I can't make any promises, but I'll think about this.

Jack: I really appreciate your reconsideration.

Jack did several important things here in his attempt to convince Cynthia to do the right thing. First, he didn't get angry. He presented his case in a logical manner while expressing understanding of Cynthia's position. He then posed a question to which he knew the answer. Seminars had not been recommended or required the prior August in his performance review. When Cynthia framed the

issue as one of self-improvement, Jack used this term to introduce the list formulated at his last performance review. While it is understood in most companies that raises should be based on improvements made in areas stipulated in performance reviews, Jack chose to gently remind Cynthia of this. He mentioned a Human Resources lecture. This implied that HR would be on his side should he decide to take the matter further. In some cases, this might be viewed as a threat, but if we assume that Jack delivered this gentle reminder to justify his attention to the performance review recommendations, it might not be perceived as such.

Jack then gave Cynthia some information that she could use to justify an additional raise. He asked if coaching might be considered similar to seminars. This allowed Cynthia a way out, so to speak. She could provide the raise on the basis of this additional information rather than on fear of Human Resources. It gave Cynthia a justification for doing the right thing. Should she follow through with the requested raise, it might very well be due to concerns about trouble with Human Resources, but she could position her decision as based on new information instead. She could say to Jack, "We reconsidered your raise on the basis of new information you provided about coaching and have decided to add another five percent." Giving people the chance to do the right thing often involves giving them a face-saving way to do it as well.

Sometimes the best approach to conflict is to share your own emotions with the other side. *Emotional admissions* can save a negotiation by providing an acceptable reason or account for seemingly threatening actions: "To be honest, I'm feeling as if you've ignored my interests here" or "I thought we'd developed a friendship as well as a working relationship, and now I'm concerned that we only have the latter" or "I'm passionate about this issue, so I may be more aggressive than is necessary." Sometimes admitting weakness makes us more human and makes others more comfortable with us, so long as we don't do it too often. Statements such as "I'm not as much of an expert on this as you are, and frankly, I'm feeling a bit out of my depth" may cause the other side to feel less threatened and even more understanding of emotional expressions that could otherwise be aggravating.

One of the best ways to avoid negative emotional sidetracks is take steps to avoid language that elicits them. Skilled negotiators are alert to clues that what they've said has negatively altered the emotional climate of a negotiation. They are students of potential affront. Penelope Brown and Stephen Levinson describe the ways in which affronts are caused. Skilled negotiators are aware of these. They know that affronts to self-esteem are very dangerous in negotiation. Brown and Levinson divide such affronts into two types:

- *Negative face:* The want of every "competent adult member" that his actions be unimpeded by others
- *Positive face:* The want of every member that his wants be desirable to at least some others[8]

We all wish to reach our goals and to have others appreciate us. To avoid affronts, negotiators need to be aware of ways in which negotiators become upset

about negative and positive face. Brown and Levinson devised a list of acts that threaten the face needs of others, as set forth in Exhibit 9.2.

Obviously, if negotiators had to avoid all of the types of actions we've reviewed, productive communication would be difficult, if not impossible. Skillful negotiation requires, instead, an awareness of which of these types of actions are likely to both elicit negative reactions and thereby impede negotiation progress. The goal is not so much to rid one's communication of potentially threatening statements as to avoid making such statements in a manner or to an extent likely

▶ *EXHIBIT 9.2*

POTENTIALLY FACE-THREATENING ACTIONS

Pressuring Acts
- Orders and requests
- Suggestions, advice
- Reminders (S indicates that H should remember to do something)
- Threats, warnings, dares

Pressuring Acts Due to Debt
- Offers
- Promises

Pressuring Acts Due to the Need for Protection
- Compliments, expressions of envy or admiration (indicating that S likes or would like something belonging to H)
- Expression of strong (negative) emotions toward H—such as hatred, anger, lust Threats to Positive Face Wants of H

Threat Because of Negative Evaluations by S of H
- Expressions of disapproval, criticism, contempt or ridicule, complaints and reprimands, accusations, insults
- Contradictions or disagreements, challenges

Threats Because of the Implication That S Doesn't Care About H's Positive Face
- Expressions of violent (out-of-control) emotions
- Irreverence, mention of taboo topics, including those that are inappropriate in the context
- Bringing bad news about H or good news about S that distresses H
- Raising of dangerously emotional or divisive topics
- Blatant noncooperation
- Use of address and status markers to make H feel inferior

Note: S = person speaking; H = person hearing.

Source: P. Brown and S. C. Levinson, "Politeness: Some Universals in Language Usage," in *The Discourse Reader,* ed. A. Jaworski and N. Coupland (London: Routledge, 1999), p. 331.

to be disruptive. It's a balancing act of considerable importance. The following case illustrates how one person achieved it.

DEALING CONSTRUCTIVELY WITH EMOTIONAL SITUATIONS

Jim Frances was new to management. He'd been a star salesman, but managing people who had once been his peers was a new challenge. His biggest problem was Lucille. She had wanted his job, and she was qualified for it. There was no denying her competence, but one problem seemed to get bigger by the day. She felt comfortable doing things her way even when they ran counter to Jim's instructions. This put him in a difficult position. He didn't want to alienate Lucille or squelch her creativity and independence, but he knew his credibility was waning with the others because he hadn't confronted her. And by failing to do so, he was telling her that she could continue to ignore his instructions.

It was time to turn things around. How could he do this, he wondered, without ruining their relationship and diminishing her output? He decided to meet her for lunch, away from the others, so that he could deal with any emotional reactions she might display.

After they ordered, he said, "Lucille, I have something to discuss with you. I'd appreciate it if you'd let me complete what I have to say before responding."

She nodded.

"You're a bright and productive person and a team player. You deserve to make decisions. But while you're off marching to your own drum, remember that I'm now the bandleader. When I say we're playing a different tune, that means you, too."

Granted, it was a bit direct, but Jim had considered the consequences of being vague. She needed to really *get* the message. By framing it in these terms, he could convey that her independent spirit was appreciated and her creativity was condoned, but she would have to learn where to draw the line or he'd draw it for her.

It worked. She started paying more attention to his instructions. An occasional reminder was needed, but that was a small price to pay to keep a talented employee.

▶ "AT THE END OF THE DAY" TEST

In negotiation, it is often useful to ask yourself these questions: What does the other side want to be able to say *at the end of the day?* Who must they appease? What stance do they wish to be seen as taking? A skilled negotiator considers these questions and does not overreact with angst when his or her position is not immediately adopted. When those on the other side are holding out, so to speak, perhaps there is a reason that does not meet the eye without some degree of scrutiny. Sometimes this takes a thorough understanding of the forces they are facing, the criticism they might receive for a hasty move.

In the Cynthia and Jack case, at the end of the day, Cynthia probably wants to appear fair. She wants to avoid problems with Jack and especially with Human Resources. Perhaps she even wants Jack to be happy. If her most pressing concern is to avoid giving the impression of being talked into a change, at least Jack's additional information about coaching allows her to justify a change in perspective as a rare event, due only to information not previously available.

At the end of the day, negotiators need to go away with some sense of having achieved their goals. They need to be able to tell those who would question their actions that they acted with good reason. As social beings, all of us have others to whom we must answer—bosses, peers, family members, friends. Give the other side ways to explain why they cooperated, without seeming to do so, and you are more likely to achieve the outcomes you desire. In the following example, a clever negotiation mediator changed the course of Middle East history by considering what a proud warrior needed at the end of the day—in this case, a face-saving opportunity.

▶ SAVING FACE AND CHANGING HISTORY

During World War I, T. E. Lawrence ("Lawrence of Arabia") supported Prince Feisal in the Arab revolt against occupying Turk forces. However, as Lawrence recalled later, King Hussein, Feisal's father, was green with envy at the acclaim his son had garnered and therefore was refusing to provide needed reinforcements. Requests for aid were met with an abusive reply. Lawrence described how he (somewhat underhandedly) defused the intended insult:

> The Arabs hitherto in their revolt had made clean history, and I did not wish our adventure to come to the pitiable state of scission before the common victory and its peace.
> King Hussein behaved truly to type, protesting fluently, with endless circumlocution, showing no understanding of the grave effect of his incursion into Northern Army affairs. To clear his mind, we sent him plain statements, which drew abusive but involved returns. . . . I had undesirable passages mutilated by rearranging their figures into nonsense, before handing them in code to Feisal. . . .[9]

Lawrence reported that this "play" of sorts went on for several days. Each time Feisal received a letter from his father, it was toned down from the original harshness. Finally a letter arrived with two parts—the first a lame apology and the second half a repetition of offenses in a new form. Lawrence went to work again, editing at will:

> I suppressed the tail, and took the head marked "very urgent" to Feisal's tent where he sat in the full circle of his staff officers. His secretary worked out the despatch and handed the decipher to Feisal . . . and all eyes were on him as he read it. He was astonished and gazed wonderingly at me, for the meek words were unlike his father's obstinacy. Then he pulled himself together, read the apology aloud, and at the end said thrillingly, "The telegraph has saved all our honour."
> A chorus of delight burst out, during which he bent aside to whisper in my ear, "I mean the honour of nearly all of us."[10]

Lawrence knew that at the end of the day, what Feisal really needed was a way to save face in front of his staff. His father was not going to change, so Lawrence took advantage of a meek apology and changed the course of history.

▶ CONVERTING DIFFERENCES TO COMPATIBLE INTERESTS

King Hussein and his son are examples of two people whose interests should have been compatible, yet somehow they found a way to make them otherwise. I've frequently seen negotiators who are locked in conflict overlook or ignore compatible interests right before their eyes. They focused instead on their differences, on the strength of their convictions, or on the superior accuracy of their arguments and evidence. Negotiation expert Leigh Thompson offered this explanation: "Recognizing compatible interests may be more difficult than recognizing differences in priorities. Because most people enter negotiation with a fixed-sum perception, the existence of compatible issues represents a violation of this perception, whereas the existence of different priorities only partially violates this perception."[11]

Skillful negotiators do not slip into the trap of fixed-sum perception. To them, negotiation is not war. This is where they hold a considerable advantage over novice and naive negotiators. They do not shoot themselves in the foot by focusing exclusively on differences.

The following case is an example of how differences can be converted to compatible interests.

Sam: We need to deliver this project on time, or we'll lose credibility with the client.

Ann: Quality is the main concern. They won't remember how late it was, but they'll remember how bad it was.

Sam: The client is extremely punctual. He keeps mentioning the deadline. I don't want to lose his respect and trust.

Ann: If that's the main concern, we should call him, tease out the degree of latitude he has on delivery, and offer to be on time but suggest that two extra days, or whatever he can spare, will give him both punctuality and added quality. That puts the ball in his court and focuses on a shared desire for a top-notch product.

Sam: I suppose it's worth a try. But if he insists on punctuality, we'll go with it.

Ann: I'll work all night if that's the case, but if I were him, I'd give us at least another day and benefit from promised additional value.

Sam: Let's see how logical he is.

In this negotiation, incompatible differences were converted to compatible ones by shifting focus to a shared goal—pleasing the client. Ann has arranged to please the client while still making it possible for her and Sam to work cooperatively. The client can still press for on-time delivery, but now Sam doesn't have to be the one demanding it. She offers the lure of additional quality. She avoids implying that product quality will suffer if the product must be delivered on time.

Identification of compatible interests is a valuable conflict resolution strategy. Sometimes it involves compromise, sometimes refocusing on a larger, overarching, shared goal. A successful search can convert a potentially negative altercation into a cooperative venture.

▶ STRATEGY SEQUENCING

Another means of dealing with conflict involves managing strategy sequences to avoid slipping into a tit-for-tat negotiation. Negotiation usually consists, to some degree, of *reciprocal strategy sequences*. Research has identified various types. The first describes patterns in which negotiators reciprocate each other's strategies by matching them exactly. A concession from one side, for example, elicits a concession from the other. Nonreciprocal sequences include the pairing of two congruent but not identical strategies, such as two moves that are competitive though different in type. Another such sequence is the pairing of two incongruent strategies, perhaps one cooperative and one competitive. One negotiator might move toward compromise, only to be faced by resistance or rejection by the other. Sometimes such nonreciprocation is intentional. For example, a negotiator may wish to convey that he or she is not easily placated; that the other side is dealing with a "tough customer." Astute negotiators faced with nonreciprocation pause to determine whether it might be strategic and then decide whether to perhaps respond in kind, deflect, ignore, or redirect.

Just as negotiators have style preferences, they have preferences for strategy and strategy sequencing. Some negotiators fall easily into patterns of distributive reciprocity, in which one win-lose move is met with another. Breaking this kind of cycle is one way of preventing the escalation of conflict to the point of diminishing returns. Although we could delve further into the research findings in this area, in essence they conclude that the kinds of patterns that negotiators fall into or choose to engage in affect their outcomes. Skilled negotiators are attentive to their actions in this regard. They realize, as researchers Mara Olekalns and Philip Smith found in their studies of negotiators, how important it is to bear in mind the potential of unexpected strategies to transform the negotiating environment. Because of this, they recommend that negotiators learn to combine the cooperative and competitive components of their strategies.[12]

How exactly do you do this? In large part, by avoiding predictability. If you always meet an attack with an attack, the other side can manage your actions. If you always meet a concession with a larger concession, the same management is facilitated. In short, the predictable negotiator is the manageable one. To avoid this, vary your approach in accordance with your desired outcomes. If, for example, you know that the overall goal of negotiation is to establish a long-term relationship, you'll gain from using mainly relationally cooperative actions. To avoid being seen by the other side as someone who wants the long-term relationship no matter what the cost, hold firm on some issues. Demonstrate your overall desire to work well together while also demonstrating that you are not desperate:

> "Like you, I value this relationship. I see us working together on a number of projects, but on this particular issue I have very little wiggle room."

> "This issue shouldn't be a stumbling block to what is clearly a strong working relationship. Perhaps there's a creative solution in here somewhere."

These approaches suggest a desire for cooperation as a context for your resistance on a particular issue. Just as journalists tend to alternate long sentences and short

ones, skilled negotiators know how to combine cooperation with resistance or competition.

In salary negotiations, employers often state that they are not at liberty to discuss the salaries of any other employees. They argue that such an approach would constitute an invasion of privacy that no reputable organization would make. This kind of criterion limitation puts the person asking for a raise in a difficult position. How can he or she justify a salary if the salaries of people who work at the same level cannot be used as criteria? In one such negotiation, a fast-track junior executive addressed this by providing salary ranges from an outside research firm. She pointed out that although discussing another employee's salary could be considered an invasion of privacy, were that person to freely reveal his or her salary, the issue of privacy would become moot. She then introduced what fellow employees had said their salaries were. The other side contended that people are prone to inflate their salaries in discussions. She argued that while that might indeed happen now and then, it would be rare indeed for a number of highly credible employees like the ones mentioned to all depart from reality. These two approaches prevailed, and she obtained an amount close to her desired salary.

This example shows that instead of arguing with the other side's reasons for refusing to accept or even hear some criteria, it is often more effective to open another door—to discover their reasons for rejecting the criteria and then work around them. In this case, the reason for rejecting a discussion of other employee salaries was invasion of privacy. Rather than attack the reasoning, the junior executive decided to find another door, a way in that wouldn't violate the rule that the other side appeared to hold dear. Had the other side shut the new door by insisting that no matter how the data were obtained, they could not be introduced, she could have asked whether they were concerned about introducing the criteria because it constituted a violation of privacy or because it would hurt their case. This moves toward hardball—a step that she was ready to take but that fortunately didn't prove necessary. Her data from highly credible sources were sufficiently persuasive.

Any successful dealing with significant conflict involves getting to the root concerns of the other side. Debating the surface issues or attending to symptoms rather than seeking a cure leads to failed negotiations. In *Must We Fight?* William Ury addresses the question "Is war on earth inevitable?" He treats violence as a virus, the spread of which depends on the work of "the third side." These are people "from the community using a certain kind of power, the power of peers, from a certain perspective, which is a perspective of common ground; supporting a certain process, which is the process of dialogue and nonviolence; and aiming for a certain product, which is a triple-win—a solution that's good for the community and good for both of the parties."[13]

Skilled negotiators seek double or triple wins. They ask themselves, *What is at the heart of this matter, this diversion, this difference of opinion, this emotional outburst?* They act, when possible, as their own "third party," stepping back at times to assess what is really going on at the heart of the discussions at hand. The *why* of negotiator actions is what the skilled negotiator seeks to understand, especially in cases of conflict or impasse. Often if they can discover the actual concerns behind actions, they can find some means of addressing those concerns. In

many cases, those means have been lost in the back and forth of negotiation, the seeking of strategies and efforts to derive desired outcomes. Finding those means again is what skillful negotiators do.

▶ FRAMING TO REDUCE POTENTIAL OR ACTUAL CONFLICT

In Chapter 7, we discussed the power of framing as a persuasive technique. We now look at framing as a means of preventing or reducing conflict. The following example demonstrates how frames can be used to alter widespread perceptions—and even to redirect people's attention away from anger by repositioning how actions might be interpreted.

Neal Gabler, a senior fellow at the Norman Lear Center at the University of Southern California, wrote of the disappearance of class warfare in an opinion piece for the *Los Angeles Times*.[14] He described how William Jennings Bryan had addressed eastern bankers with these compelling words: "You shall not press down upon the brow of labor this crown of thorns; you shall not crucify mankind upon a cross of gold." President Theodore Roosevelt railed against those who threatened to wrest power from the people, as President Franklin D. Roosevelt did three decades later when he sneered at "economic royalists." These frames were powerfully persuasive. Gabler then turned to the present-day framing that has allowed the average American income to increase by only 9 percent over the past twenty years while the wealthiest 1 percent have experienced a 140 percent increase. He attributes this condition to the subversion of class warfare (the haves against the have-nots), accomplished "through a kind of national brainwashing" by Republicans, Democrats, captains of industry, journalists, religious leaders, and radio and cable television hosts. In other words, these leaders have framed the average person's living conditions in a way that has caused them decline to fight for more.

How did this happen? Gabler described a campaign against class, which created the American dream—that anyone in America can succeed by dint of hard work. To talk in terms of class, Gabler explains, is to betray that dream. The American dream is a frame, one that Gabler contends became converted during the Reagan years into what it is today—the belief that equal opportunity already exists and that anyone who can't succeed has only himself to blame. America reached a point "at which you either decided to make a fortune or you didn't, with the promise that your own windfall might be just around the corner. This was the new economic myth that trumped economic truth."

The power of this myth is derived, in part, Gabler contends, by the American people's desire to have it be true. This frame has removed the rich as a target of class. After all, if you aren't rich, you have only yourself to blame. Gabler wrote, "Most of us believe that the rich are deserving and that, with a few breaks, we might get ours, too. Most of us believe that taxes are some kind of confiscatory scheme rather than a tool for correcting an imbalance. And most of us believe that to think in terms of class under these circumstances is to deny the ideal of individual responsibility that is the very basis of America." Gabler argued, "That is why the rich will keep getting richer, the middle class will keep losing ground, the poor will keep getting ignored, and no one will say a single word about it."

Whether you agree with Gabler or not, it is interesting to look on the American dream as a frame that guides the social and economic decisions of a country as large and diverse as the United States. It is a powerful frame, one to which most Americans pay considerable homage. Gabler describes it as a frame that has muted conflict and thereby relegated millions to a poor standard of living.

Frames can be powerful in resolving conflict. Yet as Gabler's perspective suggests, they can also suppress it by rendering some discussion and debates inappropriate and even heretical. His arguments demonstrate how a frame can be used to shape actions. Negotiators who frame effectively or who call on powerful frames to support their views have a considerable advantage. A good frame is worth a thousand words. It can take the wind out of the sails of a conflict, send it in a different direction, or escalate it. It's a tool you don't want to be without in negotiation.

Hewlett-Packard CEO Carly Fiorina used the power of framing in her eight-month battle with Walter Hewlett, son of the company cofounder, during his opposition of HP's $25 million merger with Compaq Computer. Hewlett had the clout of the company name, control of his family's financial stake, and considerable shareholder sentiment on his side. According to George Anders in *Perfect Enough: Carly Fiorina and the Reinvention of Hewlett-Packard,* Fiorina used persuasion and nostalgic photos of founders to bring shareholder sentiment to her side. She linked her leadership to the Hewlett-Packard culture and history by saying, "This company has always been about being daring." She sat down to dinner with each of HP's directors (except Hewlett) a few days before an important shareholder meeting. Instead of attempting to coerce their support, she used a "soft power" approach. She left the room for more than an hour, allowing the directors to speak candidly. When she returned, they were allied behind her. Not long afterward, Hewlett was out and the merger was on. Fiorina had won. Leadership expert Warren Bennis proposed that her success was due, in part, to her ability to build alliances. She did this by linking her goals to the company's goals and its directors' interests. It was a bold move that demonstrates the power of skillful linking and framing.[15]

The first example of framing depicts a sort of pulling of the wool over the eyes of American people, thereby preventing conflict; the second shows how redefining actions in the context of acceptable practice (Hewlett-Packard's emphasis on daring) can render them acceptable and cause conflict to dissipate. Framing can be a very powerful tool, both for avoiding conflict and for resolving it once it has arisen.

► DEALING WITH DECEPTION

As we discussed in Chapter 5, the pressures of negotiation can cause people to engage in deceptive tactics. This is especially the case in the face of conflict, so no chapter on this subject would be complete without some discussion of which types of deception deserve a strong response and which may deserve a more measured one. Since skilled negotiators expect some level of deception in negotiation, they aren't taken aback when it occurs. They know that it is common for negotiators to engage in some degree of deception. This is especially the case for people

known primarily as negotiators. As a professor of negotiation, I tend to put people on edge right from the start of a negotiation. They seem to think I'll take them in circles before they know they've moved an inch. They say things like "I know what you do for a living, so don't try any of that stuff on me." The last time a dean said that to me, when I was negotiating for a sabbatical leave, I replied, "And I too know who I'm dealing with. You're the dean. I'd say you have the upper hand." He seemed pleased with the compliment but looked directly into my eyes to determine whether I'd flattered him to relieve him of the upper hand. "Very smooth," he said, probably to cover his bases.

There is no getting around it. If you are known as a negotiator, people are going to be wary. They expect some degree of management of their actions, if not downright manipulation of them. They expect words to be selected carefully; for some degree of deception to occur. And truth be told, they're not always wrong, because most human interaction involves a level of deception.

There are various levels of deception. The first may be called relatively *benign deception*. Its purpose is to avoid offense. Such deception is often used in the service of politeness. We all engage in it; otherwise, we'd be ostracized. Society is built on a foundation of benign deception—people not saying all that they are thinking. The next level is *strategic deception*. Its purpose is to achieve some advantage through the skillful management of information sharing. It is planned rather than the result of courtesy training.

At the upper range of strategic deception, the motives behind it are more self-serving than at the lower range. The third level of deception is *ulterior motive deception*. The primary purpose of this type is to achieve some gain without apprising the other side of any intention to do so. Typically, this type of deception, if discovered, is explained in a dishonest manner, covering the true intentions with accounts such as "I did it to protect you" or "My passion to be of help got in the way of my reason." It's a slippery kind of deception, more self-serving and manipulative as it progresses along the continuum shown in Figure 9.1.

Novice negotiators often become incensed when they suspect that deception is occurring or when they actually discover it. The expert negotiator, on the other hand, knows that deception is to be expected and also recognizes that different levels of deception call for different types of responses. The following are examples of benign deception.

Benign Deception

- Building one's credibility a bit more than deserved
- Falsely implying that there is a competitor in the wings
- Giving the impression of greater knowledge on a subject than one actually possesses
- Creating the impression that something is of greater value than it actually is
- Dressing in a manner unlike your usual style, to give the impression of competence or wealth
- Disclosing information to the other side in a manner that suggests it is private

| Benign | Strategic | Ulterior Motive |

Figure 9.1 Deception Continuum.

- Omitting or downplaying some of the less attractive aspects of a product or idea

Some of these tactics are in the gray area between benign and strategic deception. For example, everyone expects people to dress up a bit when they go to job interviews. To do otherwise suggests disinterest, disorganization, or a lack of sophistication. So although dressing up doesn't present the everyday you, it presents a side of you that is attainable.

Here are examples of strategic deception in negotiation:

Strategic Deception

- Agreeing to so something you may not be able to do
- Bluffing (to a limited extent)
- Fogging or confusing an issue; using strategic ambiguity
- Misrepresenting by omission—not mentioning unfavorable information
- Making additional small requests after an agreement has been made
- Feigning scarcity of an item

As with benign deception, any of these strategies can move into the ulterior deception category. It's a matter of judgment. The negotiation context may render some types of deception "part of the game." If you don't use them, people wonder why you didn't. Business in Hollywood is a case in point. A lot goes on there that isn't considered acceptable in other contexts. Telling someone that his or her idea is "pure genius" when you don't particularly like it is common in Hollywood. Even in academia, people commonly stretch the truth. If a student is applying for a job, everyone expects that the people writing letters of recommendation will focus on the student's strong points, exaggerate them somewhat, and downplay any faults. I remember a former professor using the following phrase in a letter of recommendation I requested: "She does not yet walk on water, but she skims large puddles with ease." The people who hired me told me that phrase really made a difference. In some contexts, exaggeration is expected. In others, it is a sign of dishonesty. I'm sure that the faculty that hired me knew I have just as much difficulty with puddles as they do, but the expectation of exaggeration gave the phrase some legitimacy.

Ulterior motive deception is the kind in which lying occurs; for example, using the bait-and-switch strategy or pretending to be against an idea for a while merely so that you can later act as if you've been convinced of its acceptance. Other forms include creating obligation or pressuring people by suggesting that others will think ill of them if they don't comply. Here are a few more:

Ulterior Motive Deception

- Agreeing to do something you know you won't or can't do
- Threatening someone with power you don't have
- Switching sides on an issue to create confusion
- Suggesting that the other side will receive something you don't intend to deliver
- Offering false flattery
- Intimidating the other side with false claims
- Making intentional misrepresentations (such as lying about value)
- Pretending to be angry, insulted, or annoyed to induce cooperation

At the ulterior motive point on the deception continuum, negotiation has become unethical. Things are said, promised, and implied that are not true. When the stakes are high, though, it is not uncommon to see such practices. Negotiators must decide for themselves if they are willing to go to such lengths, to dabble or dive into falsehoods. Those who do often underestimate the intelligence of those with whom they're negotiating. They also underestimate the impact of their lies once the other side discovers them. Regaining trust is a long road. The more skilled the negotiator, the less likely he or she is to resort to ulterior motive deception. Skilled negotiators know how to manage what they say in ethical ways. They may not tell everything they're thinking at all points in a negotiation, and they may foster impressions favorable to their goals, but they are not likely to resort to out-and-out lies. Not only are such lies unethical, but they are also difficult to sustain. Most negotiation experts admit to managing their delivery of information to their advantage, but they try very hard to avoid ulterior motive deception.

Because deception is to be expected to some degree in negotiations, it's important to know how to deal with it. There are direct and indirect ways. The latter is often the preferable. It rarely helps a negotiation to say, "Obviously, you aren't telling the truth." Let's look at a few cases of deception and ways to deal effectively without eliciting excessive conflict.

CASE A: THE SLEIGHT OF HAND

You get all the way to the point of closing a deal and your counterpart sends an e-mail to you that describes how he interprets the final agreement. In it are several sleights of hand, in which he has taken what you agreed to and eked out a bit more. Do you accuse him of deceit?

A better way, especially if the other negotiator has been honorable up to this point, is to reply to the e-mail with "edits" based on "my records" or on prior e-mail interactions. If you've done a good job of keeping notes—and, ideally, shared those notes with the other side on occasion—this approach is likely to succeed. Once your counterpart knows you have some tangible evidence of agreements, he is likely to accept your "edits." If the intention was to deceive you, then the deceiver will likely take the opportunity you've offered to ignore that intent.

CASE B: DIVIDE AND CONQUER

A negotiator from the other side seems to be trying to forge divisiveness between you and your conegotiator. Her intention appears to be to divide and conquer. What are your options here?

One way is to say, "It's good that you and Jim have similar perspectives on these issues. I share several of them as well. It's good to see that we're on the same page." Another option is to take a break, during which you apprise your partner of what you believe to be the motive of the other side. Don't recommend that he suddenly cease to be friendly and agreeable, but suggest that he pepper his discussions with support of his team. The negotiator on the other side will be unsure whether her intent has been discovered but will likely cease to continue her line of attack, recognizing that the person she targeted is not likely to be accommodating.

"Divide and conquer" is not an uncommon scenario. A leading New York City–based negotiation expert told me how he makes this strategy work:

> I listen for quite a while. As I present a proposal, I watch to see if several people seem opposed to it. In that case, I do a little constructive deception. If one of them expresses some disagreement with me, I might use him to divide the group. After coaxing him to my side, I'll gradually turn against him myself. The others, who are by then angry with him, become more open to my proposal, especially if I throw in some things they want. Essentially, the person who initially agreed with me becomes the common enemy. And nothing brings people together so well as that.[16]

CASE C: FALSE INFORMATION

The other side has presented false information. You have the correct information.

Of course, you could suddenly pull out the accurate information and make the other side look small and deceitful. That may be deserved, but it isn't the best way to keep a dialogue open. Instead, pause as you consider the information they provided and then say, "I see you've done your homework. I also have some information [mention highly credible source and recent date] that paints a somewhat different picture. I can share it with you, and then we can discuss how to proceed." This approach allows the other side to save face. By framing the information as up-to-date and from a reliable source (which it should be), rather than framing yourself as more honest than the other side is, you give them an out while letting them know that you are not oblivious to their deception.

If they return to their data, you might propose an approach that accommodates a key aspect of their information while responding to yours. Alternatively, you could say, "Let's put all of this information aside and look at what we really want to achieve." This diversionary approach takes you away from a "my data are better than your data" battle and toward desired outcomes. Ask, "What do you ideally want on issue X?" Then find a way to connect your interests to theirs. "Perhaps we've spent too much time on what divides us when right before us has been considerable commonality. If it works for you, I suggest we shift our focus to that."

CASE D: THE INSULT

The other negotiator acts insulted by something you said or did. You meant no harm, but he is giving others the impression that your comments have caused him considerable discomfort.

The natural response here is to apologize. And that may be the best option, especially if you believe that the other negotiator is sincere. Before apologizing, however, you should ask for clarification. "It appears that I've said or done something that has upset you. Is that the case?" Do *not* say, "It appears that you're taking something I said very personally," or, "You seem angry." The word *upset* is more benign, less subject to negative connotations. It allows the other person to determine the nature of the upset. Accusing him of anger or some other negative state might backfire. Remember, the goal here is to gain information that will help you determine whether his reaction is real and justified, contrived to put you in a one-down apologetic position, or a little of both. You also have the option of apologizing for the existence of the situation rather than for any personal contribution to it. "I truly regret this misunderstanding" is this type of apology.

If his emotions are contrived, however, by apologizing you run the risk of appearing weak. You also run the risk of feeling obliged to provide some recompense. Bill Richardson, a seven-term congressman from New Mexico who has negotiated with hostile governments for the release of prisoners, described a meeting with Saddam Hussein in which he dealt with insult in a unapologetic way that garnered him respect:

> Dictators often try to take advantage of you at the outset. They try to catch you off guard. At the beginning of my meetings with Saddam Hussein, I crossed my legs and the soles of my feet were visible. He got up and left the room. I asked the interpreter, "What did I do?"
>
> He said, "The President was insulted that you crossed your legs. To an Arab that's a nasty insult, and you should apologize." I asked, "Is he coming back?" The interpreter said, "Yeah, he'll come back."
>
> When he did, I made the decision not to apologize. I wasn't going to grovel, say, "Hey, I'm really sorry I crossed my legs." I planted my feet and said, "Mr. President, let me resume." And I think he respected that, because the discussions got better. You try to show that you're a humble person, but at the same time you can't back down. You can't show weakness. You keep coming at them.[17]

Richardson described Hussein as a tough person with whom to negotiate. "He starts out with a very menacing image. It sets you back a bit. I remember looking at my hands, and I was sweating. I was conscious that he knew what his reputation was. And he knew that I knew his reputation."[18] Hussein probably expected Richardson to apologize. He may have walked out to exaggerate his annoyance with Richardson's inadvertent insult. If so, then Richardson's decision to do something different, to violate Hussein's expectations while still showing respect, told the dictator that he was talking with someone who was not afraid. There are people who only respond well to power, who consider apologies as weakness, and who try to intimidate. In those circumstances, it's important to make sure your cooperation and courtesy are not misinterpreted as signs of fear or weakness.

Rather than apologize in Case D, you could put the insult into a broader, positive context. Mention that your relationship has enjoyed such mutual positive regard that it would be unproductive to let a misunderstanding threaten it now. Suggest that you both back up a bit, return to the earlier discussion, essentially erase the last few minutes, and proceed from there.

CASE E: FEELING CORNERED

Essentially, the other side has presented you with a no-win option along the lines of "If you don't keep quiet about this, I'll wreck your career." Whistle-blowers face threats of this sort.[19]

It's wise to remember in situations of this type that the power someone has over you equals the amount of power you're willing to give. Often when you're cornered, it doesn't seem that way. The other side seems to have all the power, and you seem to be at their mercy. Rarely is that actually the case. There are few roads from which it's impossible to emerge somewhat victorious. Usually the last-resort option of walking away is available. Bill Richardson took this approach when negotiating in Nigeria: "My objective was to secure the release of Moshood Abiola, who was imprisoned after he won the 1993 election. But General Abacha was taking such a hard line that I didn't even get to visit Abiola. Finally I said, 'Mr. President, I'm leaving the country. Let me know if you change your mind.' You want to keep the channels open. And I've been contacted since then. They've sent messages, and I've coordinated with the State Department. I think eventually Abiola will be released."[20]

It could not have been easy for Richardson to walk out of the meeting with Abacha. He could have shouted at the Nigerian leader instead. That would have vented his emotions, but it would not have achieved what Richardson knew to be critical—keeping the channels open while letting the other side know that you are very close to closing them and taking some action that will not serve them.

Sometimes when you're feeling cornered, the better option is to *take the issue to another level*. This should not be done lightly, as in many organizations it is considered a serious offense. It must be done carefully, with political savvy, and when possible with the support of people in high places. Some years ago, a senior administrator called me into his office to inform me that a critical promotion had been denied me. I asked him to describe the basis for the denial. One of his direct reports piped up, "The quality of your research."

"Tell me something else," I said. "Tell me something believable. I've won award after award from my research."

They would say no more.

"I'll have to look into this," I said.

The senior administrator advised me that were I to complain to anyone above him, he could assure me that it would ruin my career.

"You don't seem to see," I said, with as much conviction as a young person watching her career derail before her can muster, "that you have already done that. I have nothing to lose." I then rose to my feet, bade them farewell, and headed toward the door.

"I warn you and forbid you to go above me," my detractor called as I stepped into the doorway. I turned to find his face twisted in anger, burning with indignation. There was nothing more to say.

Before taking the issue over his head, I sought information and support. It was a difficult, trying time. The situation was resolved in my favor. I paid a price. I was someone who'd challenged the system. In some organizations, you might as well wear a sign that reads "Hot Potato." No career worth having is without costs. The people I respect have never expressed anything but admiration for my decision. The others don't matter. People who threaten in the manner I experienced have something to hide. My would-be nemesis showed his hand, and it was not clean.

Now, you should use this go-to-the-mat approach sparingly and only in matters of great significance. As a rule, it's best to get out of tight spots without generating antagonism. Questions are often useful. "What do you suppose others like me will think if we go this route?" Phrase what you have to say as a point of caution, not a threat. "What long-term

consequences are we facing here?" is another option. Get the other side talking, reconsidering. In situations of no choice, find a choice. Two other options for opening the lines of communication are "If we don't do X, we'll all be faced with Y. Do you want that?" and "The options have certainly been limited, perhaps to our mutual disadvantage. Do you see what I mean?" The goal is to get the other side to reconsider their cornering tactic, not by retaliating but by providing food for thought.

▶ *EXHIBIT 9.3*

HOW GENDER INFLUENCES CONFLICT

Perhaps you've heard the story of the man who asked the Lord for a wish. Since he'd been a faithful person, the Lord agreed to grant the wish. The man requested a bridge spanning the Pacific Ocean from California to Hawaii so that he could drive back and forth. The Lord thought the wish materialistic and demanding. At the Lord's urging, the man reconsidered and asked instead if he might be allowed to understand women—why they talk as they do, what they mean when they say "nothing," what they want, and why they seem so emotional. The Lord thought for a moment and then replied, "Do you want two lanes or four on that bridge?"

Men and women are different. They're raised differently, are different biologically, and often communicate differently. In negotiation, it's wise to try to bridge these differences. A big step in that direction involves recognizing five dysfunctional communication patterns (DCPs) that often occur in male-female interactions: dismissive, exclusionary, undermining, retaliatory, and patronizing.

Dismissive DCPs usually involve interrupting, talking over, or ignoring. Research indicates that men interrupt women more often than they interrupt each other. Women often contribute to this bad habit by not insisting on retrieving the conversational lead. Many speak more softly than men and take longer to get to the main point, so men get impatient. In most cultures, men are accorded greater credibility, so people are more willing to hear them out. Negotiation success is out of reach if people constantly interrupt or are interrupted or ignored. Watch that you aren't a contributor to this type of DCP.

Exclusionary DCPs involve leaving someone out of important meetings, discussions, or social gathering. Negotiators need to be connected and need to be in on key conversations and plans. *Undermining DCPs* involve going behind the back of others or taking the wind out of the sails of their arguments in an insulting way. *Retaliatory DCPs* are attacks legitimated in the attacker's mind because he or she feels threatened. *Patronizing DCPs* occur when negotiators talk in a condescending manner to their counterparts. Again, research indicates that this happens more to women. The conversation example that follows illustrates a patronizing DCP.

Demeaning stereotypes lead to all of these DCPs. Sometimes gender differences alone are enough to elicit them. The astute negotiator watches for cues and endeavors to avoid or deal constructively with them. The conversation examples that follow show how to do this.

Kelly: The meeting time you're suggesting isn't going to work for me.

Edward: We have to schedule it then.

Kelly: Why?

Edward: Listen, Kelly, everybody knows you have a lot of outside demands with your family, so if you miss the meeting, it won't be a problem.

Kelly: My family has nothing to do with this.

Edward: You know, you look stressed and tired.

Kelly: My fatigue level is irrelevant.

Edward: I think it would be better if we talk about this after you've rested up.

In this exchange, Kelly is as much to blame as Edward. She yielded control. Here is how she could have replied instead:

Kelly: That meeting time won't work for me.

Edward: We have to schedule it then.

Kelly: Why?

Edward: Listen, Kelly, everybody knows you have a lot of outside demands with your family, so if you miss the meeting, it won't be a problem.

Kelly: Your concern for my family is noted, Edward, but let's stick with the subject of the meeting time. I have my calendar here. I see you have yours.[21]

As this example suggests, it's wise for negotiators to be on the lookout for DCPs. Break out of them. Make sure you're not being stereotyped into a corner and that you're not doing it to someone else. When it comes to gender differences, it's easy for men and women to fall victim to stereotypes. The wise negotiator doesn't let this happen.

► QUESTIONS

1. Differentiate and critique fast-slow versus slow-fast approaches to conflict.

2. Using a conversation that you have observed or in which you have participated, describe how conflict served as a cue for change. Did the people involved notice the cue? If so, what did they do and, if not, why not?

3. What are conflict choice points? Write a dialogue (real or contrived) and describe the choice points. What might one or both persons have done differently? What did they do well?

4. Interview a negotiator about how he or she handles conflict. Write a brief report or develop a presentation for class on the most interesting learning points.

5. Describe a recent conflict between you and at least one other person. What did you do well and what might you do differently based on what you learned in this chapter?

6. Use each term below in two sentences that reveal its meaning:

 Manager of conflict

 Dictator of conflict

 Giving them the chance to do the right thing

 Negative face

 Positive face

 At the end of the day test

Strategy sequencing

Deception types

7. Consider a significant conflict you were in. Analyze it in terms of potentially face-threatening actions. Then analyze it in terms of how differences might have been converted to compatible interest. Use part of the dialogue from the actual conflict to demonstrate how this conversion might have sounded.

8. Referring to the conflict scenarios (Cases A–D) in this chapter, develop two scenarios and explain how they could be resolved.

Taking Negotiation Talents Global

With the caveat that generalizations should always be suspect, we now enter into a discussion of how people from around the world think about such things as time, trust, socializing, decision authority, negotiation etiquette, tactics, strategies, gender, and emotion. There is no need to throw away all that we've discussed about preparing for and engaging in negotiation simply because we turn now to the cross-cultural version. In fact, what cross-cultural negotiation calls for, first and foremost, is greater attention to the approaches we've been discussing—more careful listening, questioning, preparing, checking of perceptions, and generally increased mindfulness and versatility.

It's important to begin with some understanding of how culture influences choice. Paul Herbig and Hugh Kramer, experts in cross-cultural negotiation, describe culture as the catalyst that transforms private meaning into public meaning so that expressions can be understood by other members of society.

> Shared cultural norms give the people of any society a sense of their common identity and a means of relating to one another. Culture consists of both explicit rules and implicit, unrecognized sets of underlying meanings through which experience is interpreted. Cultural meanings render some forms of activity normal and natural and others strange and wrong. Much of the power with which culture structures society derives from this capacity to make cultural practices seem natural and self-evident rather than arbitrary or relative; it is the system by which new information can be taken in and given meaning without continuous groping. Culture affects attitudes, and hence behavior, and explains how a group filters information.[1]

Herbig and Kramer argue that patterns of personality exist for groups that share a common culture. As they are socialized, people pick up the knowledge, ideas, values, beliefs, phobias, and anxieties of their society. While some of this is explicitly taught, most of it is absorbed subconsciously. Herbig and Kramer point to the emphasis the Japanese place on belonging to the group and on their sensitivity to obligation related to status, age, and one's place in society. Americans, by contrast, value time in terms of efficiency and strive to separate their business and

personal lives. They stress individual differences and achievements even if these sometimes fly in the face of cultural norms. The French see themselves as a reasoned people with a beautiful language and an impressive history. They are less pressured than Americans because their history has taught them that the more things change, the more they remain the same.

Such differences influence the attention negotiators give to different aspects of a negotiation. They affect their comfort level with proposals and with strategy choices. Herbig and Kramer explain, "The implementation of a business agreement may be stressed in one culture, while the range and prevention of practical problems may be emphasized in another culture. In some cultures, the attention of people is directed more toward the specific details of the agreement (documenting the agreement), while other cultures focus on how the promises can be kept (process and implementation). Americans negotiate a contract; the Japanese negotiate a personal relationship. Cultures force people to view and value differently the many social interactions inherent in fashioning an agreement."[2]

Clearly, crossing cultures in negotiation is complex. It requires extensive intelligence gathering and constant flexibility. First and foremost, however, it requires an understanding of one's own culture, the forces that impinge on one's own decisions and actions. "Know thyself," Socrates advised. This same advice is in the Bible and the Koran and is central to Confucianism and Buddhism. Freud argued that an absence of self-knowledge is at the heart of many modern problems. It is also at the heart of most cross-cultural negotiation problems.

Understanding of another culture is impossible without an understanding of one's own. It's important to understand our own points of reference and to unearth the influences that have shaped the way we think and act.[3] It isn't enough to know that the Japanese or Mexican negotiator looks at time differently from the American or the French person. We must ask, What does that difference mean in terms of choices? What obstacles does the difference present, what opportunities? So as you read this chapter, do not regard it solely as a chance to study "foreigners" but also as a chance to better understand yourself and how who you are influences the way others act toward you.

▶ THE GLOBAL MIND-SET

Probably the most important aspect of a global mind-set in negotiation is patience. Cross-cultural agreements usually take longer than those within a single culture. McDonald's negotiated for nearly ten years to open its first hamburger restaurant in Moscow. Negotiating a joint venture in China takes an average of two years.[4] In Latin America, delays of thirty minutes or more are to be expected before a negotiation gets under way. In China and the Middle East as well, there will be some time for tea. In Spain, you can expect to do business over dinner, which may begin at 9 or 10 P.M., and in Japan, a good deal of circling back to review an already discussed subject is likely to occur. Time is not linear in these cultures. It is *polychronic* or circular, with no beginning or end. Focus is on the here and now and on questions of balance, both of input and of relationship concerns with task concerns.

Time is considered external to the control of human beings; hence many unpredictable things may happen at the same time. Consider that the Chinese, for example, have five thousand years of cultural heritage that provides them with a unique perspective on time. When Mao Zedong was asked what he thought of the French Revolution, he replied, only half-jokingly, "It's too soon to tell."[5]

Germans and Americans tend to be more *monochronic* in their orientation to time. They look to the future and emphasize structure and a focus on one subject at a time. Their preference is for linearity, sequencing of events, a logical order of arguments in negotiation within a specified time period. By contrast, for example, Latin Americans may wish to discuss many topics at the same time. Negotiators from India will consider the building of relationships very important. Brazilians, Thais, Mexicans, and Spaniards are also more likely than Germans, Americans, and the British to concern themselves with relationships. Of course, the world is getting smaller, and we are all adjusting to each other's preferences. Nevertheless, it is a wise negotiator who knows that imposing time constraints on someone from a polychronic culture is likely to cause problems and that having no sense of sequential logic is likely to upset the monochronic negotiator.[6]

Each semester, at least one student asks me, "So why am I supposed to be the one doing the adjusting? Why don't they adjust to my culture?" My answer invariably begins with a question: "Do you want this negotiation to go well?" The answer is always yes. Some add that they expect the other side wants it to go well also. Therefore, the other side should do half the work in terms of cultural sensitivity. Each side should do half the work. But you have to know enough about them to know what that half should look like, and if they won't or can't meet you halfway but rely instead on stereotypes, you'll need to decide whether the negotiation is important enough for you to do the lion's share of adjusting. Also, if you're visiting their country, you'll look foolish if you don't know how their ways of negotiating differ from your own. At the very least, you need to be aware of the differences in perspective between yourself and your negotiation counterpart. People don't want to work any harder than they have to work. After all, we humans are cognitive misers. When it comes to cross-cultural negotiation, however, work is what it's all about. Bridging differences is especially difficult work because it is so easy to fall back on our cultural predispositions, to become annoyed with people who do not think as we do. Prepared negotiators realize, for example, that having the best data, the best arguments, power, or charisma is not as important in countries like India, Sri Lanka, Egypt, and Saudi Arabia as having demonstrated that you care about the relationship being forged.

It's important to point out that delay in negotiation is not always due to the type of subconscious cultural influence described here. Often it is strategic. Asians delay negotiations for a number of reasons, including to test the other side's will, commitment, reliability, and patience. Delays can be used to unsettle the other side. Americans are easily unsettled by delays and often rush to offer more in the hope of getting things back on track and brought to a timely conclusion. Delays are used by the Irish, as well as by Asians, to kill deals without losing face. If delays occur, perhaps the negotiation counterpart will walk away. Cross words will have been avoided. The relationship will not be irreparably damaged,

and future dealings will, it is hoped, not be compromised. Delays are used in many cultures, including Western ones, to suggest waning interest. Indonesians often use delay to avoid having to admit to failure or inability to deliver what is desired.

The duration of a negotiation is influenced by the number of people who must be involved in a decision and the amount of details required. The Japanese involve many people in decisions, a condition often viewed as a sign of negotiator weakness by novice American negotiators. The Japanese also spend considerable time asking detailed questions. The Chinese often delay in order to avoid being the first to show their hand.[7]

▶ ESTABLISHING TRUST

A subject invariably mentioned in observations of cross-cultural negotiation is the value placed on *trust*. All societies value trust, but they do not all measure it in exactly the same way. Americans often perceive trust in terms of accountability—who will take responsibility for making things go well and who will take it if things go wrong. The Chinese do not look at trust in this way. The "stand up and be counted" rule does not apply for them. In fact, the people in positions of authority are supposed to be protected from accountability by those below them. The Japanese are reluctant to do business with people who are arrogant or impolite, people who place blame and engage in what they see as public humiliation. They do not separate personal and business relationships in the ways more common among Westerners. They are distrustful of evidence in the absence of attention to intuition and rapport. For the Malaysians, trust means loyalty, commitment, and companionship. Koreans look to develop a pleasant rapport; Latins seek personal affinity among negotiators. This is why social interactions are so important to them and to negotiators whose cultures emphasize personal relationships as a means of determining trust.

Cross-cultural negotiation expert John Graham proposes that negotiations consist of four major processes:

1. Nontask sounding (rapport)
2. Task-related exchange of information
3. Persuasion, compromise
4. Concession and agreement

Nontask sounding relates to the establishment of a comfort level, of which trust is a significant component. During this stage, the negotiators get to know one another. Even if they have done so through past negotiations and social encounters, renewal of the relationship is essential. This is an especially important stage when the person with whom you're negotiating is from a *collectivist culture*. Collectivism refers to group solidarity, loyalty, and interdependence among members. Collectivist cultures such as Japan's draw sharp distinctions between in-groups and out-groups. Conflict is minimized, often through politeness rules, in collectivist cultures. In contrast to *individualist cultures*, in which independence

is valued along with attention to detail and control, collectivist cultures prefer general agreements based on trust. The United States, the United Kingdom, the Netherlands, France, and the Nordic countries are highly individualistic. Latin American and Asian countries tend to be collectivist.

Collectivist and individualist tendencies are manifested in the ways that various cultures view compromise. To the French, compromise is often seen as an insult to their carefully crafted logic. Why would people want to meet in the middle, to abandon their stance, when right and reason are on their side? This is a question that the French answer with an unequivocal "I wouldn't." For the Japanese, compromise may constitute a departure from company-backed consensus. Meeting in the middle, so to speak, may for them be akin to rejecting the opinions of their colleagues merely to achieve agreement. That leaves far too many people unhappy with the outcome. Americans are more appreciative of compromise as a solution to impasse. The Italians pride themselves on flexibility, as do the Spaniards, but for the latter especially, giving ground must be accompanied by a good reason that significant others will accept. Otherwise dignity is compromised more than the issue at hand. In the Middle East, compromise can have negative meanings involving a sense of giving in to the other side. Collectivist cultures are not opposed to compromise per se so much as they must be assured that the concerns of their group are addressed in reaching it and that face is not lost by those negotiating, especially the faces of those in authority.[8]

These are all generalizations and hence should be applied cautiously. Cross-cultural negotiators would do well to learn a good deal about their counterparts' cultures and also about them as individuals before making predictions regarding how they'll likely respond to a proposal of compromise. With regard to trust, it's good to remember that one's own way of measuring it may differ from the way it is measured by negotiators from other cultures. Impressive data are less likely to elicit trust from a Japanese counterpart than attention to feelings and personal considerations. This does not mean that they do not want data but rather that in the absence of a positive relationship, the data may fall on deaf ears. In the Middle East, using an intermediary trusted by both sides accompanied by demonstrations of respect and generosity is often a promising avenue. Attending to control concerns of Russian counterparts and endeavoring to assure them of respect is critical to trust. Do not expect friendship to be easily given. A warm smile and a handshake aren't sufficient in most regions of the world. Expect to work for a sense of mutual trust. Trust, American style, is often a function of staying on track and not behaving in ways inconsistent with prior agreements. Important in North America is attention to all parties involved. Address comments primarily to leaders of a negotiation team, but do not ignore other members. Include them via eye contact. Even junior negotiators will likely have input into the final decision. Americans do not like being treated as irrelevant, even if a superior is with them. The superior is likely to turn to subordinates for guidance, because Americans value teamwork. In most companies, the leaders ultimately decide, but they typically seek input from others before doing so. With Chinese counterparts, it is wise to sympathize with their views and to patiently work with them toward resolution. Do not show upset at long delays or efforts to incur obligation. They are likely

testing you. Allow "all the time in the world" for the negotiation; the Chinese build relationships over time and are impressed with tenacity.

▶ WHO MAKES THE DECISIONS?

This question should be asked in all cross-cultural negotiations. If you've done a good job of preparing, you'll know the answer. You'll know whether the people at the table are the ones who have the authority to make important decisions. If they are not, it's nevertheless important to treat them with respect because they are the ones conveying the information to the decision makers. Research has shown that individualist countries where power is shared produce negotiators who rely heavily on their own experience and training. Much power is vested in the individual. In collectivist countries, reliance on group consensus is prevalent. You can expect that collectivist negotiators will check with the home office before making significant decisions. Rather than treat this as an annoyance, the sophisticated negotiator uses this time to consider what has been achieved and what to do if counterparts do not get the go-ahead from superiors.[9]

A variety of other factors affects who makes the decisions in cross-cultural negotiations and how quickly decisions are reached. Cultural expert Geert Hofstede identified four cultural dimensions that impinge on the decision processes of negotiators.[10] These dimensions are *masculinity-femininity, uncertainty avoidance, power distance,* and *individualism.* Masculine cultures value assertiveness, independence, task orientation, and self-achievement; feminine cultures value cooperation, nurturing, relationships, and quality of life. The more masculine the culture, the more likely its members are to think of negotiation in win-lose terms. Work is a way of life in such cultures rather than a means to achieving a quality life. By this definition, masculine cultures include Japan, Latin America, and Austria; more feminine cultures include Costa Rica, Chile, and Finland.

Uncertainty avoidance refers to the level of discomfort felt in the face of risk and ambiguous, uncertain situations. Cultures comfortable with risk require less information, have fewer people involved in decision making, and act more quickly than in high-risk-avoidance cultures. The United States, the Scandinavian nations, Jamaica, Hong Kong, Ireland, and Singapore are low on uncertainty avoidance. High-risk-avoidance cultures include Greece, Portugal, Guatemala, and Japan.

Power distance refers to the acceptance of authority differences among people. Low-power-distance countries like the United States strive for equal power among people, whereas high-power-distance cultures are status-conscious and respectful of age and seniority. The lower the power-distance orientation, the greater the tendency to make decisions using a consultative style. The Anglo-American, Nordic, and Germanic cultures are low-power-distance cultures. High-power-distance cultures include Latin American, South Asian, and Arabic countries.

Individualistic cultures value independence of thinking and focus on task issues over relationship. The goals of self-actualization and self-motivation are valued in such cultures. People speak for themselves. Collectivist cultures, as we've discussed, value saving face, protecting their groups, and sharply distinguishing

in-groups from out-groups. Individualistic cultures stress linear logic, whereas collectivist cultures stress more circular reasoning and abstract, general agreements rather than specific, concrete ones. Negotiation team members from highly individualistic cultures are not averse to contradicting one another. The United States, the United Kingdom, the Netherlands, France, and the Nordic countries are highly individualistic. Latin American and Asian countries tend to be highly collectivist. It is no wonder that the Japanese and Chinese ask many questions in negotiation, especially of their individualistic counterparts. They are looking for the common agreement—some consistency on which they may rely. When negotiating with individualistic negotiators, that commonality may not be easily found. Such cultures value differences in views and encourage their expression.

It's useful to know where your negotiation counterparts stand on the four dimensions defined by Hofstede. The benefit comes not so much in terms of exact predictions of how they're likely to behave as from a general understanding of why they might, for example, delay decisions or rush them. Cultural knowledge also helps predict with some degree of certainty whether one's negotiation counterpart is likely to rely on authority figures or give free rein to the ideas, show more concern for the task or for the relationship, or speak in general terms rather than specifics. It is never beneficial to become too certain about how another person will act in negotiation. There is peril in comfort zones. Robert Reich, secretary of labor during the Clinton administration, warns of the affects of comfort. He explained at the 2000–2001 Harvard Leadership Roundtable that "comfort zones," whether born of exposing oneself only to those who share our views or of learning a little and assuming a lot, remove the "sandpaper" that forces individuals and groups to examine their assumptions.[11] It's advisable for negotiators to attend to Hofstede's four dimensions but also to remain aware of the inevitable absence of full knowledge about a counterpart. Only then can they avoid being lulled into failure.

► WHERE TO MEET

As a rule, neutral sites are best for cross-cultural negotiations. In 1989, Presidents Bush and Gorbachev met in Malta; Paris was selected for the Vietnam peace talks; and a raft in the middle of the Neman River was used when Napoleon Bonaparte and Tsar Alexander I met in 1807. While the host company or nation possesses advantages, including control over location protocols and a psychological advantage due to comfort with familiar surroundings, a neutral location suggests a desire to level the playing field.[12] It gains one points in this regard. It also relieves each country of the burden of hosting, the burden of having to make sure that everything, from soup to nuts, goes well.

There are times when it is necessary to host. If there is a series of meetings and you've been hosted by your counterpart in his or her country, then it is typically expected that you will reciprocate. With Chinese counterparts, you'll want to reciprocate in kind. Don't choose a location that is more opulent than the one they chose when hosting you. This may cause your counterparts to lose face. It's

important to research appropriate protocol when hosting to be sure that you do not insult your guests.

When you are a guest, you have the advantage of experiencing firsthand the culture of your hosts and seeing their physical facilities. Sometimes this is important to negotiation, as it provides indications of how they work. Traveling a long distance may indicate that you are serious about the negotiation and that you are willing to save them money and spare them inconvenience. These advantages should be weighed against the downsides mentioned earlier, as well as the disadvantage of travel fatigue.

▶ MINDING YOUR *P*'s AND *Q*'s

An extensive knowledge of the etiquette expectations of your cross-cultural negotiation counterpart is critical to successful negotiation. Many a negotiation has been negatively affected by the insensitivity of a negotiator who dismissed etiquette as an irrelevant issue. If you do not have the time to develop such knowledge, there are many sources of information to which you should turn for help.

I've conducted research on international business gift customs, both in the sense of what constitutes a gift versus a bribe as well as which gifts offend and which impress in various regions of the world. Give a clock in China, and you run the risk of considerable offense. An experienced international negotiator told me that one of his biggest mistakes was to send a clock as a wedding gift for his Chinese negotiation counterpart. The association of clocks as gifts with death or the termination of relationships made it a most inappropriate wedding gift. The parents of the bride sent the gift donor some money for the clock, which made it a purchase rather than a gift. They also never communicated with him again. Give a leather-framed painting in India where cattle are sacred, and the same negative result may obtain. Knives and other sharp instruments can offend in parts of Latin America, where they may represent the severing of ties. Bringing wine to France may prove insulting, as the French are proud of their own wines. Even the color of flowers can be offensive in various regions of the world.

The when, where, and to whom aspect of gift customs is important as well. Don't expect your Asian counterpart to open a gift in front of you. Receive a gift in Japan with two hands. Express appreciation, but do not do so excessively. Open the package later, when you are alone. When you give a gift in Japan, understate it. "This is just a token of our appreciation" will do. Gifts incur obligation in much of Asia and should not be treated as something for which the recipients owe you a favor. Gifts representative of your country are often appreciated. In the Middle East, men should not bring gifts for the wives of their negotiation counterparts. Something for the children is fine and often very much appreciated, especially if you've done some research regarding the children's interests.[13]

If you're traveling to Asia, be prepared to produce your business card in a relatively formal way. Bring many of them with you. It is considered inappropriate to arrive without them. Shake hands and bend slightly from the waist if your counterpart does so. Present and receive business cards with both hands. When a person gives you a card, take a few minutes to read it carefully. It represents the

person and so should be respected. Recipients may say your name as they read your card. You may do the same if you are meeting for the first time. Don't put the card in your wallet and then in your back pocket. Watch to see what your hosts do. If they place your card in front of them on the negotiation table, lined up according to the seating position of you and your team, do the same. If not, after stepping away, put the card in a cardholder and place it in a vest pocket. Westerners are very informal with business cards. Some toss them across a negotiation table to people on the other side. They write additional information on the back or even on the front. They may cross out information that has changed, such as phone numbers and titles. The more sensitive they are to other cultures, the less likely they are to do such things.

It is important to watch what you say about a country and its relationship to its neighbors. Making comparisons between North and South Korea or between Japan and Korea can cause offense. Americans may have forgotten that Japan occupied South Korea from 1910 to 1945, but the Japanese and Koreans have not. Do not treat everyone in Asia as if they are the same. Learn some history. Do not ask people in Northern Ireland about the tension between Catholics and Protestants. Avoid questions about religion and territorial struggles in the Middle East and in countries once part of the former Soviet Union. Try to speak the language. Learn some words and phrases; this is usually seen as a sign of respect. If you use an interpreter, look at the person to whom you're speaking, not at the interpreter.

▶ THE ROLE OF EMOTION AND AFFECT IN CROSS-CULTURAL NEGOTIATION

In a fifteen-year study of negotiation styles in seventeen cultures, cross-cultural negotiation expert John Graham concluded that the variation across cultures is greater with regard to structural aspects of language and *nonverbal behaviors* than it is in the area of verbal content in negotiation. For example, in his research, Japanese negotiators behaved the least aggressively, while the French were the most aggressive. The Japanese used fewer threats, commands, and warnings; instead, they used positive promises, recommendations, and commitments. Their conversational style was polite, with infrequent use of *no* and *you* and more periods of silence. The French used more frequent threats and warnings, more interruptions, facial gazing, and abundant use of *no* and *you*. Brazilians were also aggressive, using more physical touching. The British and Americans were in the middle and used fewer interruptions. Graham advises that negotiators can improve their skill and increase the likelihood of effective negotiation if they teach themselves to attend to not only what is being said but also to how it is said.[14]

Research on affect has shown that the presence of one form of negative affect increases the likelihood of the presence of others. If, for example, a person expresses sadness, other negative affect forms, such as anger and fear, are likely to co-occur. Similarly, positive affect states, such as joy, tend to co-occur with other positive affect states, such as excitement and confidence.[15]

Skilled negotiators recognize when negative affect conditions are emerging and, unless these suit their needs, endeavor to alter those conditions with more positive affect on their part. The challenge is exacerbated in Asian cultures, where facial expressions are controlled. The private self is hidden, with expressions truncated during negotiations. North Americans, by contrast, reveal much of what they're thinking through facial expression. They deliver serious points with stern faces, whereas Asians making the same kinds of points may smile or give a short laugh to soften the directness and avoid confrontation. Christopher Engholm, in his book *Business East Meets Business West*, describes how facial expressions belie and disguise thought in various regions of the world:

> When Filipinos laugh during a negotiation, they may be indicating that they are stating something vital to the discussion, not something frivolous. Filipinos use a smile to apologize, to praise, or to show poise, but they also smile when they are angry or embarrassed. In Thailand, the "land of smiles," a smile or a laugh may not indicate amusement or mirth, especially during a business meeting. A short laugh may mean that a Thai is embarrassed by something that has been done or said. Thais smile at conflict rather than confront it; they are likely to smile at Westerners when disagreeing with them, which can be disarming and disconcerting for the more overtly aggressive North Americans.[16]

Nonverbal expressions used in one culture may mean an entirely different thing in another. Those who understand this can manage emotion to facilitate success. What was dubbed the "Blair Flair" in 2003 can be described as the ability of Great Britain's Prime Minister Tony Blair to use humor at just the right time, to ease the angst being expressed by members of Parliament. As a matter of course, he shifts the affect conditions to positive, which in turn elicits other positive affect states in the people around him. What seems mysterious, to some charismatic, is in part this ability to sense that the negative affect from others has reached a point where it will spiral out of control unless some balancing actions are taken. Skilled negotiators have this flair. They nurture affect blends during negotiation that facilitate acceptance of their positions rather than resistance.

Some people are prone to negative affect; others are more to positive affect. The more negative a person's affect tendency, the more likely he or she is to experience negative moods and emotions and tend to promote negative affect. Such people feel negative about themselves and others and experience distress in the form of nervous, scornful, distressed, hostile, and fearful states. Those who are more positively inclined are predisposed to experience positive moods and emotions. They feel good about themselves, self-efficacious, and enthusiastic. They tend to see others in a positive light and enjoy social interactions. They elicit these feelings in others as well.[17]

What researchers have discovered about positive-affect negotiators and negative-affect negotiators, expert negotiators know from experience. They are in touch with the mood states of others on their team and of their negotiation counterparts. Their task is made more difficult in cross-cultural negotiations, in which the rules for emotional expression often differ between negotiators of different

cultures. Negotiators raised in cultures that encourage emotional reserve are likely to react negatively to those from cultures in which emotional expression is encouraged. Negotiators unfamiliar with cultures outside of their own tend to be unsettled by reactions and responses that don't fit their expectations. Certain habits of voice tone, speed, volume, directness of comments, formality, and other manners of speech, often referred to as linguistic style, can be perfectly fine in one culture and offensive in another. When this occurs, adept negotiators pause to ask themselves whether what they're hearing and seeing might be the product of culture rather than a reason to dislike or distrust the other party or team. When negotiators fail to do this, they risk slipping into the kind of dysfunctional communication patterns that occur across genders, described in Chapter 9. It is important in cross-cultural negotiations to keep an eye on the affective dimension and to avoid allowing one's own stereotypes and expectations to create impressions deleterious to achieving positive outcomes.

Don't assume that because a counterpart is Asian, all emotional expression will be suppressed. Korean negotiators can become very emotional during the course of talks. They tend to be more direct than the Japanese and Chinese in addressing issues that may be regarded as sensitive. They tend to arrive at decisions more quickly, usually because their negotiation teams are smaller than those of the Chinese and Japanese and because the decision-making power is solidly vested in senior people who can be consulted rather quickly. Human relations are, however, still very important to Koreans. They are sensitive to connections between people. Among themselves, blood relation, school ties, and geographical connections are important. Since most negotiators cannot achieve such connections, it's wise to find intermediaries who can do so.[18]

Researchers have found that emotional states affect not only how we interpret the actions of others but also how we process information of all types. Especially when confronted by new and extensive information, as is often the case in negotiation, emotions play a key role in which aspects of that information we will attend to and which we will ignore. Being in a positive mood can make people more receptive to positive information—and a negative mood can make them less receptive. This is why it is often a good idea to halt substantive discussions to deal with emotional issues. Otherwise, the emotional backdrop for the reception of information may predispose one or both sides to reject important information. Negative moods often lead to subsequent negative interpretations and close the mind to positive ones. A vicious circle of negativity results.[19]

The kind of skill I'm describing is indeed of the tall-order type. The ability to assess on both nonverbal and verbal levels is a rare talent. This is why most people aren't good negotiators. The best negotiators are multitracked. They interpret on many levels. This talent truly separates the more astute negotiators from the less astute. So where can the less astute start in acquiring this skill? First, study how communication works in other cultures. Learn how the people of those cultures think, what they value, what kinds of linguistic styles they tend to employ, their attitudes toward emotional expression, and what makes them comfortable. Next, observe people from other cultures in the course of speaking and negotiating. What do they do differently? How might you interpret such actions were you un-

aware of the cultural background of these people? Then comes practice. Without this, awareness of cultural differences makes you a more intellectually mature negotiator but not more mature in terms of actual hands-on interaction. Practice altering the emotional climate. See if it gives the other person—and you as well—greater inclination to listen and learn, to hear things that may even challenge currently held views. This is the real test of such skill.

► *EXHIBIT 10.1*

DON'T FORGET THAT ORGANIZATIONS HAVE CULTURES TOO

It's easier to remember that negotiation counterparts come from a different national cultural than it is to remember that they also come from a different organizational culture. It isn't unusual for negotiations to be thrown off stride because a negotiator doesn't know how things are said and done in the counterparts' organizational culture. In the common vernacular, *organizational culture* means "how things are done around here," including how things are said, who talks with whom, office arrangement, jokes people tell, the working atmosphere, and relations among people. As Stanford University researcher Joanne Martin explains, culture is a lens through which organizational life can be examined.[20] Organizational culture is often manifested in stories. Martin describes several types. One of the more typical involves a lower-level employee following the rules, even when confronted by a superior. The story that follows, told by a plant supervisor, exemplifies how cultural messages are passed from person to person in a wide variety of organizations large and small:

> I started on a plant tour with him [the president], having planned the route we would take throughout the plant. He, however, took me wherever he wanted to go—in this case, the production line. He rolled up his sleeves and leaned over one of the assembly line workers and asked her how things were going. She interrupted him abruptly and said firmly, "I'm sorry, but you can't come in this area without your safety glasses." He apologized, red with embarrassment, went back to get his safety glasses, then came back and complimented her on her guts. They chatted for quite some time. He was very impressed that she had challenged his behavior without being intimidated.[21]

Rule-conveying stories like this abound in organizations, telling the recipients that the behaviors displayed in the "scripts" should be remembered as guidelines for how things are done and what is appreciated in the organization and in this case telling them that even the president can be corrected on important matters. Martin has developed a typology of story types told in organizations. Knowing such stories gives the organizational outsider important information about how negotiation counterparts are likely to act. For example, if it is well known that an organization punishes those who don't win, fires at will, and is intolerant of mistakes, a negotiator representing this organization is under considerable pressure to at least leave the negotiation table with evidence of important victories. When dealing with a counterpart from such an organization, the astute negotiator will gladly give whatever victories she can without jeopardizing her own goals, especially if the relationship is likely to be long term.

In addition to stories, organizations foster certain ways of talking. As Martin points out, learning an organization's favorite jargon terms may seem a trivial strategy, but perceptive negotiators know it's an important one. Learning such terms actually develops important insights into the way members of organizations and groups think. "Working the issue" was a favorite expression used in one of the organizations Martin and her colleagues studied. It referred to the value placed on confronting disagreement and continuing discussion until consensus could be reached. A negotiator who knows that this approach is valued can reasonably expect that negotiators from that company will be at least somewhat willing to wrangle with issues. If they are not, it could prove useful to provide a gentle reminder: "I thought at your company you work the issues; I had hoped we could do that here as well."

The more you learn about the organizational culture of the other side and the pressures they're under, the more prepared you will be to respond to diversions. If you know, for example, that your counterpart works for an impatient boss, you also know that if something you want to do appears to be slowing up progress, an objection is likely. If you can alter that perspective by suggesting that the steps you're proposing will actually bring about a quicker solution or that they will only add thirty minutes but will save time in the long run, you're likely to substantially improve your chances of keeping the negotiation on track.

Source: J. Martin, *Organizational Culture: Mapping the Terrain* (Thousand Oaks, Calif.: Sage, 2002).

▶ USEFUL STRATEGY CONSIDERATIONS

Once you've gained an appreciation for the psychological, historical, emotional, and etiquette dimensions of cross-cultural negotiation, you can consider strategic moves on substantive issues. What types of actions are likely to constructively move the negotiation forward in the Middle East? How do these differ from those that could do the same in Latin America? How should time be handled in Europe as opposed to Asia? In what countries is the quality of the outcome more important than timing? Where is relationship building critical to success? Most sources of information on strategy regale the readers with lists of dos and don'ts. These can be helpful. Yet the actual give and take of cross-cultural negotiation requires more pliable guidelines that can be tweaked according to the situation at hand. Cultural expert Stephen Weiss has provided this type of aid. Using familiarity with a counterpart's culture as a barometer of sorts, he provides a number of strategic suggestions.

Weiss recommends that in cases of *low cultural familiarity,* the wisest course may be to employ an agent, adviser, or mediator. Unless you're familiar with a negotiation counterpart's culture, going it alone is not a wise move. Naiveté or arrogance leads unsophisticated negotiators down the dangerous path of individualism. *Mano a mano* is not for the uninformed. If, however, the other side is familiar with your culture, an option is to encourage them to operate within the confines of your cultural rules. Weiss advises that negotiators requesting such an approach should convey that it is in no way due to a lack of respect for the counterparts or their culture. If you make such a request, be sure that they realize that

you are grateful for the effort they'll need to make to step out of their cultural comfort zone. And be careful, throughout the negotiation, not to assume that they know your culture so well that misinterpretations will not occur; in all likelihood, they will. One approach to this problem is to say something like "As you may know, in my country, we regard time pressure as less important than quality of delivery. This may explain my hesitancy to rush."

Moderate cultural familiarity allows the negotiator to adapt to a counterpart's culture or to arrange a blend of both cultures. This is where some dos and don'ts can come in handy. If, for example, you are American and understand a fair amount about the Japanese culture, you will not expect to get down to business right away; rather, some socializing and exchanging of gifts may be in order, as well as a considerable amount of evening socializing. You'll anticipate that questions may be repeated that you believe were already answered. You'll be sure that your counterparts know who leads your delegation and that efforts to treat everyone the same should be curtailed, as that is not the Japanese way. You'll accord respect to issues of status, and instead of boasting about accomplishments, you'll use more moderate indicators of accomplishment, through the presentation of data. These are only a few steps you could take to adapt to the culture of the other side. Recognize, too, that they will likely expect you to slip out of your contrived role at times, because it's never easy to stay in the culture of another during negotiations. We are always pulled back toward our own scripts, our own comfort zones.

In cases of moderate familiarity, another option is to coordinate an adaptation approach, in which both sides give a little in terms of relinquishing their normal modes of operation. Essentially, the negotiators acknowledge their limited understanding of each other's culture and negotiate a process of meeting more or less halfway. In advance of the actual talks, you can negotiate such issues as which language to use, who should speak with whom, how much each side should expect to achieve, how flexibly or stringently the agenda will be followed, and the manner and extent of information sharing.

High cultural familiarity can allow a negotiator to unilaterally adopt the other side's culture (to actually "do as the Romans do"). If *both* parties are highly familiar with each other's cultures, they can improvise a procedure allowing for a personalizing of the negotiation. In the first case, a negotiator must understand the other's cultures so well that differences of that nature become secondary or irrelevant, giving way to focus on the counterpart as an individual. Weiss provides this example: "During the Camp David 'peace' talks between Egypt, Israel, and the United States in the late 1970s, then President Jimmy Carter set up a one-on-one meeting with Prime Minister Menachem Begin to try to break an impasse. Carter took along photos of Begin's eight grandchildren, on the back of which he had handwritten their names. Showing these photos to Begin led the two leaders into talking about their families and personal expectations and revitalized the intergovernmental negotiations."[22]

This type of strategy, if carefully employed, can transform the negotiation from one in which cultural differences are in the forefront of negotiators' minds to one in which the greater emphasis is on dealing with each other as individuals.

It can facilitate the development of empathy, especially in cultures that hold relational aspects of negotiation in high regard. However, it is risky, especially if a negotiator overestimates his or her knowledge of the other's culture or individuality.

In what Weiss calls *effect symphony*, both parties transcend exclusive use of their home culture by exploiting their high familiarity capabilities. They may jointly improvise an approach, create a script, or use an approach not typical of their home cultures. Essentially, the negotiating parties recognize their cultural differences and opt either to draw on them to create a new way of dealing or to put them aside altogether. Obviously, this is a high-level skill. Think of it in terms closer to home. If you have an altercation with a family member, you likely know his family culture well. Rather than deal with him within the rules of that family, you might both decide to use a different model. You might create one (for example, "What if we don't look back, don't place blame, and instead talk only of the future?") or borrow one (for example, "We could try Mike's approach to differences by taking one issue at a time, not bombarding each other with irrelevancies, and instead seeking a workable solution for both of us"). These are coordinated procedural guidelines like those in Exhibit 10.2. This is the essence of the effect

▶ EXHIBIT 10.2

EXAMPLE OF COORDINATED PROCEDURAL GUIDELINES

Although the following list may be too long and direct for some cross-cultural negotiations, it demonstrates how rules outside of one side's culture or normal mode of operation can be used to construct guidelines to bridge the gap between the two sides. If both sides are involved in the construction of such guidelines, the wording can be direct, and should problems arise during the course of negotiation, either side can refer to the guidelines.

1. Data will not be withheld because they may be "negative" or "unhelpful."
2. Concealment will not be practiced for concealment's sake.
3. Delay will not be employed as a tactic to avoid an undesired result.
4. Unfair "tricks" designed to mislead will not be employed to win a struggle.
5. Borderline ethical disingenuousness will not be practiced.
6. The motivation of adversaries will not unnecessarily or lightly be impugned.
7. An opponent's personal habits and characteristics will not be questioned unless relevant.
8. Wherever possible, opportunity will be left for an opponent's orderly retreat and "exit with honor."
9. Extremism may be countered forcefully and with emotionalism where justified, but will not be fought or matched with extremism.
10. Dogmatism will be avoided.
11. Complex concepts will be simplified as much as possible so as to achieve maximum communication and lay understanding.
12. Effort will be made to identify and isolate subjective considerations involved in reaching technical solutions.

13. Relevant data will be disclosed when ready for analysis and peer review—even to an extremist opposition and without legal obligation.

14. Socially desirable professional disclosures will not be postponed for tactical advantage.

15. Hypothesis, uncertainty, and inadequate knowledge will be stated affirmatively—not conceded only reluctantly or under pressure.

16. Unjustified assumptions and off-the-cuff comments will be avoided.

17. Interest in an outcome, relationships to a proponent, and bias, prejudice, and proclivity of any kind will be disclosed voluntarily and as a matter of course.

18. Research and investigation will be conducted appropriate to the problem involved. Although the precise extent of that effort will vary with the nature of the issues, it will be concomitant with stated overall responsibility for the solution of the problem.

19. Integrity will always be given first priority.

Source: M. R. Wessel, *The Rules of Reason: A New Approach to Corporate Litigation* (Reading, Mass.: Addison-Wesley, 1976).

symphony strategy. It allows the parties to draw on special capabilities involving a stretching of their home culture styles.

▶ TEN GENERAL RULES FOR CROSS-CULTURAL NEGOTIATION

The strategies discussed in this chapter are easier to describe than they are to implement. Practice is the key. Some missteps are inevitable in cross-cultural negotiation. Gentle reminders during negotiations of the agreed strategy approach can help negotiators avoid slipping into dysfunctional scripts. No matter which strategy approach you choose, keep the following general advice in mind.

1. Before arriving for talks, learn as much as possible about each member of the other side's team. Know their interests and status concerns. Do not fixate on these differences but use them as guides in your strategy decisions. Be sure to have your business cards readily available and know how to present them in your counterparts' culture. Try to bring along the same number of negotiators as they plan to bring. Be sensitive to status considerations and who should sit with and talk to whom. Avoid substitutions of team members, as this will be disruptive to forming and maintaining relationships. Bring suitable gifts, and present these at culturally appropriate times; learn a few words of greeting if you do not speak your counterparts' language; and be sure you know how to engage in appropriate greetings (handshakes, bows, hugs, kisses on both cheeks, and so on).

2. Be prepared for differences in concerns about time, punctuality, and logical process. In some cultures, agendas should be used as informal guidelines. Bear in mind your own cultural biases in these areas, and be careful not to impose them on your counterparts. When in doubt, discuss cultural differences and

decide how to proceed based on what is learned. And don't neglect organizational cultural differences—they may prove crucial to the selection of effective strategies.

3. Remember that relationships are critical to success in most regions of the world. Treating contracts as binding legal instruments can be insulting and detrimental to relationships (particularly in China, Japan, and Korea). Treating them too informally in structured cultures can be detrimental as well (as in the United States, Germany, and Britain). It's important to do your homework here.

4. Don't automatically treat compromise as the answer to impasse. Esteem for this solution varies widely.

5. If you do not speak your counterpart's language, find a good interpreter, and practice with the interpreter. But when you meet with your negotiation counterpart, speak to the counterpart, not to the interpreter (yours or hers). Ask your interpreter to help ensure that your counterpart's interpreter is translating accurately. Get your interpreter's impression of what is not being said but is implied or hidden. Do not use lengthy sentences loaded with information. Break information down into translatable segments, and end with your strongest claim.

6. Be sure the others know your accomplishments and experience, but do not boast. You could send a biographical sketch in advance, along with some information about your company or a proposed list of key topics. Especially in Asian countries, it is important for negotiators to know your status and what you've achieved. This is a must for women, who might otherwise find it difficult to be taken seriously. Being a woman can actually be an advantage in cultures not used to female leaders. As one business negotiator told me, "When a woman is leading the team or even on it, the males on the other side pay closer attention and are less likely to expect our team to spend the entire evening socializing. Those are two very important advantages." This advantage does not accrue in every part of the world, however. It's wise to know how gender differences are treated and how that affects dress and demeanor before leaving your own country to do business elsewhere.

7. Be patient. If questions are repeated or topics reemerge, it may be a test of your knowledge, sincerity, or commitment to the work and the relationship. Your counterparts may be buying time while they obtain instructions from more senior decision makers. Be ready to spend time socializing, and don't reveal when you plan to fly back to your country. Offer to stay as long as required or for as much time as it takes to negotiate the stage at hand and to experience the beauty of the country. Above all, do not appear desperate, under siege, or at a disadvantage. Turn such impressions on their heads, so to speak. Tony Fang, author of *Chinese Business Negotiating Style,* tells a story passed down through the ages that demonstrates this strategy:

> During the Three Kingdoms period (A.D. 220–265), Kung Min sent his troops to battle. His city was left without good protection. His greatest enemy, Si Ma, the commander of the army of Wei, made an unexpected approach while Kung Min was in this vulnerable position. But Kung Min used the empty-city strategy to defend the

city. He sent an old man to open the city's front gate and sweep the entranceway. Kung Min then went to his tower to prepare food and wine. He played a musical instrument and sang poetry as if he had not a care in the world. Commander Si Ma approached the city gates, but hesitated to enter. He was wary of tricks and feared a trap was waiting because of this obvious lack of security. Si Ma ordered his troops to retreat and wait so he might discover the true situation. While Si Ma waited and wondered, Kung Min's soldiers returned from their campaign, and the city was once more defended.[23]

8. Prepare, prepare, prepare. Think in terms of four stages of intercultural negotiations: relationship building, task-related exchanges of information, persuasion, and concessions and agreement.[24] Give each considerable attention, and after your plans are firmly in place, remember to remain flexible. Negotiation is a process of ups and downs, surprises and sharp turns. As mentioned in Chapter 1, the skilled negotiator doesn't fight them but bends into the sharp turns, rides the ups and downs, and even enjoys the challenge of the occasional surprise.

9. If misunderstandings occur, slow things down. Do not demand that the discussion return to a prior tone; instead, attempt to decipher where that problem arose and work with the other side to rectify it. Check your own contribution as well as that of the other side. As in all relationships, it usually takes two to cause difficulties.

10. Use the strategies you've learned here, but be sure to balance attention to your goals with attention to your level of adaptation. Some negotiators become so concerned with adapting that they forget what they want to achieve. The best negotiations consist of attention to differences as a means of achieving goals, not at their expense.

▶ QUESTIONS

1. Choose a country with which you are unfamiliar. Study its customs with regard to etiquette, greetings, business card format and exchange, commonly used negotiation strategies, and how casually or formally are contacts viewed compared with your culture? Write a 2-page report or prepare a 5-minute presentation based on what you learn.

2. Interview someone highly familiar with another culture (possibly a family member). Prepare a brief report on "What anyone traveling to _____ should know."

3. Define the following terms:
 Monochronic
 Polychronic
 Four major processes of cross-cultural negotiation
 Collectivist culture
 Individualist culture
 Decision-making authority
 Hofstadter's four cultural dimensions
 Cross-cultural DCPs

Organizational culture
Rule conveying stories
Low cultural familiarity
Moderate cultural familiarity
High cultural familiarity
Effect symphony
Coordinated procedural guidelines

4. Read the intelligence-gathering case below. Apply it to another cross-cultural peace-making endeavor by describing the cultural differences that stand in the way of successful negotiation.

5. Describe monochronic and polychronic, collectivist and individualist with regard to cultures, and then describe how they do or do not apply to your own culture and to another culture with which you are familiar.

6. Read the case below. Analyze it based on what you learned in this chapter and from class discussions:

▶ INTELLIGENCE-GATHERING BENEFITS IN A CROSS-CULTURAL CASE

Negotiation experts are often called in as facilitators or mediators in conflict-laden situations to help disputants establish a workable negotiation process. These third-party consultants intervene to reduce confrontation and improve the chances for a constructive settlement or agreement. Such practitioners face many choice points during an intervention, say Benjamin J. Broome and John S. Murray, professors of communication and international relations respectively at Arizona State and Syracuse universities[1]:
A partial list they have developed includes:

- Who should we interview to design an effective process?
- What information is essential to this design?
- Should the parties meet initially together or separately?
- What is a good agenda for the first gathering?
- How can we turn expressions of anger, fear and frustration into constructive steps for resolving differences?
- When are the parties ready to consider options for solving their problems?
- Would a brainstorming format be useful at that time?
- Will a single-text process help the parties at this point move toward agreement?
- What follow-up steps can support smooth implementation of an agreement by the parties?

During two years as Fulbright Scholar in Cyprus during the mid-1990s, Broome himself worked with a group of Turkish Cypriots and Greek Cypriots who were committed to "citizen-based peace building activities" on the militarily and politically divided island

[1]Improving third-party decisions at choice points: A Cyprus case study, Benjamin J. Broome and John S. Murray, Negotiation Journal, January 2002, pp. 75-98.

where the communities were separated by a buffer zone bordered by barbed wire fences and military checkpoints. While waiting for the necessary permissions to have a joint meeting with both groups—and ever aware that he was working under time constraints—Broome faced a choice point: wait for permission or find a way to act while motivation remained strong?

He decided to meet separately with both groups to identify obstacles to peace building and to build a structural map of how those issues inter-related. Serendipity prevailed, and Broome also gained valuable insights into the different ways the Turkish and Greek Cypriots viewed their shared history and the status quo. He also met individually with members, gleaning opinions on how the collective task should proceed. Broome was also able to see internal issues developing: "differences in political orientations, various views about the meaning of 'peace' with the other side, insufficient level of trust, competition for leadership of the group, and other potentially divisive matters." All the above, even before the first joint meeting! Broome took the opportunity to work through those issues, which may well have proven counterproductive or at least distracting once the "real" work had gotten underway.

Broome did not give the groups any preview of each other's projects, a choice that in retrospect he feels may have been incorrect. At the first joint session all three parties were surprised when the Turkish and Greek Cypriots differed greatly not just in their views of the issues structure, but also in their very reactions to that difference. The Greek Cypriots, proactive and future-oriented, were disappointed and became discouraged at prospects for progress. The past-oriented Turkish Cypriots gleaned satisfaction from seeing their counterparts realize, many for the first time, the extent of the historical differences between the communities. Intensive one-to-one meetings were required to rebuild momentum.

Another defining moment, as Broome saw it, occurred at the next inter-group meeting. Noting the pronounced differences the peace groups perceived in each other, he decided to highlight what he believed were significant overlaps in elements of the two groups' issue structures. Doing so, he hoped to encourage progress. When he presented the commonalties, the Greek Cypriots became enthusiastic but now the Turkish Cypriots showed concern. In subsequent discussions he learned that the overlap threatened the Turkish-Cypriot view that there were huge differences in world and future views between the communities, and they were ready to withdraw from the talks or change their direction. The Greek Cypriots, on the other hand, had taken encouragement from the commonalties and were now eager to move ahead with the process.

Broome faced a "serious dilemma." How could the groups develop an agenda for joint projects when they had such contrasting views of the future—when findings that encouraged one side seemed always to discourage the other? Rather than discussing a possible change in direction in order to minimize group differences, Broome made the crucial decision to move ahead with joint development of a vision statement as he had originally intended.

"As I thought might happen, we got off to a rocky start. A lot of discussion took place between members of the Turkish-Cypriot Group, pitting those who wanted to emphasize the differences against those who wanted to emphasize their commonality with the Greek Cypriots. I remember clearly the moment the confrontation came to a breaking point. Two members of the Turkish Cypriot group, both of whom were closely tied to the political leadership structure, decided they could no longer take part in an exercise that would result in a collective vision statement. They pressured publicly, in the joint session, the other Turkish Cypriots to join them in leaving the workshop. To my great relief, no one joined them and even others who were also close to the authorities stayed to continue the work. This was a bold move . . . and was recognized as such by the Greek Cypriots.

"From that moment, the atmosphere in the group changed dramatically…the group no longer thought of itself as two separate community groups but as a single entity working toward a common set of goals, and a confidence developed among the group members, who had survived one of the strongest threats yet to its existence. The work then progressed in smooth fashion, at least until it hit the next 'bump in the road.'"[2]

Constantly the focus of efforts by both community groups to take their "side" in personal disputes, complaints and competition both within and between the groups, Broome strove to remain unaligned and to assure balanced representation in the discussions. He dealt with the issue by scheduling time for "check-ins" and "check-outs" before and after meetings, which "allowed individuals an opportunity to share feelings about a number of issues, including group dynamics. This gave us a way to gauge whether we needed to schedule a special time to discuss the progress of the group, which we did from time to time."[3]

In studying the history of Cyprus before his arrival there, Broome learned that "Cypriot society has long been characterized by internal infighting and struggles for influence and control. Similar to what I had learned from the time I spend in Greece earlier, I found that no one wants to work 'under' another person, and nearly everyone believes they can do a better job than the person in charge. As in many Middle Eastern and Balkan countries, leadership roles are not viewed as 'service' positions, and often the person doing the best job is criticized most severely. This often leads to a destructive pattern involving attempts to pull down whoever takes on a leadership role. This pattern carries over into the peace-building groups, making it difficult for any meaningful form of organizational structure to be sustained over long periods."[4] Broome dealt with this by focusing on equal participation and avoiding formal leadership positions. Instead, leadership was enabled on a project-by-project basis, which enabled people to assume leadership roles on specific tasks and then step back into their group before recriminations could develop.

[2]Broome and Murray, 2002, p. 92.
[3]Broome and Murray, 2002, p. 87.
[4]Ibid. p. 87-88.

Summary Remarks

After reading a book like *Becoming a Skilled Negotiator* comes the challenge of remembering what you have learned. The mind can accommodate just so much information and, as we've discussed, would just as soon not tax itself. Learning new skills can be daunting. It's a considerable challenge for most of us to learn even new accents—as an article in the *Wall Street Journal* has proposed[1]—let alone new ways of talking, as described in this book. Linguistic accommodation—the process of adapting to new ways of speaking—is extremely difficult for most people and often only partially accomplished by those who lack a predilection for such adaptation.

These summary remarks are therefore provided as an aid to your negotiation strategy and language repertoire development. Review them before you embark on a negotiation. As needed, return to more extensive strategy descriptions and language examples in Chapters 1 through 10 and especially to Exhibit 3.1, "Steps in Preparing for Negotiation," in Chapter 3. For many situations, however, attending to the following review will raise your chances of achieving positive negotiation outcomes.

▶ VERSATILITY

Enter negotiations ready for surprises, using assumptions but treating them as tentative. No matter how well you know the other person or team, the key early in any negotiation is to *gather intelligence* in the service of developing and maintaining a *versatile frame of mind.* Identify the other side's *interests* and the *issues* they view as relevant to them. Discover their *priorities* in both regards. What do they care about most, and therefore, which issues relevant to satisfying those interests must you address? What are your interests and accompanying issues, and how might you find a way to jointly prioritize—perhaps by *folding issues together*—so that both sides believe that their concerns will be addressed? Recall the "house of negotiation opportunity" images in Chapter 3, depicting the many ways that a subject can be approached. Look for hidden options. They're there. Remember that some issues may be *emotion driven,* and these may be even more important than ones driven by logic. Keep in mind the *ICE model,* which depicts how each set of perceptions on any issue is composed of interests, concerns, and emotions in varying degrees. Attend to all three aspects. If the *E*'s are looming large, emotions cannot be suppressed or ignored. They will emerge one way or another, so be prepared to deal with them, perhaps before they become evident.

▶ DEFINING GOALS

Once you've identified interests, relevant issues, and their priorities, articulate for each of the high-priority issues one or more *ideal outcomes, contingency goals, and BATNAs.* For each of these, develop major *claims* that you'll advance. Be sure to check the strength of the *data, warrant,* and *backing* you have for each claim. Play the devil's advocate, or have someone else challenge your reasoning. Locate the holes in your case by considering what the other side might say in response to your claims and their supporting structure. Perform the same exercise for what you believe will be your counterparts' major claims. Where are the strengths and weaknesses in those? Consider whether your claims will clash with theirs or how your claims may be advanced without appearing as an obstacle to the other side. When deciding how flexible you'll be in designating priorities, think about the importance of your *relationship.* If an issue is potentially explosive or some past history might cause both sides to be on edge, make the resolution of such relational issues one of your key goals. At the very least, acknowledge the differences that might prove to be obstacles. You might say something like "No relationship is perfect. Ours has weathered some ferocious storms. If we focus on the positive here today, if we listen carefully to each other's concerns, there'll be fair skies ahead" or "We've hit some potholes in the road, largely of our own making. Today's a chance to find a new way around them."

▶ SETTING THE AGENDA

Develop and propose the order in which issues will be addressed and claims advanced. A good *agenda* avoids extensive discussions of *clutter issues.* It is based on sound intelligence gathering and reflects sensitivity to the other side's main issues and goals. It's not merely a laundry list of topics but a strategic device in itself, indicating to the other side what issues matter to you, to them, and to both parties. If you anticipate considerable resistance on an important issue, placing it first could be detrimental to the negotiation. On the other hand, placing it last could leave a significant item to a point in time that may never arrive if other issues take up more time than planned. Be sure to estimate the *amount of time* each agenda item should be allocated, to help avoid giving too much time to issues of lesser relevance and too little time to issues of greater relevance. If possible, *connect* success on one issue to the introduction of another; for example, "The next issue is of the same type as the first, one on which we share considerable previously unacknowledged agreement."

▶ FRAMING

Word your positions on key issues in ways that are memorable and persuasive. Use analogies, images, and stories. *Frames* help demonstrate the existence of *linkages* between seemingly disparate positions. A statement like "When issues are as important as the ones we'll discuss today, differences are bound to be expected" proposes a view of conflict as something natural rather than abnormal

and therefore nonthreatening. For each key issue, develop some frames that present your thoughts in goal-facilitating ways. Use frames to which you could return later in the negotiation. If you say early on, for example, "In any healthy debate, there are moments of dissension, but there is always respect," you could return to that frame if personal attacks occur. Experiment with framing, even if it feels awkward at first. It's an important negotiation tool.

▶ PERSUASIVE OPENING

First impressions are crucial, especially when negotiating with people who formulate assumptions quickly and fail to question them. Carefully consider how you'll introduce issues. Here again, framing is important. The opening is an opportunity to discuss issues of importance to both of you, to grapple with some problems that have slowed progress, to clear the air, or perhaps to develop an effective means of working cooperatively. By providing an overarching perspective on the entire negotiation—especially one that advances your goals—you can help set the negotiation on a constructive course.

Before choosing an opening, be sure to identify the *negotiation style* preferences of your counterparts. Do they clash with your own? Can you stretch to accommodate their preferred and backup styles so that your ideas are expressed in ways of interest to someone who is largely either an *Achiever,* an *Analytical,* a *Mediator,* or a *Motivator?* Many negotiations fail before they've even truly begun because of style differences that could have been addressed.

▶ CHOOSING KEY STRATEGIES

Sometimes the goal of negotiation is *compliance*—getting the other side to merely go along with a proposal. More often, especially in long-term relationships, the goal is gaining *private acceptance*—personal commitment to a belief, attitude, value, or mode of action. Because people tend to prefer the status quo, achieving private acceptance requires skillful persuasion. Several strategies for this were introduced in Chapter 7, along with the *ACE model,* a means of identifying the strategies likely to work with a particular negotiator or team. The ACE model guides strategy choices according to the other side's concern for thinking and acting in ways that are appropriate (what significant others would do or respect), consistent (what is in accordance with one's self-image or desired self-image), and effective (what will lead to desired outcomes). Consider which of these approaches is likely to influence the other side, and select strategies associated with that approach or combination. For example, if your counterpart is highly influenced by the opinions of others, give extra weight to appropriateness strategies as lead options, but also prepare appeals to consistency and effectiveness to use in case you've misjudged. Be prepared with *concessions* you'd be willing to make to advance your goals. Before conceding, however, consider whether another strategy might work. Negotiations, like all human interactions, consist of *choice points* at which a new approach could be taken. Keep your options open. Don't become desperate, as it will weaken your stance, and do not allow yourself

to slide into unethical strategies. If you believe that your counterpart is prone to using such strategies, consider developing, early on in the negotiation, an *ethics agreement* that commits both sides to aboveboard actions.

▶ HANDLING CONFLICT

Conflict is natural in negotiation. Resources are usually scarce, and often one or both parties believe that any gain for one is a loss for the other. It's important to treat conflict as a cue for change rather than as a threat. If you've prepared effectively, you will know which issues are likely to elicit conflict. Have in mind conflict-resolving statements such as those introduced in Chapter 9. Remember that each of us wants to protect our *face.* Teach yourself some face-saving ways to handle *benign, strategic,* and *ulterior motive forms of deception.* The three forms are quite distinct and thus require different types of responses. The main idea is that when faced with potential or real conflict, it is better to *respond* than to *react.* Don't get pulled into *dysfunctional communication patterns.* Skilled negotiators are not *predictable.* They have at their disposal a repertoire of responses. Study the ones in Chapter 9, develop more of your own, and have them ready to use should conflict become a detriment to progress.

▶ CROSSING CULTURAL DIVIDES

When negotiators leave the relative comfort of their surroundings for other countries, they must pay greater attention to differences. Our cultures shape the way we see the world, what we think, and what we say. Our views of time, trust, decision making, etiquette, emotional expression, and other important aspects of negotiation are affected by the environment in which we live and work. A *global mind-set* is required for effective cross-cultural negotiation, one that is attentive to and respectful of differences. Never enter into a cross-cultural negotiation without prior study of the country of your counterpart. Know, for example, whether it is *collectivist* or *individualist* in orientation, whether time is perceived in *monochronic* or *polychronic* fashion, what the expectations are regarding manners, the cultural perceptions about trust and the use of contracts, and the predispositions toward strangers. In work-related negotiations, understand the culture of your counterpart's company. Be careful of unchecked cultural assumptions. People are influenced by their cultures, but they are not totally shaped by them. We are all individuals; remember to respect that as well.

In general, skilled negotiators are more observant than those who are less effective. They are more versatile and have a repertoire of available responses to a wide variety of situations. They are confident but not arrogant. Learning never stops for them. Experimentation is how they master their craft. They realize that negotiation is one of the most complex forms of human communication. And because all human communication is complex, there is no end to what can and should be learned if negotiation mastery is the goal. In this book, the main focus has been on the language of negotiation: how strategy is converted into words.

The more practiced you are and the more you learn from mistakes, the more skillful you will become in knowing what to say. Some negotiations are simple and require little risk, but most, as described in Chapter 1, are much like roller-coaster rides, varying in speed and in the number of unexpected drops and sharp turns. The key is to approach them incrementally, gaining experience and confidence on the tamer ones until you're ready for the most hair-raising. The goal is not to seek out such extreme experiences but rather to be ready for them. Fortunately, negotiations are rarely death-defying, but most include some sudden, surprising turns. For the skilled negotiator, the one who knows what we've discussed in this book, that's a good part of the fun.

Notes

CHAPTER 1

1. C. Handy, "Viewpoint: Charles Handy," *Business: The Ultimate Resource* (London: Bloomsbury, 2002), p. 75.
2. Ibid.
3. W. Bennis, "No Lone Rangers," CIO Insight, May 23, 2003 [http://www.cioinsight.com/article2/0,3959,1102476,00.asp].
4. E. Langer, "Be Aware of Life's Mindfields," *Los Angeles Times,* Aug. 14, 2003, p. B15; E. Langer, "Rethinking the Role of Thought in Social Interaction," in *New Directions in Attribution Research,* ed. H. Harvey, W. Ickes, and R. Kidd (Hillsdale, N.J.: Erlbaum, 1978), vol. 2, pp. 35–58.

CHAPTER 2

1. D. G. Pruitt and S. A. Lewis, "The Psychology of Integrative Bargaining," in *Negotiations,* ed. D. Druckman (Thousand Oaks, Calif.: Sage, 1977); R. E. Walton and R. B. McKersie, "The Framing of Decisions and the Psychology of Choice," *Science,* 1981, *40,* 453–463; R. E. Walton and R .B. McKersie, *A Behavioral Theory of Labor Negotiations: An Analysis of a Social Interaction System* (New York: McGraw-Hill, 1985).
2. M. Olekalns and P. L. Smith, "Understanding Optimal Outcomes: The Role of Strategy Sequences in Competitive Negotiations," *Human Communication Research,* 2000, *26,* 527–557.
3. L. M. Rinehart and T. J. Page, Jr., "The Development and Test of a Model of Transaction Negotiation," *Journal of Marketing,* 1992, *56,* 18–32.
4. M. C. Bateson, "Embracing Continuity and Change: The Power of Lifelong Learning," plenary session presentation, International Communication Association Conference, Chicago, May 28, 1999.
5. B. Dervin, "Audience as Listener and Learner, Teacher and Confidante: The Sensemaking Approach," in *Public Communication Campaigns,* ed. R. Rice and C. K. Atkin (Thousand Oaks, Calif.: Sage, 1989), pp. 67–86; see also http://communication.sbs.ohio-state.edu/sense-making/bib/biblist.html.
6. K. E. Weick, "Leadership as the Legitimation of Doubt," in *The Future of Leadership,* ed. W. Bennis, G. M. Spreitzer, and T. G. Cummings (San Francisco: Jossey-Bass, 2001), p. 94.
7. C. Cellich, "Communication Skills for Negotiations," *International Trade Forum,* 1997, *3,* 22–27.
8. G. G. Tharp, "No-Lose Negotiating," *Commercial Investment Real Estate,* July–Aug. 2000, pp. 16–19.
9. Ibid, p. 18.
10. M. Foucault, *Power/Knowledge: Selected Interviews and Other Writings, 1972–1977* (New York: Pantheon, 1980).
11. L. L. Putnam, "Challenging the Assumptions of Traditional Approaches to Negotiation," *Negotiations Journal,* Oct. 1994, p. 341.
12. J. Carlin, "Freed to Live Up to His Legend," *Independent* (London), Feb. 12, 1990, p. 19.
13. Ibid.
14. G. W. Bush, "Remarks Addressed to the United Nations General Assembly," New York, Sept. 12, 2002.

CHAPTER 3

1. R. M. Peterson and G. H. Lucas, "Expanding the Antecedent Component of the Traditional Business Negotiation Model: Pre-Negotiation Literature Review and Planning—Preparation Propositions," *Journal of Marketing Theory and Practice,* 2001, 9(4), 37–49.
2. S. Harish, B. A. Weitz, and N. Kumar, "Learning Orientation, Working Smart, and Effective Selling," *Journal of Marketing,* July 1994, pp. 39–52.
3. See R. J. Lewicki and J. A. Litterer, *Negotiation* (Homewood, Ill.: Irwin, 1985); M. E. Roloff and J. M. Jordan, "The Influence of Influence, Effort, Experience, and Persistence on the Elements of Bargaining Plans," *Communication Research* 1991, *18,* 306–332.
4. J. C. Freund, *Smart Negotiating: How to Make Good Deals in the Real World* (New York: Fireside, 1992).
5. H. Mintzberg, "The Strategy Concept II: Another Way to Look at Why Organizations Need Strategies," *California Management Review,* 1987, *30,* 25–32.
6. R. Redford, B. Fryer, and D. Meyerson, "Turning an Industry Inside Out: A Conversation with Robert Redford," *Harvard Business Review,* May 2002, pp. 57–62.
7. Ibid., p. 59
8. Ibid., p. 59
9. S. E. Toulmin, *The Uses of Argument* (New York: Cambridge University Press, 1958).
10. T. Buzan, *The Mind Map Book: How to Use Radiant Thinking to Maximize Your Brain's Untapped Potential* (New York: Penguin Group/Dutton, 1993).
11. D. Kipnis, *The Powerholders* (Chicago: University of Chicago Press, 1976); G. L. Frazier and J. O. Summers, "Interfirm Influence Strategies and Their Application Within Distribution Channels," *Journal of Marketing,* 1984, *48,* 43–55.
12. A. Rao and S. M. Schmidt, "A Behavioral Perspective on Negotiating International Alliances," *Journal of International Business Studies,* 1998, *29,* 665–693.

CHAPTER 4

1. See R. Fisher and W. Ury, *Getting to Yes: Negotiating Agreement Without Giving In,* 2nd ed. (New York: Viking Penguin, 1991).
2. K. K. Reardon, "The Memo in Every Woman's Desk," *Harvard Business Review,* Mar.–Apr. 1993, pp. 4–8.
3. Ibid.
4. J. Adair, *Effective Teambuilding* (London: Pan Books, 1987), pp. 60–64.
5. J. Lipman-Blumen and H. J. Leavitt, *Hot Groups: Seeding Them, Feeding Them, and Using Them to Ignite Your Organization* (New York: Oxford University Press, 2001), p. 3.

CHAPTER 5

1. D. Dooley, "Expanding an Island Ethic," in *Ireland: Towards a Sense of Place,* ed. J. Lee (Cork, Ireland: Cork University Press, 1985), p. 47.
2. Ibid., p. 56.
3. M. Warnock, *An Intelligent Person's Guide to Ethics* (London: Duckbacks, 2001), p. 32.
4. R. A. Friedman and D. L. Shapiro, "Deception and Mutual Gains Bargaining: Are They Mutually Exclusive?" *Negotiations Journal,* July 1995, pp. 243–253.
5. R. Lewicki and R. Robinson, "Ethical and Unethical Bargaining Tactics: An Empirical Study," *Journal of Business Ethics,* 1998, *17,* 665–682.
6. R. Volkema and M.T.L. Fleury, "Alternative Negotiating Conditions and the Choice of Negotiation Tactics: A Cross-Cultural Comparison," *Journal of Business Ethics,* 2002, *36,* 381–398.
7. "Under the Microscope" byline—Daniel Kadlec pp. 27–33 and "Enron Spoils the Party" byline—Michael Duffy and John F. Dickerson, pp. 19–25. *Time,* Feb. 4, 2002.
8. M. Elliott, "The Incredible Shrinking Businessman," *Time,* Feb. 4, 2002, p. 26.

9. R. J. Lewicki, "Lying and Deception: A Behavioral Model," in *Negotiating in Organizations,* ed. M. H. Bazerman and R. J. Lewicki (Thousand Oaks, Calif.: Sage, 1983), pp. 68–90.

10. R. A. Friedman, *Front Stage, Backstage: The Dramatic Structure of Labor Negotiations* (Cambridge, Mass.: MIT Press, 1994).

11. K. K. Reardon, *Persuasion: Theory and Context* (Thousand Oaks, Calif.: Sage, 1981); K. K. Reardon, *Persuasion in Practice* (Thousand Oaks, Calif.: Sage, 1991).

12. For example, the Joseph and Edna Josephson Institute of Ethics in Los Angeles, California.

13. N. Machiavelli, *The Prince* (Chicago: Great Books Foundation, 1955; originally published 1532).

14. P. J. Kalbfleisch, "The Language of Detecting Deceit," *Journal of Language and Social Psychology,* 1994, *13,* 469–496.

15. Aristotle, *The Ethics of Aristotle,* trans. J.A.K. Thomson (London: Penguin, 1976), pp. 108–109.

16. Ibid., p. 109.

CHAPTER 6

1. M. A. Neale and M. H. Bazerman, "Negotiating Rationally: The Power and Impact of the Negotiator's Frame," *Academy of Management Executive,* 1992, *6*(3), 42–51; M. H. Bazerman and M. A. Neale, *Negotiating Rationally* (New York: Free Press, 1992); G. T. Fairhurst and R. A. Sarr, *The Art of Framing: Managing the Language of Leadership* (San Francisco: Jossey-Bass, 1996).

2. E. Goffman, *Behavior in Public Places* (New York: Free Press, 1963).

3. A. Kendon, "The Negotiation of Context in Face-to-Face Interaction," in *The Discourse Reader,* ed. A. Jaworski and N. Coupland (London: Routledge, 1999), p. 372.

4. Adapted and abridged from F. Cooren and G. T. Fairhurst, "The Leader as a Practical Narrator: Leadership as the Art of Translating," in *Management and Language: The Manager as a Practical Author,* ed. D. Holman and R. Thorpe (Thousand Oaks, Calif.: Sage, 2002), pp. 85–103.

5. A. Bourke, *The Burning of Bridget Cleary* (London: Pimlico, 1999).

6. W. Benjamin, "The Storyteller," in *Illuminations,* ed. H. Arendt (New York: Harcourt, 1968), pp. 89–90. (Written in 1936)

7. Bourke, *Burning of Bridget Cleary.*

CHAPTER 7

1. G. Marwell and D. R. Schmitt, "Compliance-Gaining Behavior: A Synthesis and Model," *Sociological Quarterly,* 1967, *8,* 317–328; G. Marwell and D. R. Schmitt, "Dimensions of Compliance-Gaining Behavior: An Empirical Analysis," *Sociometry,* 1967, *30,* 350–364; see also G. R. Miller, F. Boster, M. E. Roloff, and D. Seibold, "Compliance-Gaining Message Strategies: A Typology and Some Findings Concerning Effects of Situational Difference," *Communication Monographs,* 1977, *44,* 37–51; M. J. Cody and M. L. McLaughlin, "Perceptions of Compliance-Gaining Situations: A Multidimensional Analysis," *Communication Monographs,* 1980, *47,* 132–148; and W. J. Schenck-Hamlin, R. L. Wiseman, and G. N. Georgacarakos, "A Model of Properties of Compliance-Gaining Strategies," *Communication Quarterly,* 1982, *30,* 92–100.

2. K. Kellerman and T. Cole, "Classifying Compliance Gaining Messages: Taxonomic Disorder and Strategic Confusion," *Communication Theory,* 1994, *4,* 3–60.

3. M. E. Roloff, "Validity Assessments of Compliance Gaining Exemplars," *Communication Theory,* 1994, *4,* 75–76.

4. Ibid., p. 76.

5. Reardon, *Persuasion in Practice.*

6. Ibid. Book copy not available.

7. R. Sanders and K. Fitch, "The Actual Practice of Compliance Seeking," *Communication Theory,* 2001, *11,* 266.

8. Ibid., 270.

9. See C. Gilligan, *A Different Voice* (Cambridge, Mass.: Harvard University Press, 1982), and K. K. Reardon, *They Don't Get It, Do They?* (New York: Little, Brown, 1995).

10. D. E. Ifert and M. E. Roloff, "Understanding Obstacles Preventing Compliance: Conceptualization and Classification," *Communication Research*, 1998, *25*, 131–153.

11. M. S. Poole, D. L. Shannon, and G. De Sanctis, "Communication Media and Negotiation Processes," in *Communication and Negotiation, Sage Annual Reviews of Communication Research* (vol. 20), ed. L. Putnam and M. E. Roloff (Thousand Oaks, Calif.: Sage, 1992), pp. 46–66.

12. J. M. Purdy and P. Nye, "The Impact of Communication Media on Negotiation Outcomes,"*International Journal of Conflict Management*, 2000, *11*, 162–187.

13. K. Kiser, "The New Deal," *Training*, Oct. 1999, pp. 116–126.

14. Fisher and Ury, *Getting to Yes*.

15. M. Albright, *CNN News*, Dec. 17, 2002.

16. D. Kahneman, J. L. Knetsch, and R. H. Thaler, "Experimental Tests of the Endowment Effect and the Coase Theorem," *Journal of Political Economy*, 1990, *98*, 1325–1348.

17. L. Thompson, *The Mind and Heart of the Negotiator* (Upper Saddle River, N.J.: Prentice Hall, 2001).

18. E. P. Hollander, "Conformity, Status, and Idiosyncrasy Credit," *Psychological Review*, 1958, *65*, 117–127.

19. E. Goffman, *Interaction Ritual: Essays on Face to Face Behavior* (Garden City, N.Y.: Anchor/Doubleday, 1967).

20. M. H. Gonzales, J. H. Pederson, D. J. Manning, and D. W. Wetter, "Pardon My Gaffe: Effects of Sex, Status and Consequence Severity on Accounts," *Journal of Personality and Social Psychology*, 1990, *58*, 610–621; T. Holtgraves, "The Linguistic Realization of Face Management: Implications for Language Production and Comprehension, Person Perception, and Cross-Cultural Communication,"*Social Psychology Quarterly*, 1992, *55*, 141–159.

CHAPTER 8

1. See L. Thompson, *The Mind and Heart of the Negotiator* (Upper Saddle River, N.J.: Prentice Hall, 2001).

2. K. Krippendorf, "Undoing Power," *Critical Studies in Mass Communication*, 1995, *12*, 101–132.

3. R. Lakoff, *Talking Power* (New York: Basic Books, 1990), p. 13.

4. H. D. Thoreau, *Walden* (Boston: Houghton Mifflin, 1964). (Originally published 1854)

5. I. W. Zartman and J. Z. Rubin, "The Study of Power and the Practice of Negotiation," in *Power and Negotiation*, ed. I. W. Zartman and J. Z. Rubin (Ann Arbor: University of Michigan Press, 2000), p. 7.

6. J. Pfeffer and R. Sutton, "The Small Talk Trap," *Harvard Business Review*, May-June 1999, p. 136.

7. J. Lipman-Blumen, remarks at Festshrift for Warren Bennis, Marina del Ray, Calif., May 6, 2000; see also Lipman-Blumen and Leavitt, *Hot Groups*.

8. Reardon, *Persuasion in Practice*.

9. R. Greene, *Power* (New York: Penguin, 1998).

10. J. H. Frost, and W. W. Wilmot, *Interpersonal Conflict* (Dubuque, Iowa: Brown, 1978).

11. R. A. Heifetz and M. Linsky, "Pacing the Work," *Leadership on the Line* (Boston: Harvard Business School Press, 2002).

12. M. Gladwell, *The Tipping Point: How Little Things Can Make a Big Difference* (New York: Little, Brown, 2000), pp. 150–151.

13. R. E. Petty and J. T. Cacioppo, "The Effects of Involvement on Responses to Argument Quantity and Quality: Central and Peripheral Routes to Persuasion," *Journal of Personality and Social Psychology*, 1984, *46*, 69–81.

14. Olekalns and Smith, "Understanding Optimal Outcomes."

15. Greene, *Power*, p. 52.

16. See P. Watzlawick, J. Beavin, and D. Jackson, *Pragmatics of Human Communication: A Study of Interactional Patterns, Pathologies, and Paradoxes* (New York: Norton, 1967), and subsequent works in the field of communication on rules and patterns of interaction.

17. See Gilligan, *A Different Voice*, and Reardon, *They Don't Get It, Do They?*

18. J. L. Badaracco Jr., *Leading Quietly: An Unorthodox Guide for Doing the Right Thing* (Boston: Harvard Business School Press, 2002).

CHAPTER 9

1. D. G. Ellis, "Language and Civility," in *The Language of Conflict and Resolution*, ed. W. F. Eadie and P. E. Nelson (Thousand Oaks, Calif.: Sage, 2001), p. 106.
2. P. Harris and B. Reilly, eds., *Democracy and Deep-Rooted Conflict: Options for Negotiators* (Stockholm, Sweden: International IDEA, 1998).
3. Ibid.
4. Ellis, "Language and Civility, p. 110.
5. K. K. Reardon, *The Secret Handshake: Mastering the Politics of the Business Inner Circle* (New York: Currency Doubleday, 2001), pp. 98–99.
6. Ibid., pp. 99–100.
7. Putnam, "Challenging the Assumptions," p. 343.
8. P. Brown and S. C. Levinson, "Politeness: Some Universals in Language Usage," in *The Discourse Reader*, ed. A. Jaworski and N. Coupland (London: Routledge, 1999), pp. 321–335.
9. T. E. Lawrence, *Seven Pillars of Wisdom* (London: Jonathan Cape, 1990), p. XX. (Originally published 1926).
10. Ibid.
11. L. Thompson, "An Examination of Naive and Experienced Negotiators," *Journal of Personality and Social Psychology*, 1990, 59, p. 88.
12. Olekalns and Smith, "Understanding Optimal Outcomes."
13. W. L. Ury, *Must We Fight?* (San Francisco: Jossey-Bass, 2002).
14. N. Gabler, "Class Dismissed," *Los Angeles Times*, Jan. 27, 2002, p. M6.
15. G. Anders, *Perfect Enough: Carly Fiorina and the Reinvention of Hewlett-Packard* (Steamboat Springs, Colo.: Portfolio Press, 2003); W. Bennis, "No Lone Rangers."
16. Reardon, *Secret Handshake*, p. 215.
17. J. Martin, "How to Negotiate with Really Tough Guys," *Fortune*, May 27, 1996, p. 173.
18. Ibid., p. 174.
19. "Persons of the Year," *Time*, Dec. 30, 2002, pp. 60–62.
20. Martin, "How to Negotiate," p. 174.
21. Reardon, *They Don't Get It, Do They?* pp. 61–62.

CHAPTER 10

1. P. A. Herbig and H. E. Kramer, "Cross-Cultural Negotiations: Success Through Understanding," *Management Decision*, 1991, 29(8), 19–31.
2. Ibid., p. 19.
3. D. A. Foster, *Bargaining Across Borders: How to Negotiate Business Successfully Anywhere in the World* (New York: McGraw-Hill, 1992).
4. M. Mayfield, J. Mayfield, D. Martin, and P. Herbig, "Time Perspectives of the Cross-Cultural Negotiation Process," *American Business Review*, Jan. 1997, pp. 78–85.
5. Ibid.
6. E. T. Hall, *The Silent Language* (New York: Doubleday, 1973); L. E. Boone and D. L. Kurtz, *Contemporary Business Communication* (Upper Saddle River, N.J.: Prentice Hall, 1996); W. B. Gudykunst and Y. K. Young, *Communicating with Strangers: An Approach to International Communication*, 2nd ed. (New York: McGraw-Hill, 1992).
7. N. J. Adler, *International Dimensions of Organizational Behavior*, 2nd ed. (Boston: Kent, 1991); P. N. Ghauri, "Guidelines for International Business Negotiations," *International Marketing Review*, 1986, 3(3), 72–82; J. L. Graham and Y. Sano, *Smart Bargaining: Doing Business with the Japanese* (New York: HarperBusiness, 1989); Mayfield, Mayfield, Martin, and Herbig, "Time Perspectives."
8. Herbig and Kramer, "Cross-Cultural Negotiations"; Foster, *Bargaining Across Borders;* R. Lewis, "A Clear-Cut Case for Compromise," *Management Today*, Aug. 1995, pp. 72–73.
9. M. H. Bond and P. B. Smith, "Cross-Cultural Social and Organizational Psychology," *Annual Review of Psychology*, 1996, 47, 205–235.

10. G. Hofstede, *Culture's Consequences: International Differences in Work-Related Values* (Thousand Oaks, Calif.: Sage, 1980).

11. R. Reich, "Leading When Everyone's a Free Agent," remarks to Harvard University Leadership Roundtable, 2000–2001, cited in E. Pruyne, *Conversations on Leadership* (Cambridge, Mass.: Center for Public Leadership, John F. Kennedy School of Government, 2001), pp. 62–69

12. J. Mayfield, M. Mayfield, D. Martin, and P. Herbig, "How Location Impacts International Business Negotiation," *Review of Business*, 1998, *19*(2), 21–24.

13. K. K. Reardon, *Gift Giving Around the World* (Stanford, Calif.: Passepartout, 1986); K. K. Reardon, "It's the Thought That Counts," *Harvard Business Review*, Sept.–Oct. 1984, pp. 136–142.

14. J. L. Graham, "A Comparison of Japanese and American Business Negotiations," *International Journal of Research in Marketing*, 1984, *1*(2), 51–68.

15. J. M. George, G. R. Jones, and J. A. Gonzalez, "The Role of Affect in Cross-Cultural Negotiations," *Journal of International Business Studies*, 1998, *29*, 749–772.

16. C. Engholm, *When Business East Meets Business West* (New York: Wiley, 1991), p. 133.

17. See R. Buck, "The Communication of Emotion," New York, Guilford, 1984; Daniel Goldman, "Emotional Intelligence," London, Bloomsbury, 1995.

18. R. L. Tung, "Handshakes Across the Sea: Cross-Cultural Negotiating for Business Success," *Organizational Dynamics*, Winter 1991, pp. 30–40.

19. George, Jones, and Gonzalez, "Role of Affect"; J. P. Forgas, "Mood and Judgment: The Affect Infusion Model (AIM)," *Psychological Bulletin*, 1995, *17*, 39–66; R. S. Adler, B. Rosen, and E. M. Silverstein, "Emotions in Negotiations: How to Manage Fear and Anger," *Negotiation Journal*, April 1998, pp. 161–179; R. Kumar, "Affect, Cognition, and Decision Making in Negotiation: A Conceptual Integration," in *Managing Conflict: An Interdisciplinary Approach*, ed. M. A. Rahim (Westport, Conn.: Praeger, 1989), pp. 1986–1994.

20. J. Martin, *Organizational Culture: Mapping the Terrain* (Thousand Oaks, Calif.: Sage, 2002).

21. Ibid., p. 73.

22. S. E. Weiss, "Negotiating with 'Romans': Part 1," *Sloan Management Review*, 1994, *35*, 51–61.

23. T. Fang, *Chinese Business Negotiating Style* (Thousand Oaks, Calif.: Sage, 1999), pp. 305–306.

24. Graham, "Comparison of Japanese and American Business Negotiations."

SUMMARY REMARKS

1. S. Stecklow, "Bloody Sticky Wicket: Americans in Britain Often Blow the Accent," *Wall Street Journal*, Sept. 30, 2003, p. 1.

Index

195